☆☆ WHEN ☆☆
DUTY
CALLS

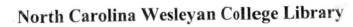

WHEN DUTY CALLS

A Handbook for Families Facing Military Separation

Carol Vandesteeg

LIFE JOURNEY®
Bringing Home the Message for Life

COOK COMMUNICATIONS MINISTRIES
Colorado Springs, Colorado • Paris, Ontario
KINGSWAY COMMUNICATIONS LTD
Eastbourne, England

Life Journey® is an imprint of
Cook Communications Ministries, Colorado Springs, CO 80918
Cook Communications, Paris, Ontario
Kingsway Communications, Eastbourne, England

WHEN DUTY CALLS

Cover Design: Michael Regennitter
Cover Photo/Flag: ©PhotoDisc

First Printing, 2005
Printed in the Canada

Printing/Year
1 2 3 4 5 6 7 8 9 10 / 10 09 08 07 06 05

Library of Congress Cataloging-in-Publication Data

Vandesteeg, Carol.
   When duty calls : a guide to equip active duty, guard, and reserve personnel and
their loved ones for military separations / by Carol Vandesteeg.
      p. cm.
   Includes bibliographical references and index.
   ISBN 0-7814-4288-5 (alk. paper)
   1. United States--Armed Forces--Foreign service--Handbooks, manuals, etc. 2.
Military spouses--United States--Handbooks, manuals, etc. 3. Military depend-
ents--United States--Handbooks, manuals, etc. I. Title.
U113.V34 2005
355.1--dc22
                              2005015621

To the ONE
who prepared and
equipped me

and
to the three most important men in my life:
Ren, Mike, and Dan

CONTENTS

Support Group Information
Resources for Helping Children

SECTION V. THE TOTAL FORCE

Army
Air Force
Navy
Marine Corps
Coast Guard
Separate Branches, but Parallel in Organization
Military Offices and Services
Private Organizations

Reserve Components
National Guard

Resources for Single Military Members
Resources for All Military Personnel and Their Families
Resources for Parents of Military Members
Army Resources
Air Force Resources
Navy Resources
Marine Corps Resources
Coast Guard Resources
Resources for Reserve and Guard Personnel and Their Families
Army Reserve Resources
Air Force Reserve Resources
Naval, Coast Guard, and Marine Corps Reserve Resources
National Guard Resources

ACKNOWLEDGMENTS

First I want to acknowledge Cyndi Anderson, who facilitated my connection with Cook Communications. Thank you for your interest and confidence in *When Duty Calls*, which resulted in bringing my work to the attention of Mary McNeil. Thank you, Mary, and your team of editors, as well as the publicity and marketing teams who make this resource available to readers. Thanks also to everyone on staff at Cook Communications who worked on some aspect of *When Duty Calls*. May God bless your efforts.

Thank you to those who referred me to resources or made me aware of corrections to be made to earlier editions. A special thanks to those who have shamelessly and generously spread their personal recommendations of my work. May God bless you for your kindness.

Thanks to each reader, for whom *When Duty Calls* is written. It's a blessing to hear your stories and appreciation for this book. May you be blessed as you serve our country and endure the family separations.

Last, and closest to my heart, thank you, Ren, Mike, and Dan, for your constant and continuing love, encouragement, and support—and for the special contributions you've made to this new edition of *When Duty Calls*.

Thank you, Lord, for all!

PREFACE

◪

In the uncertain political climate of our world today, readiness is foremost on the minds of a large number of our military personnel and their families. If they haven't thought about it already, now is certainly the time for them to begin! The demands of America's military mission are more intense now than they have been in recent years, as servicemen and women deploy to locations around the world. Active Duty personnel cannot accomplish the mission alone; Guard and Reserve personnel mobilize to contribute to the mission on a full-time basis instead of the part-time contributions that they've previously made. Reserve and Guard members may not know how or where to begin to prepare themselves and their loved ones for deployment. Some Active Duty families haven't given readiness much thought either.

I've been privileged to speak about preparation for deployment at military installations in the continental United States and Alaska and overseas in Germany, and I find that families *are* concerned about whether they're equipped to deal with the stress and uncertainty that result when a loved one is deployed. It's normal to wonder how you'll handle family separation and to have concerns about one another's safety and well-being while you'll be apart. I know firsthand how that feels. My husband, Ren, served in the Air Force. We've lived through TDYs and deployments.

Our most dramatic family separation was Ren's deployment to Operation Desert Shield/Storm in 1990 on only two hours' notice. The Air Force had little to offer family members to prepare them for deployments back then. Now military installations in each component of the Armed Forces have programs or resources to help families during duty-imposed separations from their military sponsors. However, information can be difficult for family members to find, and not everyone is comfortable attending the pre-deployment meetings that are held. Sometimes the resources are given to the military member, who is expected to share them with his or her family, but the resources don't always make the trip home or find their way into the families' hands. *When Duty Calls* helps bridge that gap. In fact, a number of military units now use this book to help their personnel prepare for deployments, as well as for reunion after the deployments.

When Duty Calls helps military members and their loved ones discover ways to prepare for and equip themselves for times of family separation. I wrote this guide from the perspective of the traditional two-parent family in which the male is the service member, because that is my experience. I recognize that the military includes male and female members, married and single, as well as dual-military career couples and single parents, and I address each in this book. Where there are references to the military member as the male or father, I do not mean to exclude females or mothers. The terminology I use reflects my experience, not any bias. I support and I am proud of all of our military members. I feel indebted to them for their service on behalf of our country.

If you're a military family member who doesn't feel comfortable attending the support group meeting around you or using the military resources available to you, I hope that reading this book will encourage you to get more involved in your military community. Please use the facilities and benefits that are offered to you. Regardless of your branch of the military, you can use resources and become involved in programs at any military installation.

You don't have to get through deployments all by yourself! This book will help you discover what the military offers to you and will give you ideas that you can apply to your family's need as you face family separation. If you are a civilian, *When Duty Calls* will help you understand loved ones or friends who are living with the stress that goes along with the military lifestyle.

Carol Vandesteeg
San Antonio, Texas

I

PREPARING FOR FAMILY SEPARATION

1/1: YOU'RE GOING WHERE? WHEN?

◩

It was August 3, 1990. Just as I did every Monday, I was working at the base hospital pharmacy when, unexpectedly, my husband, Ren, came hurrying into the building.

He probably wants to meet me for lunch today, I thought.

As he approached the window, I said, "Hi, sweetie."

"Hi. Is there someone who can take over the window for you? I need to talk to you."

"Right now?"

"Yes. Hurry. I'm going to Saudi Arabia."

"When?"

"Today."

The pharmacist, Major West, said, "Let him in."

The door opened and Ren stepped inside.

"I have to be at the mobility center and ready to go by noon. Can you leave now so you can help me pack?"

It was 10 a.m.! Someone must have taken my place at the window, but all I heard was the Major saying, "Can they do that?"

I fumbled for my purse, still not believing my ears. "Saudi Arabia." "Today." "Can they do that?" "Noon."

Ren had been in his office, counseling, when Chaplain Jeff Timm opened the door. "Ren, could you step out into the hallway?" asked Jeff. "I need to talk to you."

"I'm counseling," Ren responded.

"Ren, I have to talk to you *now*."

The sudden interruption stunned Ren. Jeff knows better than to violate professional courtesy like this. He's more sensitive than that. What's going on? This better be important, Ren thought. Apologizing to the couple in his office, he stepped into the hallway with Jeff.

The door was barely closed when Jeff began to speak. "Ren, you're being deployed to Saudi Arabia."

"When?"

"Today."

"When?"

"Noon."

As he absorbed the shock, Ren thought out loud, "But I'm not even the mobility chaplain."

"You were asked for by name by SAC [Strategic Air Command] Headquarters," Jeff said. "Maybe they asked for you because you were in Saudi before."

Jeff handed Ren a checklist of personal items he had to take along with him, and as Ren stared at it, Jeff said, "Just go home and get packed, and we'll meet you at the mobility center with the chapel trunk."

When we got home, we went down the list and mechanically began to fill Ren's duffle bag. I quickly threw a load of his underwear into the washing machine. Would there even be time for it to wash and dry before he had to leave?

Meanwhile, Ren woke up Dan, our sleepy-eyed sixteen-year-old son, and sent him to the Base Exchange (BX) to get some shaving cream and a straight-edged razor.

"Do you have an extra bottle of shampoo and some deodorant for me to take along?" Ren called from the bedroom.

"I think so." But I didn't find any. "I'll call Dan at the BX and ask him to get that too."

The duffle bag was almost full as the three of us gathered in the kitchen around 11:15 a.m. Ren wanted to call Mike, our oldest son, to say good-bye, but Mike was working on a construction site in California, and there was no way to get through to him until evening. (In 1990 people didn't carry cell phones.) With Mike on our minds, we sat at the kitchen table to pray. We brought our confused emotions to God, asking him to help us sort out our thoughts and to give each of us strength, protection, and a clear sense of his presence until we would be reunited. We had no idea when that might be.

The mobility center was not very busy. McConnell Air Force Base (AFB) did not deploy many people at a time, mostly weathermen and firemen—and a chaplain and chaplain's assistant.

Dan and I weren't allowed to walk inside with Ren, but we decided to wait in the car in case he could come back out before he left. After only a short wait, our patience was rewarded when Ren ran out with a short message for us. "It doesn't look like I'm going to Saudi after all," he said, "but I can't tell you where I am going. It's classified. Just thought you'd like to know. I'll contact you when I can. I love you both."

After a quick kiss, we said the final good-bye and he was gone again. I ached inside as he walked away from the car. Dan and I looked at each other and sat in silence for a minute.

"Now what?" I asked.

"Well, we have to be at school by 1:30," my son said. That was Dan's assigned time to register for his junior year of high school.

"Want to go to McDonald's for lunch first?" I suggested.

"OK."

We didn't talk a lot at lunch or in the line for registration at school. The excitement of the students being reunited surrounded us but seemed out of place. Didn't they know this wasn't a happy day?

It may not have been a happy day for us, but it was for them. They were renewing relationships with friends they hadn't seen all summer. Dan and I had to adjust to life without Ren and trust that eventually we'd feel like laughing again too, even though we didn't feel jovial that day.

Dan's Perspective

On a lazy summer morning, I was awakened by a loud rap on my door.

"Get up, Dan, I'm going to war," my father said.

My first reaction was, *why do I have to get up early during the summer? I don't want to do anything but be lazy.* I was bummed enough by having to go to school that afternoon to register for classes. Now my life was being interrupted again.

Once I realized what was going on, I got out of bed and got dressed. My dad handed me a shopping list of things he needed, and I headed out to the store, a little bit in a state of shock.

I got to the store (BX) and was gathering everything on the list, wondering if everyone around me realized that I was on a mission and that my father was being sent to the Gulf. A voice came over the intercom saying that I had a phone call. Surprised, I wandered around and finally found a customer service desk; I was connected to my father, who had remembered that he also needed a specific type of razor blade.

After completing my shopping and returning home, the three of us (Dad, Mom, and myself) sat at the kitchen table for a quick word of prayer. I was sinking further into disbelief.

Moments later we were at the flight line, and my dad, dressed in camies and carrying his duffle bag, was in the processing line.

Mom and I waited in the car to see if he'd be able to come back to say good-bye again and possibly tell us where he would be going. He did return for a second and said he was going to California and would be directed from there. So, in less than two hours, I went from sleeping to seeing my dad go to war.

A bummer, indeed, but at least I got to see him. My brother was off to college in Michigan. [At that exact time, his brother, Mike, was still working in California, and shortly afterward went from California to Michigan for his first year in college.]

The next couple of hours were rather quiet. My mom and I went down to school so that I could register for classes. I was totally zoned. I went right through a red light without realizing it until my mom mentioned what I had just done. She wasn't angry, though, which surprised me. That was pretty cool. Breakin' the law and my Mom didn't care. That was a once-in-a-lifetime thing!

In everything I did for the next few days, all I could think was, "Do people realize the crisis we're going through—does it show?" No one could tell, and I wasn't about to show them.[1]

Dan and I weren't the only ones going through crisis. While Ren went through the whole experience, he had a lot of conflicting feelings too. I asked him to tell the story in his own words to express what military members may feel like when they're deployed. Here's his recollection.

WHEN DUTY CALLED

The date is indelibly impressed in my memory: 13 August 1990. For me, it was like the phrase President Roosevelt used in describing the attack on Pearl Harbor when he called it "a day that will live in infamy." This was to be my day "in infamy."

It was 10 a.m., and I was in my office at the McConnell AFB

chapel, counseling a couple who were having marriage problems. While we were in deep, sober conversation, I heard a knock on my office door. Before I could even get out of my chair to answer the knock, my boss and senior chaplain of the base opened the door and told me (he didn't even have the courtesy to ask, I thought at the time) to step out into the hall because he wanted to see me immediately.

I told him the obvious, "I'm counseling," hoping he'd catch the hint that we clergy had professional ethics and *never* interrupted one another while counseling.

He ignored what I said and repeated that he "needed to see me immediately."

I apologized to the couple, strode out the door, closed it, walked a few yards down the hall, and then faced my boss. I noticed he was visibly upset as I asked him what was going on.

He said, "You know you asked me a few days ago, when Iraq invaded Kuwait, if I thought we might go to war and what the chances were of your deploying to the AOR (Area of Responsibility—war zone) because you had been in Saudi Arabia before?" (I had been in Saudi from 1984 to 1985.)

I said, "Yes, I remember."

He said, "Well, you're going."

Shocked, I asked, "When?"

He said, "Today."

Again, I asked, "When?"

He said, "Two hours from now. That's why I had to interrupt your counseling session, because you have to be on the deployment line immediately and off base by 12 noon."

Since it was 10 a.m., he told me to "get going" and that he would take care of the couple who was waiting in my office for me.

I scampered to get my Bible and ear plugs from my desk. Then I ran to my car and drove to the base hospital where Carol was work-ing in the pharmacy as a volunteer, to tell her I was deploying.

When I walked in the front door, she was standing at the phar-macy window and saw me immediately. In her sweet, happy, bubbly way, she said, "Good morning." Then she saw the look on my face. I didn't even acknowledge her greeting, and I said, "I need to talk to you right away. Where can we talk?"

She told me to meet her at the side door, which was locked and for pharmacy personnel only. The head pharmacist saw that something was wrong, and he let me in even though it was against regulation.

I then told Carol "I'm deploying to the Middle East and have to be off base within two hours."

We both drove home as quickly as possible, our minds racing ahead to what we needed to do next. I had never been in this predicament before and didn't have time to ask anyone what the "proper procedure" might be. All I knew was that I needed to pack my duffle bag with all my uniforms and a few civilian changes of clothes.

As we entered our house, I told our son Dan that I was deploying and that I had to be off base in two hours. I hurriedly gave him $40 to go to the BX to buy toiletries and some sundry items while Carol and I packed.

Trying to keep my cool, and watching to see how Carol and Dan were doing, I got to packing. In what seemed like a whirlwind, the duffle bag got full too quickly, and then I remembered something else I needed Dan to buy, so I scrambled for the phone to call him at the BX to tell him what else I needed.

Once he returned, we finished packing and threw my bag into the car. Then I thought, *I don't care how pressed for time I am, we're taking a few minutes to pray.* So the three of us sat at the kitchen table, and as I put out my hands to hold theirs, I noticed I was trembling. As calmly as I could, I said a prayer, and we all got into our Ford Taurus to drive to the deployment center on base, where I processed through the deployment line.

I was so concerned about Carol and Dan. We were all overwhelmed, but they handled it by being quiet and efficiently doing what had to be done at the time. I felt so sad for them, yet I was proud of them because they were so strong.

Our other son, Mike, wasn't at home at the time, because he was working on a construction crew for his Uncle Al in California. I didn't have time to call him to tell him what was going on, but Carol called him after I left. I felt rotten that I couldn't tell him I was leaving and that by the time he got the news, I'd already be gone. I thought that was a terrible surprise for him and very unfair that it happened to him this way. I knew how Carol and Dan were taking the news, but I wondered later, as I was flying to Castle AFB, which was our staging base to go overseas, how Mike would receive the news.

Well, once we got to the deployment center, I said good-bye to Carol and Dan. We hugged and had misty eyes and lumps in our throats, not knowing when we might see each other again—or if. No one wanted to talk about that possibility. Then I said, "If I can find anything out as to where I'm going, or if I might get some time to see you again, how about waiting here and I'll see if I can get back to you?" They agreed, and with that I went into the building and started to process through the deployment line.

Among other things, I had to sign a form stating that I had a will and a power of attorney. I received my orders, which were "open-ended" because they said I would be gone for ninety days or the duration of time needed for the contingency. (I returned 215 days later—after almost 8 months.) I also became a human pin cushion, as I got several shots. I received $200 cash for "incidentals" and my commercial plane tickets. I was issued an "A" bag, which contained a sleeping bag, mess kit, helmet, and other "stuff." I was also issued a "C" bag, which contained everything I needed for chemical warfare—things like a gas mask and syringes containing atropine, which counteracted most chemicals.

I checked in all my bags, loaded them into a van, and then went into the briefing room. After waiting for what seemed like hours, finally a Commander walked in and briefed us about when and where we would be deploying to. It was all classified, so we couldn't give any information yet to our families if we saw them before we left. After the briefing we were quarantined until flight time. During that waiting period, I and several others got permission to say one final good-bye to our families, so I rushed outside to see if Carol and Dan might still be waiting in the same spot where I had left them.

Sure enough, there they were! I was relieved, and rushed over there. I told them I had only a few minutes but had gotten permission to see them. I told them I knew where I was going and wanted to tell them, or at least give them some hints as to where I was headed, but I couldn't. As I was talking, Dan interrupted me and said, "Dad, don't tell us; we shouldn't know." I responded that he was right, and I couldn't tell them even though I wished they could know where I was. I appreciated his integrity, that in the middle of this rushed day he had the strength to say what he did. What a son! One last time, we hugged, and I turned to leave.

Shortly after, I was getting into a van with about five other troops and all of our gear, and we were on our way—for an indefinite time. I had had no chance to even say good-bye to my oldest son.[2]

After we got home from registering Dan for school that day, Dan asked me if we were still going to Michigan. We had been planning to leave on Wednesday to visit relatives in Michigan for two weeks. We looked forward to seeing Grandma and Aunt Dena, who were coming from the Netherlands.

"Yes, Dan, we'll still go. Dad just won't be there with us," I said.

"It doesn't seem fair, does it? The one time his Dutch relatives will be there, he can't come along. He couldn't even say good-bye to Mike!" Dan said.

After a long pause, we looked at each other and said in unison, "Life isn't fair."

Ren and I had taught the boys that life doesn't always deliver what we expect and that sometimes events may not seem just or right, but we still have to live in those circumstances. We might feel let down when life doesn't seem fair, but that's precisely when we can find grace and strength if we turn to the Lord. So in our family over the years, "Life isn't fair" eventually became another way to say, "We may not understand, but God does."

Later that day, I had to call Mike and tell him that his dad had been deployed. It wasn't an easy call to make or to receive.

MIKE'S STORY

I was in Chino, California, working for my Uncle Al for the summer between college semesters. I had spent the day working, went back to my uncle's, and was relaxing for the evening. My uncle and aunt were out at an Angels game, my cousin Carla was out, and the only other person in the house was a college volleyball teammate of Carla's, and she was sleeping in one of the recliners.

Just about every television station was showing footage of Iraq's invasion of Kuwait, and that's what I was watching when the phone rang. On the other end was my very tearful mother, who did her best to keep her composure and explain that my father had just been deployed a few hours earlier. At that time, Dad was stationed at McConnell Air Force Base, just outside of Wichita, Kansas.

Mom could only tell me that Dad was interrupted during a counseling session, sent home to get his field bag together, and deployed on just two hours' notice. She couldn't tell me where he was going, so I was left to imagine. One thing I remember saying was, "That must be where God wants Dad to be." After a few minutes of talking and reassuring each other as best we could, we hung up the phone.

Not two minutes after hanging up, my phone rang again. It was an operator, and before she could finish asking if I'd accept the charges, I said a very emphatic, "Yes!" I knew it was my dad waiting on the other end of the line. He was calling to tell me what my mom and brother had just told me. He said that his destination was

classified and that he was in a staging area at Castle AFB, which
was north of where I was in California. I asked how long he
thought he would be there and told him I'd drive up there to see
him, but he told me there wasn't enough time for that.

After hanging up the phone with my dad, I decided to go out
for a walk. I walked for about two hours. During that walk I was
confused and rather unsure, and at times I verbalized my displeas-
ure about the whole thing to God. When I was almost back to my
uncle's house, I suddenly felt a strange peace that I could not
explain, coupled with what I believe was God saying, "Do you *really*
trust me? Your dad is in my hands, and he will be just fine." That's
exactly what I heard. I was at peace but still a little uneasy.[3]

God's care got us through Ren's rushed deployment and each day of the
family separation. We didn't have time to prepare for the time apart—just
enough time to react to it. Fortunately, most people have more than two
hours of notification when they're deployed.

1/2: ARE YOU READY?

◪

Is family separation part of your military experience? If it isn't yet, get ready, because it will be soon! Family separation is an expected part of the Active Duty military lifestyle. "Not in a million years did I think it would really happen to me…. But, regardless of your [military] specialty, enlisted or officer, the fact that you wear the uniform means the [military] may need you to deploy, with little notice, to anywhere in the world."[1]

Unexpected deployments with varying amounts of notification are common. According to the Office of the Secretary of Defense for Reserve Affairs, the same thing is true for those who serve in the Reserves (they make up half of the total military force).[2] The military has been reduced by about 40 percent since 1990, but the number of deployments has increased by about 400 percent. The reality in today's military is that we should expect longer work hours and more frequent deployments to affect families of every military component.

Each component tries to meet the increased demand efficiently. For example, the Air Force established ten main expeditionary groups to take turns covering deployments. Air Force Reserve and Air National Guard personnel are included in the rotations. However, many Air Force families live with more frequent and longer separations than projected.

In addition to deployments, Active Duty military members face temporary duty away from home, field exercises, or unaccompanied tours of duty that separate them from their families. Additionally, spouses don't always move with their loved ones when they get permanent change of station (PCS) orders. They may want to pursue their own careers or keep their children in the same schools, or they may need to stay behind to sell houses. So families may live in two separate locations. Sometimes that choice is preferable to uprooting families, and more military couples make the sacrifice of living apart now than have in the past. These separations, like deployments, require preparation and adjustment and must be planned for carefully.

FAMILY SEPARATION AND STRESS

Even when family separation is expected, it is not routine, and each separation is unique. Researchers say that the most severe stress a military wife and her children face is forced separation from their husband and father.[3] That stress can be minimized by preparation. Part of preparation is believing that you will successfully deal with the challenge. Capt. Stan Beach, a retired Navy chaplain, said, "When family separations come, we aren't suddenly sprinkled with stardust from heaven. We either have the right stuff, or we don't."[4] You can decrease your need for stardust from heaven by beginning to prepare yourself now for the inevitable deployment or mobilization.

If your husband came home today to tell you that he was about to deploy or be mobilized, how would you feel? Wives who are new to the military may feel like they've already lost the closeness of their relationships with their parents, relatives, and friends, and now the only person close to them, their husbands, will leave them alone in a new environment. Other women may have established relationships in their military or civilian communities that they know they can rely on when their husbands are gone. They may feel ready for the challenge of the separation. Some wives have such mixed emotions when they get news of deployment that they don't know *what* they're feeling. They may forget that their husbands also feel stress when they are deployed.

One Sergeant looked at his baby, who was sucking her pacifier and holding an American flag in her little hand, and said, "It's something that you plan for but you never really think it's going to happen."[5] He was about to deploy for sixteen months. Military servicemen and women feel stress because they want to do their jobs well, and they also want to be at home to care for their families. They may feel guilty about leaving their families to deploy. The demands of deployment or mobilization seem to force them to choose between family and career. One deploying mother said, "I had such a strange dichotomy of feelings. The mother in me and the soldier in me were at war. I wanted to serve my country; that's what I've trained for. But it came at the worst possible time."[6] She didn't look forward to telling her family that she had to be separated from them because of military duty. When Sgt. Patrick Dawson deployed from Fort Hood in support of the war on terrorism, he said, "It's hard to leave your family. It's the hardest part of my job, I reckon."[7]

Staff Sgt. Daniel Diaz-Centeno agrees. He said, "There's never going to be enough practice to where you get used to being away from your family."[8] It's hard to leave your family to go to war, on a peacekeeping mission, on a humanitarian mission, on a Navy cruise, or on temporary duty assignment.

EXPECTING SEPARATIONS

When you volunteer to join any component of the military, you and your family must accept the fact that you could be called to go to war. Active Duty, Guard, and Reserve families may have to consciously remind themselves that their military spouses could be called away. Thinking of separation as an inevitable part of military life gives families better attitudes when they face deployment or mobilization.

Whatever the reason for the family separation, the ability of the family to communicate freely and carry on daily routines is interrupted. Interruption may make adjustments necessary, but problems and adjustments don't have to be seen as bad. They may not be pleasant or be our choice, but we can endure them and emerge better than we were before.

TRAIN YOUR FAMILY

The attitudes of parents set the tone for how children respond to separations, and children often mimic the behavior patterns or attitudes toward separation that they see in their parents. For this reason, if there is enough advance notification, husbands should tell their wives about deployment or mobilization in private so they have time to talk and get used to the idea before they tell the children. Then, when the time is right, the parents can have a positive attitude about what is ahead as they give the news to their children. When everyone in the family gets used to the reality of the deployment, the family can take steps to prepare for the time apart.

As you think about how to prepare your family for a military separation, it may help to think of the military's training system as a model to follow. The first thing a person does after enlisting in the military is go to basic training to learn how to work and survive in the military environment. Basic training may be the first experience of family separation that the military imposes on you. Military members learn to live without their families as they are trained. The family needs basic training[9] to handle the military lifestyle too. Active Duty, Reserve, and Guard members and their families all need to know how the system works and what it has to offer them.

Ralph F. Nelson's book *The Sailor's Savvy Spouse* is one good resource to help military families learn the military system. Another is *Today's Military Wife: Meeting the Challenges of Service Life* by Lydia Sloan Cline. Spouses need to be self-reliant enough to take care of family business if that becomes necessary. They need to be aware of the fact that "at times like this, it may seem the service is coming before the family. It is. It has to. It won't work any other way.... You can send him away complaining or send him away with a kiss. Either way, he has to go."[10] Expect separation as part of family life rather than as a traumatic interruption.

Valorie Torbert and her two sons hugged Sgt. First Class Kenneth Torbert good-bye, and as he departed she said, "We just do what we've got to do with the belief that they're coming back real soon. I'm glad he's going; he's going for all the right reasons. This is his job. I knew that when I married him."[11] Valorie's good attitude must have made it easier for her husband to leave and provided a positive perspective on family separation for her and their sons. She knew they would survive the deployment and she was ready to face it. You can decide to have the same perspective toward your deployments.

I/3: PREPARING SINGLE MILITARY MEMBERS FOR DEPLOYMENT

◩

If you are single and don't have children, you don't have the same concerns as service members who have dependents, but you must still prepare yourself for deployments. There may not seem to be many issues for you to deal with, but Ralph F. Nelson, in his books *The Savvy Sailor, The Savvy Naval Officer,* and *The Savvy Marine Officer,* does a great job of presenting issues, prioritizing needs, and leading readers through financial and life planning. If you aren't in the Navy or Marine Corps, don't be put off by the titles. These books are for everyone. You'll find information about how to get these great resources in chapter I/12 under "Resources for Single Military Members."

Nelson uses a very practical and easy-to-follow approach to help you plan for the future, financially and in every other way. You have bank accounts to take care of, bills to pay, and mail, among other concerns. You may want to consider the following questions to be sure you are ready to be deployed:

- How will your bills be paid if you are suddenly deployed? Do you have arrangements to pay your car payment, insurance (auto, health, life, household goods), club membership, credit-card payments, department store layaway, Deferred Payment Plan (DPP), and loan payments? Are any of your payments made automatically by allotment? What would happen if you were gone and the allotment was late? Do you have a backup system? If not, how will you avoid late payments and late-payment charges?

- When do your car license, inspection, insurance, and installation registration need to be renewed? Who will take care of it if you are gone? Who will take care of your car while you're gone?

- Do you have car payments? How will they be made? Who will be responsible for your car? You may want to put it into storage. It's possible that you can save on your insurance if you store your car while you're deployed.

- Have you assigned power of attorney (POA) to someone to do the specific things that you need to have taken care of?

- Do you need to give someone POA to conduct your banking? Carefully consider who you will give access to your bank account. If the account is listed in only your name, do you have a beneficiary listed on the account?

- Do you have a will? Who will take care of your things if you do not return? You may not own a lot of things, but the decisions about who will get them are yours to make.

- Is your emergency data card up to date?

- Who will take responsibility for your personal possessions while you are gone? Do you have your stereo equipment, computer, or other items of value insured? Be sure they are secure while you're deployed.

- Will your home be empty while you're away? Will you leave a key to your room, apartment, or house with anyone? It's a good idea to notify your housing office, landlord, or the police that you'll be away so people will look in on your place while you're gone.

- How will you file and pay your income taxes while you are gone?

- Do you need to disconnect your phone service—either landline or cell phones?

- Do your friends and relatives have your deployment address?

- Do you have someone designated to pick up your mail, or will you have it forwarded to you? You have to fill out a request form if you want the post office to forward your mail. If you ask someone to pick up your mail, he or she will need POA.

- Do your relatives know how to contact you in case of emergency? Do they know how to contact the Red Cross for emergency notification?

- Do your relatives have the names and phone numbers of your First Sergeant and Commander?

- Do your First Sergeant and Commander have your parents' names and phone numbers?

- Do you have pets or plants that will need care while you are gone? Who will take care of them? (See chapter I/7, "Deployment & Pets.")

- Do you have a second job? If so, does your employer know that you will be deployed?

- Do you have a list of things you will need with you on your deployment? Where is your immunization record? Do you have any health records that must be carried with you?

- Do you have a backup plan for the care of your mail, housing, car, etc., in case the person you designate is unable to follow through on helping while you're gone? Sometimes people who are designated to help are deployed during the time they are helping someone else.

- Review all of the above every year to be sure it is still effective.

Attend pre-deployment briefings if they are offered in your unit or elsewhere on your installation. Do you have a boyfriend or girlfriend, parents, or other friends or relatives who are close to you whom you could invite to the pre-deployment briefing? The information given at the meeting may be important to those who are close to you and may help them feel connected to you after you leave. They will probably be grateful for the opportunity to be introduced to your military lifestyle and to the people who will be available to give them information about you after you're gone.

Although most of this book is written for families, you will find a significant amount of information that you can apply to your situation as a single person, so I encourage you to read further. And, don't forget to pick up a copy of *The Savvy Sailor, The Savvy Naval Officer,* or *The Savvy Marine Officer*!

WILL YOU MARRY BEFORE YOU DEPLOY?

If you decide to get married before you deploy, be sure to get all of your records updated immediately, before your departure. Here are some of the things you'll need to do:

- Change your official records to show you're married and list your spouse as "next of kin" on your record of emergency data.

- Be sure your spouse is listed as beneficiary on any insurance policies you may have and on your will.

- Apply for an identification (ID) card for your spouse and enroll him or her in the Defense Enrollment Eligibility Reporting System (DEERS).

- Apply for your basic allowance for housing (BAH) and start any allotments that you may need to for your spouse.

- Be sure all bank accounts and automobile ownership documents are joint.

- Be sure your unit knows you're married and has contact information for your spouse.

- Be sure your spouse knows how to contact your unit.

- Take your spouse to a pre-deployment meeting, if possible.
- Introduce your spouse to the Family Support Program to be sure that in your absence he or she can use the available benefits.

I/4: PREPARING YOUR FAMILY FOR DEPLOYMENT

COMMUNICATE EARLY

Although preparing for deployment does help reduce stress, no amount of preparation can entirely erase all the stress. "But the perception of even some control can be enough to lessen most negative responses and become a base for building positive coping behaviors."[1] Knowing what to expect and having open communication about the feelings of all family members are good places to begin to find a perception of control. You may want to set aside an evening or weekend to talk about the possibility of deployment with your family. Tell them that it's likely that you'll be deployed, although you don't know when. Talk about what would happen if you were deployed so they will be ready if you are called. Make sure they know that you may be given advance warning or that you could be deployed without notice. Ask each member of the family to share his or her concerns and feelings.

When you have advance notice of a family separation, having a series of family meetings during the weeks leading up to the deployment will keep concerns out in the open where they can be addressed. The emotions of family members will probably be strained just before the separation. Many families experience frustration, because the deploying family member has to take extra time both at work and at home to prepare for the separation, which can result in longer work hours and less family time when the family wants more time together.

The decrease in the time families have left together can also cause wives to dwell on the deployment, wonder how their families will survive separation, or even doubt that they can survive alone. As the time for the husband's departure approaches, the wife may gradually pull away in order to protect herself from hurt, without even realizing why. The husband may become totally involved with his work just before he leaves. The wife may feel like it's her husband's fault that the family doesn't have more time together before he leaves. Disagreements and tears may become more frequent, children may misbehave more, and little irritants may become major issues. Family members may build walls around themselves to hide the pain of the departure, and that breaks down communication.[2] If reactions like these are recognized as responses to the deployment, they will be less likely to cause major problems in families.

COMMON CONCERNS

Most families say that deployment hasn't caused serious problems for them. The concerns voiced most often by military members include the family's safety in the event of war; the family's safety in the community; the children's health, well-being, and day care; money to pay bills; and whether the family car and household repairs would be taken care of.[3] Everyone who deploys or mobilizes and leaves loved ones behind has concerns about his family's welfare and how the absence will affect them.

The concerns of every family member are important, and families deal with separations more effectively if each person knows that the rest of the family cares about the issues that are important to him or her. Don't avoid sharing your feelings; make a conscious effort to be open and honest in your communication with each other. A husband may want to tell his family that he knows it won't be easy for them when he's gone but that he has confidence in them and knows they'll be OK. He might want to mention things that individual members in the family can do to show them how they can solve problems that could come up in his absence.

Preparing for deployment may remind a couple or family that they have not been communicating well and may help them begin to give more attention to communication. *Don't assume anything* if you want your relationship to be strong enough to get through tough times. Talk about concerns or problems as they are brought up by both spouses. For example, recognize that after the husband leaves, social life will be different for the wife, because married friends will probably not include her in as many activities as usual, and even if they do, she may feel awkward about being alone; she will not feel totally comfortable with single people either. When a wife thinks about that and has the opportunity to talk to her husband about it, she can feel more comfortable about expecting less group social activity during the separation.

See if there are any misunderstandings between husband and wife about what each of you expects during the separation. Try to understand your husband's feelings and how he approaches the deployment. Many wives find that when they talk about their feelings, their husbands will share that they find separation difficult too. Wives can discover that though their husbands are well-trained and prepared to go to war, they are concerned about their families' welfare in their absence. Husbands can discover what their wives feel insecure or apprehensive about and fortify those areas with moral support.

Some military members are married to spouses whose first language is not English. If that is true in your family, does your spouse speak and understand English well enough to be self-sufficient while you are gone? If her command of the language is limited, ask her whether she wants or needs help with understanding and translation while you are gone. She may be more comfortable if there is someone who knows both languages whom she can go to for assistance when she needs it, even if she can communicate sufficiently in English. Sometimes it's just easier to think and speak in a native language during times of stress, so try to make that possible for those whose first language is not English.

If you discuss these things before you're notified of deployment or mobilization, your family will have more time to enjoy each other before the military member leaves, because the issues will already have been settled. Your last days together can then be used to reassure each other and show confidence in each other's ability to get through the family separation in spite of hardships that may come.

CONNECT WITH YOUR UNIT

Hardships may seem easier to handle if your family knows they're not alone. Your family may want to try to develop relationships with the families of people at work. Many military units deploy as units, so relationships formed with coworkers continue during deployments. The husband will have friends to relate to as he deploys, and the family at home will have relationships with their families. If you don't already know the families of the people you work with or who work with your military spouse, invite them over for a visit or go on a family outing with them to get acquainted.

If your unit has family days to introduce your family to what you do at work, attend them as a family. The more your family knows and understands about your job and how it fits into the mission of the military, the more they can appreciate the role you play and envision you at work when you are gone. If it's possible, have someone take pictures of you with each family member at your work station. Your family can keep the pictures when you are gone and feel your care and presence when they look at them. A connection between your care for your family and your work will make the separation more bearable for both you and your family.

Some units are creative in their efforts to meet the needs of military family members. For example, the Texas National Guard gave children of deploying soldiers Future Soldiers Foot Locker Kits. The kits provided a connection between the children and their parents while they were apart.

McConnell AFB in Wichita, Kansas, held a mobility line to show family members what the servicemen go through when they deploy. Their program included signing in, a briefing from a unit deployment manager, preventative health assessments, and boarding buses to the mobility center. At the mobility center, attendees processed through a line where they were asked to show their ID cards and immunization records, and they learned about the Military Personnel Flight. They met representatives from the same squadrons who are present in real-world mobility lines and received an intelligence briefing about their simulated deployed location.

The Maryland Air National Guard's 175th Wing held a similar event. Although their Family Deployment Day didn't include waiting in mobility lines, it gave families a good perception of what happens when military members deploy. Family members had the opportunity to see airplanes, work centers, and booths representing organizations that play a role in mobility, such as insurance, legal, pay, and family readiness.

The 176th Wing at Kulis Air National Guard Base in Anchorage, Alaska, held a weekend readiness conference to introduce family members to their mission and teach them how to prepare for deployments. While the military members performed their drill weekend, family members saw the aircraft, had lunch in the chow hall, and learned about the military structure and benefits. Their briefings included presentations about the commissary, the First Sergeant's role, OPSEC (Operations Security), COMSEC (Communications Security), military pay, family programs, and legal and other military benefits and services, in addition to presentations that addressed preparing for deployments, getting through family separations, and reunion.

The 436th Wing at Dover AFB, in Delaware, held a mock deployment readiness exercise for children. The children had a briefing about what their parents do when they deploy and had a hands-on demonstration to reinforce the briefing. Children lined up to get their own dog tags and "passports." They stopped at mobility line processing stations, such as immunizations, finance, legal, and chaplains. Each station made its own impression: The health representatives gave them fly swatters, suntan lotion, and insect repellent; the legal representatives gave them candy; the chaplains offered them Bibles or prayer books; the finance representatives gave them pencils and their own leave-and-earnings statements. An Airman showed the children how to dress in a chemical suit, and he told the children how the suit protects their parents. They also saw the contents of each type of mobility bag, including cold weather gear, desert BDUs (battle dress uniform, which is the camouflage work uniform, normally worn in shades of green and in shades of tan for the desert), sleeping bags, and eating utensils. The children tried MREs (meals ready to eat).

All of the activities helped the children understand deployment better. They also gained a feeling of security by learning how their parents stay safe when they're deployed. The Dover AFB program was such a success that they held a follow-up program some months later. The second program took children to a mock deployed location. There were tents set up to simulate a deployed tent city, and children were taken to see everything in the camp. They saw tents with cots and sleeping bags, where parents would sleep during deployments. They saw the mess tent where their parents would eat. There were port-a-potties. They saw camouflage netting covering vehicles. Some of the Airmen were dressed in Middle Eastern clothes to give a feel for being in that part of the world. The children learned a lot about what life is like for their parents when they are deployed.

Operation KUDOS (Kids Understanding Deployment Operations) is a program that originated at Tinker AFB in Oklahoma. When the Kansas Air National Guard's 190th Air Refueling Wing in Topeka, Kansas, held their Operation KUDOS, children ages three to thirteen went through the whole deployment cycle. They had an intelligence briefing, went through the mobilization processing line, and carried packed duffle bags to ship out. A bus took them to a hangar. There they toured a KC-135 tanker and went on a pretend mission. When the children came out of the hangar, their parents met them with welcome home signs.

Many of the mock deployments and family days incorporate the same ideas, but each unit emphasizes their own part in the military mission. I've given mostly examples from flying wings, but the same principles can be used to plan an event in any of the military environments. If you have the opportunity to attend an event like those I mentioned, participate with your family. The events are usually open to children as well as adults and provide a learning environment that is a lot of fun. An important part of the learning is the *visual image* of their loved ones' military duty that these events give families. The visual image and experience help families feel connected to military members when they're away during deployments.

If your installation or unit doesn't offer events like family days or mock deployments, perhaps you can ask your Commander or family support personnel to consider holding one. The connections and bonds that these events create are well worth the effort it takes to plan and present them.

PLAN FOR FAMILY UNITY AND SUPPORT

Help your family find creative ways to maintain closeness during the separation. Ask each family member which methods of long-distance communication are most meaningful to him or her and how often he or she would like to hear from you while you're deployed. Different family members may prefer cassette-tape exchanges, photographs, letters—or maybe greeting cards, postcards, videos, encoded messages, or puzzle messages. Others may prefer unique stationery or paintings or drawings by young children or artistic family members. If you know what means something to each family member, you'll be able to communicate with him or her more effectively while you're away. And if you tell them what you'd like to hear about or receive when you're gone, they'll have an opportunity to do the same for you.

Deployment disrupts life and causes pain for everyone in the family. Instead of giving in to the temptation to think that conditions are rougher for one person than the others during those times, families should find ways to help and support one another through them. Before you are deployed, whether you are Active Duty, Reserve, or Guard, make sure your family knows that there is someone they can call who will help them. It will be most helpful if the person they call knows and understands the military system. If there are pre-deployment briefings offered at your unit or installation, take your family to the meetings. Friends and relatives who are close to you may also benefit from the briefings. These meetings will give your family, parents, and friends a means to feel connected to you while you are gone.

Some units designate a rear detachment when a large number of personnel deploy from one organization. The rear detachment are the military personnel who stay behind to take responsibility for personnel, equipment, and family-readiness duties during the deployment. They provide support to the families in whatever manner they are able. They may help with getting information out and supplying rumor control. They may muster a Family Readiness Group (FRG) if there isn't one established. In areas where Reserve or Guard personnel are mobilized, the FRG may send a newsletter to families who live too far away to come to meetings at installations. FRGs provide support in an environment in which there is no rank. They are grassroots groups of people who care about each other and network together to get through the issues of military duty and family separation.

Anything that your family can do to build a bridge to the Active Duty, Reserve, and Guard communities will give them less of a feeling of isolation or alienation when the family is separated. Preparation for the inevitable military family separations helps your family appreciate the military lifestyle even during unpleasant times. The Family Service or Support Center at your installation will help you prepare for separations, and you can also do many things to help yourself get ready for deployment.

Do you remember the reference to the military's training system as a model to prepare families in chapter I/2? Comparing the family to the military structure may help service members understand the importance of preparing their families for separation. "As an effective military officer you know the value of training and encouraging a staff, particularly the Deputy or Executive Officer. Your wife is your Deputy in the family; she is your 'Vice-Commander.' When you are separated from your family because of military duties, she must be equipped and motivated to carry on your family training program. How can you help her do this?"[4] Lt. Col. Ward Graham suggests that one way to help prepare the family is to develop a "briefing guide" for their use. His suggestion is a great idea, limited only by your family's imagination. Maybe you'd like to make your own family deployment guide (see chapter I/5 for further information).

Whether you include them in a family deployment guide or on a separate list, gather important phone numbers that your family may need while you are gone,. The list should include the numbers of your First Sergeant, Commander, police, fire department, ambulance, and hospital emergency room. Be sure that your family, parents, and in-laws know how to reach you while you are deployed. Do you have an address to give them for correspondence? If there is an emergency and they need to reach you, do they know how to do it? Do they know how the Red Cross is used for emergency notifications and aid?

Be sure that your family is able to receive *all* of the information and support that your installation offers. One Lieutenant Colonel filled out the pre-deployment questionnaire at his base Family Support Center and checked "no" for the "May we contact your family?" line of the form. When asked why, he said, "My wife does just fine.... She knows about taking care of herself." His wife happened to walk in as he said this, and she was not happy. "What on earth did you say that for? Do you think I can't answer a phone and decide for myself if I want to get involved in a program? Did you know that 90 percent of you men do this?" As I travel to speak at spouse support groups, readiness workshops, and conferences, I am consistently told that military members forget to ask their spouses for input.

Unfortunately, that wife was correct in saying that most men decide for their wives that they don't need to be contacted during deployments. Why *wouldn't* a husband want his wife to experience as much support as possible? *Please check "yes" on forms that request permission to contact your spouse when you're deployed!* If your spouse doesn't want to be involved, she will say so, and she won't be bothered with phone calls that she doesn't want. But, let *her* make that decision!

PLAN TO SHARE HOUSEHOLD CHORES

Some families help their children visualize the comparison between the family and the military lifestyle by having a family change-of-command ceremony before deployments. They prepare a list of responsibilities and chores for each family member. If you like that idea but you aren't sure what household jobs children of different ages are ready for, here are some examples: Three- and four-year-olds can put away toys, dust, feed a pet, or empty small wastebaskets; five- and six-year-olds can make their beds, tidy up a room, set the table, make a sandwich, help with cooking and cleaning up afterward, and fold clothes; seven- through nine-year-olds can clean the tub and sink, wash clothes, and vacuum; ten- through twelve-year-olds can wash the car, entertain younger children, fix simple meals, and clean up the house.

You may want to have a family planning meeting to draw up the lists and plan your change of command. Children can help; they like to be included in planning, and they may be more enthusiastic about taking on some of the family responsibilities if they have a voice in making the lists of jobs for the family. When you have your ceremony, hand family members their lists and small flags after you've read the lists out loud. This signifies that they accept the responsibilities delegated to them. You may even want to have a cake and punch reception after your ceremony to make the atmosphere similar to a real change-of-command celebration.

Your family may choose to make a family duty roster that resembles a military roster. A two-column chart might list in one column what each family member's jobs are now in one column and in another column list the jobs that each will have while Dad is gone. Dad's job could be listed as his military mission or as the long-distance communicator—be creative. You may want to add a slogan, such as "All valued members of the family team working together," to your chart. The chart could be hung on the refrigerator or somewhere that the children will see it every day.

Each deployment is different, and changes occur from one year to another, so even if you've prepared for previous family separations, it's necessary to prepare yourselves for the one coming next. Your plan probably needs to be revised and updated. Military families need to "be flexible in everything. Military life has no room for rigidity.... Military service isn't a job. It's a lifestyle."[5] The lifestyle affects the whole family, and preparing for each new experience will help them enjoy—and sometimes endure—the unique life of the military family.

PREPARING YOUR CHILDREN

Children don't like change. They can sense when something like a family separation is about to happen and will respond better if they are included in the preparation in at least a small way. Children always watch their parents and imitate aspects of their behavior. That's one way that they learn. They will watch you respond to the impending separation too, and your response will show them how to act. If possible, involve them in your plans for the separation. You may want to go to the library to check out books that deal with family separations or changes or look for information on the Internet together. For example, read the story of Mr. Roundhead at www.tckworld.com, or look at the Web sites operated by the National Institute for Building Long Distance Relationships. (For more information about these resources, see "Resources for All Military Personnel and Their Families" in chapter V/5.)

If you do things with your children to help them understand what family separation is like, they may realize that they will be able to adjust to the changes. Books can help them understand that they don't have to be afraid when a parent goes away and that the parent still loves them. *When Dad's at Sea* by Mindy Pelton is an excellent book that communicates that message loud and clear to children ages four to ten. *When Dad's at Sea* is written from the Navy perspective and also features the daughter of a Marine sailor. I'd recommend it for children in any military component because of the sensitivity and the honesty of the portrayal of feeling that is involved in family separation. Dads may want to buy the book as a gift to their children and record their own voices reading it before they deploy.

You can also use books or the Internet to find information about where Dad is going. Children will enjoy learning what the place is like, what customs people there have, and what kinds of foods they eat.

Maybe before you deploy you could spend time with each child, doing what that child likes to do and possibly have a picture taken of you during the activity. For small children, the activity may be going to the park to swing or going to the zoo. For some, it may mean going to a pizza place and playing video games. Others may want to go bike riding, play catch or basketball, or go to a mall. Doing things together that the children like to do makes it easier for them to talk about what's on their minds, because the adult is entering into *their* world of interest. You may want to make a "date" with them to do the activity again as soon as you return.

INVOLVE THE CHILDREN IN YOUR PLANNING

Children need to know that you'll be thinking about them while you're gone. They may enjoy preparing a Deployment Calendar so that they can mark off the days while Dad is gone. (Scriptographic Booklets has a coloring calendar for military families called "Deployment Days." For ordering information refer to "Resources to Help Children" in chapter I/12.) If children have a way to measure how long Dad will be gone, they may be able to accept his absence better, because they are reminded that it will end.

Children may enjoy writing letters to Dad while he is gone and will look forward to receiving mail from him. Dad may want to buy cards, postcards, and stamps to take along so that he can send personal greetings to each child and to his wife. The Write Connection letter-writing kits are designed to facilitate adult and child pen pal relationships. Channing-Bete offers a "Write from the Heart" kit for children. (If you want to know more about these kits, refer to "Resources to Help Children" in chapter I/12.)

Dad may want to write small messages to each child that can be put into capsules and given to the children like a daily or weekly vitamin pill from Dad. Children may want to help by addressing envelopes for Dad to take along and putting stamps on them. Dad may want to buy some gift certificates to his children's favorite restaurants, such as McDonald's, to take along to mail to the children during the deployment.

Before leaving, Dad or Mom could lie down on a piece of paper and let the family draw his or her outline. Then each day that he or she is away, the children could add a decoration to the outline by coloring with markers or stickers. The children could lie down on the outline and pretend they're getting their daily hug from Dad or Mom.

Maybe your family would enjoy making T-shirts with each family member's handprint on them to wear for family solidarity during the deployment. Knowing that Dad or Mom has his or her shirt along on the deployment may make this a child's favorite shirt to wear.

Some families find that if Dad makes each child a chart to record his or her daily chores, behavior, or activities, the children feel connected to him. If Dad is on a Navy cruise, a cruise map could be made so that the family can mark his progress during the separation. Including pictures of Dad at work, using colorful stickers, and following Dad's travel route with a marker can make the project more fun. The children learn geography in the process and might even want to take the chart to school for show-and-tell.[6] If Dad is not on a ship your family can still use the cruise map idea, revising the map to fit your circumstances. Maybe your map will have airplanes or tanks on it to mark where Dad is located.

Any map or chart that Dad prepares for use during the separation will help children feel closer to him after he's gone. As they use the visual aid, they will remember the preparation of it and that Dad cares so much about them that he wanted to do something special for them before he left. You can find more ideas to help you stay close to your children in *The Business*

Traveling Parent by Dan Verdick. This book is available in most bookstores; if the bookstore near you doesn't have it, you can order it.

Before Dad leaves, both parents and children should have a clear understanding of family rules and methods of discipline. Then, when he is gone the family patterns can continue smoothly. There are some excellent books available to help parents decide how to build their family rules and communicate them to their children. Two of the best are *Dare to Discipline* by Dr. James Dobson and *Withhold Not Correction* by Bruce Ray. They are both available in libraries or can be purchased in bookstores. These books stress what separated families soon discover: Developing and maintaining a predictable pattern of routine and discipline helps children feel secure.

Children appreciate being included in preparing for Dad's departure. Maybe your children could help you pack (roll up your socks, fold towels or handkerchiefs, etc.). Ask each child if he has something that he'd like to give you to take along to remind you of him while you're gone. Just be sure that it isn't valuable or too large to fit into the duffle bag. Maybe he has a favorite picture you could take, a small plastic toy, a favorite washcloth or towel for you to use, some stickers, or a few of his favorite decorative Band-Aids for blisters.

Try to give each child something of yours to help her remember that you think of her individually while you are gone. You might want to give her your baseball cap, an old military hat, a uniform patch or pin, a key ring, a handkerchief with your initial on it, or anything else that represents a special connection between you and that child.

The deploying parent may want to buy a teddy bear or other cuddly stuffed animal for each of the children so that they can relate that particular toy to the love of the parent during the separation. Your military clothing sales store or exchange may have teddy bears dressed in military uniforms. Many children have been tremendously comforted by their "Daddy Bears" when they don't have Daddy at home to hug. Older children might relate better to GI Joe soldier action figure that represent Daddy to them. See "Relating to Dad" in chapter II/6 for more ideas.

Spouses naturally think of equipping each other with a phone list before they deploy, and the person who is deploying may even tell his family how to get in touch with someone in the unit, but what about the children? Can we assume correctly that since a parent is there with the children, they'll have all the support they need? Don't forget that a parent is also missing, and the child feels that void. The parent who is at home may not be able to fill that void alone. If a single parent is deployed, the void is intensified for children. Before you deploy, help your children understand that after you leave there are people they can talk to or do activities with, and be sure that they feel comfortable approaching those people and know how to contact them.

SENSITIVITY TO CHILDREN'S EMOTIONAL RESPONSES

Children resist change and don't always understand how to express their fears and feelings verbally. The first thing you can do to prepare them emotionally for separation is to tell them what will happen. When you tell them about a deployment early, they will have time to think about it and adjust to the idea. If your children are old enough to understand it, tell them the purpose of your deployment. They need to know that you are leaving because you have to work in a different place for a while and that you leaving home has nothing to do with anything they did. Children need reassurance of both parents' love for them; they need the security of knowing that love does not change when you are separated. Find time to get your family together to talk about it. Older children might be able to tell younger brothers and sisters what a previous deployment was like.

Explain at each child's level why you are leaving, where you are going (generally, if not specifically; depending on the security of your orders, you may have to say only that you are going overseas, or you may be free to tell them exactly where you'll be), who you are going with (maybe they have a friend whose parent will be deploying with you), and how long you expect to be gone (you may not know, in which case you should tell them that you don't know but you hope to be home before some date or celebration that they can relate to and that they look forward to every year). Always use your most *pessimistic* estimate of the amount of time you'll be away—it's better for children to be surprised at an early return than disappointed that you didn't return when you said you would.

Children may think their parent is leaving because of something they did or that they are being abandoned by him. Taking time to prepare children for family separations helps them understand that they aren't being deserted and that they aren't responsible for Mom or Dad's absence. Whatever their level of understanding, try to help them relate your absence to your work.[7] It helps children to visualize what that means if you've taken them to a family day or have pictures of your workplace.

It can help your children if you voice your own ambivalent feelings about being separated. Then your children know that you have feelings like theirs, and they can see you model appropriate ways to release feelings by talking about them.[8] As they talk about their feelings, be a sensitive listener. You don't have to answer all of their questions; it's all right to admit that you don't have all of the answers. They need you to be honest with them and sensitive to their reactions to change.

When we got orders to go to Okinawa, our oldest son, Mike, who was in junior high at the time, said that he wasn't going, so we didn't need to get him a plane ticket. We asked him why, and he said that he didn't want to live outside of America, especially so far away where people didn't speak English. After a few weeks went by, we told Mike that we'd be picking him and Dan up from school a little early the next day so that we could get our passports. He said that he didn't need one, because he wasn't going. We asked him whether he thought he might like to come to visit us sometime while we lived over there, and after he thought about it for a moment, he said, "Well, I guess so."

"Then you'll need a passport, Mike."

"OK, but I'm not going to Okinawa, so don't get me a plane ticket! I'll only get the passport for a visit."

Well, by the time we had to get the plane tickets and board the plane, Mike was ready to go. I think he knew all along that he wouldn't have a choice, but he needed time to express and process what he was feeling without being told that he shouldn't feel like he did or being judged or disciplined for his response. Give your children time to process their emotions.

Open communication helps your children understand that they're important to you. So does spending time with them. Before you leave on your deployment, make it a priority to spend time with each child doing the things that he or she enjoys doing with you the most. If someone can take pictures of the two of you during the activity, the picture will be a special memory for the child to hold on to while you're gone.

There are some very helpful resources available on the Minnesota National Guard Web site that any family can use at www.dma.state.mn.us. On the site home page, click on "Family Programs." From that page click on "Soldiers and Families," and then click on "Youth and Development," followed by clicking on "Youth and Deployment." There you'll find Discovery Guides and Emotional Intelligence Activity Books that you can download and print. They talk about deployment and help children understand and deal with their emotions.

The Army Community Service (ACS) Web site (Virtual ACS), www.armycommunityservice.org, also has downloadable children's workbooks. When you go to the Web site, on the left side of the home page click on "Deployment Readiness" then "Deployment Tools" then "Download Center." When the page comes up, click on "Children's Workbooks." You'll see the titles available as you scroll down; open and view them and print them out. It's that easy!

All of these resources will be helpful regardless of which branch of the military you belong to or whether you're full- or part-time military families. If you feel like you need more help preparing your children for a family separation, there are organizations that can give you advice or provide activities to help your children. Among them are the Family Service or Support Center, chapels or churches, recreation centers, youth centers, child development centers, schools, libraries, civilian boys or girls clubs, the Red Cross, the YMCA, mental health clinics, and counseling centers.

I/5: FAMILY DEPLOYMENT GUIDE

◩

Families may want to develop checklists of things to do to prepare for military separations. This is important for Reserve and Guard families as well as for those on Active Duty. Checklists should be reviewed every year to ensure that they are still effective.

Where do you start? If you put all of your ideas into a notebook or an accordion file, it will be easier to organize the information into a usable format. You may want to divide your information into topical sections. Here are some ideas that you may want to include as you consider making a deployment guide for your family.

FINANCES

One of the most important places to begin can be the family budget and financial practices. The financial circumstances of military families can change frequently because of their mobile lives, and their financial plans should be flexible.

Ralph F. Nelson wrote three books—*The Savvy Sailor, The Savvy Naval Officer,* and *The Savvy Marine Officer*—that contain the best financial planning guides, tailored specifically for the military, that I've ever seen. If you aren't in the Navy or the Marine Corps, don't be put off by the titles; these books are for everyone. They give information to help you plan for cash management, budgeting, investing, home buying, estate planning, insurance, retirement, and more. I can't recommend these resources highly enough! Every military family needs what Nelson offers. (See chapter I/12 under "Resources for Families" for ordering information.)

As Nelson points out in his books, budgets must be continually revised and updated to remain useful. How sensitive to change is your financial plan? Who takes care of the bills? Do both spouses know how to do it? If the one spouse is deployed on short notice, there may not be time for him or her to show the other spouse how to pay the bills before leaving. Be sure that both spouses have a list of all passwords, PINs (Personal Identification Number), and user IDs that either of you use. You must each be able to access all of your accounts whether you're together or apart. Husband and wife should be equally qualified and knowledgeable about how to run the household finances. Specifically, they should each know the following:

BANK ACCOUNTS

- Account number, type of account, bank's name, address, and telephone number for each bank account (checking and savings). Do you both know how to use automatic teller machine (ATM) cards?

- Do you have a safe deposit box? Where? Does your spouse know how to get into it?

- What investments do you have? List the agents, companies, and account numbers for investments, including stocks and bonds. Remember to include the Thrift Savings Plan (TSP) information for federal employees if you participate in that plan. What percentage of your pay is deducted into your TSP account, and how is it invested? Be sure that your spouse knows where this information is located.

- What loans do you have? When and where do you make payments? What is the minimum payment that can be made? Will deployment affect the amount of payment or rate of interest? You may want to ask your lender those questions.

- Do you know how to balance the checkbook to the monthly statement and maintain the checking account? Who do you call at the bank if there is a problem balancing the account? Be sure to keep track of your checking account balance. Bounced checks cost you money and damage your credit, and knowingly writing a check with insufficient funds is a violation of the Uniform Code of Military Justice (UCMJ) and will result in harsh penalties.

- Is the checking account in both spouses' names? It is better if the account is registered in *both* names and set up so that if one party should die the account is automatically the property of the other. In some cases, an account registered in two names must go to probate in case of death. You may want to ask your bank about your account to be sure that your money would be immediately available to the remaining spouse if one of you died.

- How does your pay get into your account? Do you have direct deposit? If you don't have direct deposit, visit your military finance office immediately to get it started. You are allowed allotments to other accounts if you don't want all of the pay to go into a single checking account.

- How do you order new checks when they are needed? How many do you order, and is it important that you keep the same type of checks?

- Where do you keep the monthly leave and earnings statement (LES)? Is it mailed to your home or work address? If you are deployed, will your spouse still regularly receive the LES?

Each military family should have a plan for handling the finances in case of a sudden deployment and be ready to activate it on a moment's notice. You may not have enough notification to get a plan together before a spouse leaves.

However, deployment isn't the only reason to have a plan for handling finances from separate locations. Many military members frequently go on temporary duty (TDY or TAD) away from their families. Along with deployments, temporary absences may increase due to recent changes in the military.

You may want to have a separate account to use as the temporary duty or deployment account to keep your household financial plan flexible and efficient. Open the account in the names of both spouses, so that both will have access to it. You may want to keep only the minimum balance in the account when the military spouse is not away from home, but try to keep a balance in the account that will give him enough money for at least the first month that he is gone. You can decide what that amount should be for your family. If both names are on the account, the military spouse can take the checkbook along when he or she is deployed, and the other spouse will be able to make deposits as necessary (keep deposit slips on hand, so they aren't all deployed with your spouse), depending on the length of the separation. Your family might prefer to have a regular allotment going into the account. Set up the allotment now; it often takes a few months to get an allotment working smoothly.

Many military members have government credit cards that *must* be used for official travel and expenses. Remember that the government credit cards *must* be paid in full when the bill comes each month and that they are not for personal use. If you decide to open a TDY/deployment checking account, you may want to use that account to pay the government credit card bill when it comes. If the military member is gone for an extended period of time, the bill may arrive before the deployment or TDY is complete, but the bill must still be paid.

Talk to your military finance office about how to keep your account current. You may be eligible for an advance in pay to cover the bill or an automatic payment to the credit card account. Your spouse can write a check to pay the bill but cannot conduct any other business related to the card, including talking to the finance office about how to keep payment current or changing your address. The regulations regarding use of these credit cards are strict, and you don't want misuse or late payments to mar your credit rating *or* your military career.

HOUSING

- Do you own a home? When and where do you make payments? Are taxes and insurance paid separately or included in your payment? If separately, when are they due?

- If you are renting, who is your landlord and when is your rent due? Keep the landlord's address and phone number available. Did you sign a lease? Will it expire while you are deployed? If so, does your spouse need power of attorney to renew it?

- Are you on a waiting list for military housing? What will your family do if they are offered housing while you are gone? Can they accept it and move in? If they accept government housing in your absence, they will need power of attorney to accept the house and arrange the move. If they are offered housing and turn it down, will you still be eligible to receive quarters later? How would a turn-down affect your place on the waiting list?

- What is the process for moving your household goods? If it became necessary to move without you, does your spouse know how to handle it?

- Where are the rental or lease agreement, the deed to your home, your real estate records, and appraisals or mortgage information?

BILL PAYING

- Do you know what bills to expect on a monthly basis and how to pay them (by mail, at the bank, at the place of business, etc.)?

- Who owes you money? Whom do you owe? When and how are payments made?

- Do you have any purchases on layaway or Deferred Payment Plan (DPP)? How do you keep them current?

- Make a record of credit card numbers and their issuers' phone numbers and addresses (and similar information for anything else in your wallet, such as ATM cards and PINs for accounts); include instructions for reporting lost cards.

- When do annual, semiannual, or quarterly payments or bills come due and how are they budgeted to be paid?

- Do you know how and where to file federal, state, and city income tax forms? Who prepares your tax forms? Remember to allow time to mail the tax return back and forth for both spouses' signatures, and always make copies in case forms are lost in the mail.

- Do you have a cell phone that you won't need during the deployment? Will you cancel that service? Who do you call to activate or deactivate your cell phone service?

- Do you live in an area where you use ration cards or gas coupons? Will they expire during the separation? How are they renewed, obtained, and used?

- What insurance policies do you have? List insurance policies for coverage of life, automobile, home, household goods, property, long-term care, and medical, along with the policy numbers and expiration dates of each policy. Include the insurance agents' names, phone numbers, and addresses.

- Do you have a budget to help you spend your income wisely? Monthly expenses that you may want to consider including in your budget are: housing, house repairs, utilities (gas, oil, electric, coal, water), telephone (local and long-distance carriers and cell phone), food (including school lunches, eating out, groceries/meat, pet food, holiday treats), babysitters, clothing, dry cleaning, debts (payments, loans, car, credit cards, layaway, DPP purchases), club memberships, car upkeep and gas, insurance (car, household goods, life, health, long-term care), school (books, fees, tuition, general supplies), children's allowance, music lessons or instruments, recreation (entertainment, travel, parties, sports activities or teams that children are involved in), cable TV, Internet charges, savings, investments, holiday gifts and spending, emergencies, gifts, etc. Having at least a guide for your budget will help ensure that you plan properly for your expenses. Added expenses during deployment might include extra uniforms, food, telephone calls, postage and stationery, toiletries, and entertainment and personal expenses for your deployed spouse. Are you prepared for those extra expenses or planning how to meet them?

When both spouses are equipped to handle ongoing financial matters in the home, they may want try to develop a system in which they take turns paying the bills so that they are both comfortable with their ability to handle the process. They should both be familiar with the family checking account and the account that you may use for temporary duty or deployments. As you consider the balance that you will keep in your deployment or temporary duty account, remember that your budget may be tighter while you're separated.

Even if your spouse is deployed in tent conditions and field rations, he will want and need money for things like writing materials, postage, and personal hygiene items, and your family's needs at home will also go on. Expect the deployment to strain your budget and add to your costs. If you plan for a tighter budget before it is necessary, you and your family will be able to deal with it better if it costs you more to live apart than it does for you to live together.

If the financial strain of a deployment becomes great enough that you fall behind on a scheduled payment, write a letter to the company explaining your situation and try to make at least a partial payment. Although you'll have to pay more interest and service charges, the company will likely extend the payment period because you are making an effort to pay what you owe them.

Your installation has financial counselors to help you plan your budget and teach you how to manage when the strain becomes too much. You can ask your Family Support Center or Family Service Center for help. You can also contact the aid societies (the Army Emergency Relief [AER], the Air Force Aid Society, the Navy-Marine Corps Relief Society, and the Coast Guard Mutual Assistance) for help with budgets. There's a description of these agencies in chapter V/2, and contact information for each society is listed in chapter V/5. Ralph Nelson's books, which I discussed earlier, may also equip you to draw up your own plan. (See chapter I/12 for ordering information.)

You may decide to keep your entire household budget and your financial matters separate from your family deployment guide, but be sure that both spouses agree to and understand your plan. Then learning how to do everything and finding out where everything is will not be part of the goodbye process.

Important Papers

Each family has important papers that need to be organized and accessible to the spouse who remains at home during a military separation. It may be most helpful to keep them in a safe place and list them in your family deployment guide, along with the location of each document. You may want to put a copy of each document in your family deployment guide, including instructions for finding the original. If you don't have everything on the following list, you may want to begin to accumulate them if they apply to your family situation. Know where these documents are and keep them available.

Legal records

- Is your record of emergency data at your military personnel office up to date and correct? You may want to review it to be sure.

- Power of attorney: There are general and specific POAs. A general POA allows the person you designate to have unlimited authority to sign your name or act on your behalf. It should be used cautiously, because it allows another person to do any legal act in your name. A special POA is more limited and gives the person you designate power to do only what you specifically request him or her to do. You might use a special POA to enable someone to cash your checks, secure a loan, ship your household goods, sign damage claims, accept quarters, sign agreements for home rental or purchase, give your consent for someone to obtain medical care for your children, or other specific acts that you may need to have accomplished. The special POA should be used whenever it meets your needs.

POAs are valid only while the person granting the POA is alive. POA cannot be used to start, stop, or change your military pay allotments. Because some organizations hesitate to accept a POA, make your POA as specific as possible to increase the possibility that it will be honored. Remember that POAs expire and must be updated yearly. Your legal office can help you determine what exact POAs you may need.

- List the names and phone numbers of your personal lawyer and/or any trusted friends who may be consulted about your personal or business affairs in your absence.

- Both spouses should have a will. The wills should be reviewed and updated periodically. Situations that require updating your will include when there is a substantial change in the value of your assets (such as receiving an inheritance), the birth or death of an immediate family member, when there is a change in your state of legal residence, when your executor dies or is no longer competent, when a guardian must be appointed for your children, when there is a change in marital status, when certain provisions need to be changed, or when there are changes in property ownership. You may also want to consider having a living will. A living will informs a hospital of your wishes regarding your medical treatment if you become incapacitated. To be sure that your will is honored according to your wishes, find out whether your state of residence or home of record has any special requirements. Consider:

- What burial instructions do you have? Do you own a cemetery plot?
- Marriage license, divorce decrees, court orders relating to children, prenuptial agreements.
- Death certificates.
- Birth certificates, baptismal certificates, adoption papers.
- Citizenship papers, naturalization papers.
- Social Security cards and numbers for each family member. Keep a separate list of each person's Social Security number (SSN).
- Discharge papers (DD 214).
- In addition to the passports, keep a list of each person's passport number, where it was issued, the date it was issued, and the date it expires. You need that information to replace or renew passports.
- Copies of your current military permanent change of station (PCS) orders and your deployment orders. Include privately owned vehicle (POV) shipping documents, if applicable.

HEALTH RECORDS

- Health and immunization records for family pets. (See chapter I/7 for more information about deployment and pets.)
- Immunization records for each family member, health records for any family member with special requirements (including chronic health problems, allergies, etc.), as well as the location of each family member's medical records. Are immunization records up to date?
- Copies of eyeglass prescriptions and records of medications that are regularly taken by anyone in the family.
- Do you know how to use the military medical and dental facilities? Keep

central appointments, emergency, and other applicable phone numbers where you can find them easily. If you have civilian medical or dental care, what doctors does each family member see for care? Keep a list of names, phone numbers, addresses, and insurance information that relates to the care each provides.

- When do your family members need their next dental or orthodontic visits? What providers do you go to? If you do not receive care in a military facility, how is payment made? Do you have insurance to help cover the cost?

- Do you know how to get medical care when you need it? Do you know procedures for using military medical treatment facilities and for using TRICARE? If you know how to use these benefits and have the paperwork available, then when a need arises and your sponsor is gone you will not have trouble getting the care you need.

- Do you have medical insurance, including secondary policies such as Civilian Health and Medical Program of the Uniformed Services (CHAMPUS) or TRICARE supplemental policies? Do you know how to file claims and where to mail them?

PERSONAL RECORDS

- Keep a record of the military ID card numbers and their dates of expiration for each family member. Do they need to be renewed soon? If they expire in the sponsor's absence, do you know how to get them renewed?

- Are your dependents all enrolled in DEERS?

- Copies of temporary or PCS orders.

- Résumé of each spouse and transcripts (or addresses of school[s] to which the request for transcripts would be sent), if applicable. Are you or your spouse taking any classes? Will you try to continue them, or will you have to drop them? Talk to your school representative as soon as you are notified of your deployment.

- School record of each child, listing names, addresses, and phone numbers of each school that each child has attended and report cards.

- Income tax records.

- Official military records or documents, including copies of requests for allotments and information about your TSP account, if you have one.

- Automobile or motorcycle title and registration for each vehicle. Do you have a boat or other type of recreational vehicle that you need a title or registration for?

■ Do you have extra keys for your car, house, or safe deposit box? Where are
   they kept?

HOUSEHOLD MANAGEMENT

As you continue to prepare your family deployment guide, include a separate page or section for household items that may need attention or maintenance during the separation. You may want to consider the following items as you do this:

AUTOMOBILE CARE

■ Automobile (list separately for each car): What kind of gas does your car
   use? Does your family know how to check the oil and tires? How much air
   goes in the tires? Can each driver change a flat tire? When does the oil need
   to be changed? How much and what kind of oil does it need? What about
   filters? How often does the car need to be tuned up? Do you have a maintenance schedule for the family to follow? What kind of battery does the
   car need if it needs to be replaced? What size and type of tires do you use?
   How can you tell if they need to be replaced? Where should they be
   bought? What kind of muffler does your car have? If it needs to be
   replaced, where should it be purchased? Where should the car be taken for
   repair if there is a breakdown (list the name, phone number, and address)?
   When does the vehicle registration tag (military installation sticker) and
   inspection or safety sticker (where required) expire? How can it be
   renewed? When do your license plates need to be renewed? Does your
   family know how to do that, where to go to do it, and what paperwork or
   fees they'll need to take along? Who is your automobile insurance agent
   (list the agent's name, phone number, address, and your policy number)?
   Does each driver know what to do in case of an accident? Where, how
   much, and when do the insurance payments need to be paid? Is the car
   paid for? If so, where is the title? If not, who holds the lien? When and
   where are loan payments made and how much are they?

■ Are you living in an area where you use gas coupons, or do you pay for
   gas with cash or a credit card? How and where do you get gas coupons?
   What paperwork is needed? What kind of gas does your car use?

■ Do you belong to an auto club? Do you have towing service? What are the
   phone numbers for these services? When are dues payable, how much are
   they, and where are payments made?

■ Do you have a first aid kit, a flashlight, maps, and extra water or other weather-appropriate supplies in your car?

HOME MAINTENANCE

- Lawn care: Does the family know how to operate and maintain the lawn mower? Do they know what kind of oil and fuel it uses? If your family isn't sure, take them outside for a lesson or make a plan together for how the yard will be cared for. If the lawn mower breaks down, where do they take it for repair?

- Furnace/air conditioning maintenance: Does your family know how to check and change the air filters? What type and size filters are required? Do you have extras available? Where do you go to buy them? How often do you change them? Does the unit need servicing periodically? How often and when? How is your system fueled? Do you need heating oil or coal? Where do you get fuel? Who does the servicing and maintenance (list the service company's name, address, and phone number)?

- If you have a gas water heater, furnace, or fireplace, do both spouses know how to light them and operate them? Who do you call for help?

- Be sure to keep your dryer free of lint. You may want to check the accordion hose behind the dryer for lint periodically to prevent a house fire.

- Do you have power outages periodically because of wind or severe weather? Be sure that you have candles, flashlights, and fresh batteries available. Do you have a non-cordless phone (landline) or cell phone to report power outages? Most cordless phones do not work at all without electricity. You may want to have a backup plan for phone use so that you don't feel isolated if the electricity goes off.

- Computers: Do both spouses know how to operate and take care of the computer and change ink cartridges in your printer? What type of ink cartridge does your printer use? Where do you buy them? Do both spouses know how to prevent and eliminate viruses on computers? Who will you call for help with computer issues during deployments?

- Household inventory: Do you have a list of your household items, appliances, and electronic equipment and their serial numbers? Most insurance companies recommend that you take pictures of electronic equipment and appliances that have serial numbers and keep the pictures with those serial numbers. You also need this information for military moves. Some items you may want to check for serial numbers are refrigerators, ovens, portable dishwashers, TVs, VCRs, CD players, DVD players, other stereo component parts, all computer components, sewing machines, bicycles, treadmills or other sports equipment, lawn mowers, and humidifiers.

■ Do you have a list of repair services to call if anything in the house breaks down? (These might include plumbing, heating/furnace maintenance and repair, air conditioning, electrical, washer and dryer, water heater, dishwasher, garbage disposal, oven, microwave, refrigerator, computer, stereo equipment, bicycles, etc.)

■ Does the family know the location of the fuse box or electric control panel for your house or apartment? Do they know how to operate the breaker switches and change fuses? Do you have extra fuses?

■ Bicycles: Do the family bicycles need to be registered or licensed? If so, when do they expire and how will they be renewed?

■ Home security: Do all of your windows have locks that work? Does your family know how to test the smoke alarms and turn them off if they go off accidentally? Is each family member careful to keep the home secure—do they lock the house if no one is at home and during the night?

■ Do you live in a climate that makes use of screens or storm windows as seasons change? Do you know how to change them and where they are stored? If they need repair, who do you call?

■ Do you know how to check your roof for leaks and keep rain gutters cleared of leaves? Who do you call for roof repairs?

■ Do you have a fireplace? Do you burn wood, or is it gas? Where do you get and store your firewood? Does your family know how to use the fireplace and ventilate the smoke correctly? Who do they call if they need to have the chimney cleaned? It should be checked every year if you use the fireplace regularly. Does everyone in the family know how to clean the hearth and safely dispose of remnants from the fireplace?

■ Do you have a pool or spa? Is your family safety-conscious about its use? Do they know how to care for it and treat it with chemicals? Where do you buy chemicals? Does it matter what brand you use? Who is responsible for regular maintenance? Does it need to be drained or treated for seasonal changes throughout the year? Who do you call for service or problems?

■ Where are your family's tools? Does everyone know how to use tools (flashlight, hammer, wrench, regular and Phillips screwdrivers, pliers, etc.) for basic repairs?

■ Where does your family keep extra light bulbs and batteries?

FAMILY MANAGEMENT

■ Key phone number list: You may want to keep a list of telephone numbers for key military installation facilities near your telephone. Many military Family Support Centers provide a magnetized list of all installation and civilian key telephone numbers for families to put on their refrigerators. The numbers listed may include the hospital emergency room, poison control, Security Forces/Military Police, the fire department, the installation operator, the chaplain (including where to reach the chaplain during non-duty hours), the Red Cross, the Family Support Center/Army Community Service (ACS), your First Sergeant, your Commander, the hospital central appointments, the vet clinic, and vendors for household maintenance. You may want to include names and numbers of neighbors, friends, or relatives.

■ Emergency numbers: Do you have a list of all phone numbers that might be needed to take care of an emergency located near your phone? Remember that if a babysitter takes your children to a hospital, he or she must have a power of attorney along with proper ID in order for your children to receive care. Have you provided for that possibility?

■ Household chores: Do both parents know what must be done to keep the house clean and orderly? Do both parents know what chores are suitable for each child by age and which chores the children do regularly? Do you have a schedule for routine chores? If the person who likes to do the cooking is deployed, what plan will your family follow for meals? Who will cook and do the grocery shopping?

■ Laundry: Do you know how to sort and wash the clothes? What laundry products do you use? Do you know what things have to be machine or hand washed? Do you know when to use hot or cold water? Do all of your clothes dry in the dryer? At what settings? If they don't go in the dryer, what care do you give them? What has to be ironed? How hot should the iron be? Do you use steam? What water do you use for the iron? Read labels on clothing for help.

■ Hygiene: Do you normally wash your children's hair, bathe them, or supervise their tooth care? Are they brushing every day? If a child is too young to fix her own hair, do both parents know how to do it?

■ Clothing: Do both parents know what stores to shop at for clothes for each of the children? Do both know what amount of clothing each child needs at one time and any special requirements they might have (for ballet, soccer, band, etc.)?

1/6: PREPARATION FOR SINGLE-PARENT AND DUAL-MILITARY FAMILIES

◪

If you are a single-parent or dual-military family in which both spouses are vulnerable to deployment, perhaps this book will be most useful to you if you think "caregiver" when you read *spouse*. As you prepare to deploy, you have to answer many of the same questions as your married coworkers. Does your unit know how to contact your relatives and your children's caregiver? Do you have someone to take care of your car and your mail while you are deployed? What about finances? Perhaps you have only your own name on your checking account. Who will pay your bills for you while you're gone? Things such as car payments, insurance, and credit-card statements will continue. Should you add someone's name to your checking account or get someone a power of attorney to take care of your bills? How will you file your tax forms while you're gone? If something happens to you, does your will specifically designate what your wishes are for your finances?

Even more important than that, however, is the care of your children. The military requires you to designate someone to care for your children if you are deployed or separated from your family. Your family care plan may need to be revised every time you move to a new duty assignment. If the plan you make won't work, your family will suffer when you're deployed. Make sure that your plan is workable—without depending on your Commander to tell you what parts of your plan need improvement.

Your plan should provide for both short-term and long-term care of your children in your absence. You should have an alternate caregiver selected in case your primary caregiver becomes unable to take care of your children. Can you financially meet the demands of the plan you have? If you can't afford to send your children to the person you choose as caregiver, your plan won't work. Remember to consider everything, including costs, as you make your decisions.

Some parents decide to send their children to grandparents, aunts and uncles, friends, or ex-spouses. Choose carefully who will care for your children, and as you consider who to ask, think about your children's relationship with the person you select, as well as that person's ability to provide long-term care for the children. You want to choose someone who will care for your children lovingly and who will keep you informed about how things are going. Many of the parents who left children with ex-spouses were disappointed afterward, because they didn't receive the communication they wanted during the deployment. You have to know the personality and reliability of the potential caregiver before you make such an important decision.

You've probably already filled out a dependent care certificate, but if you haven't, do it now. Do you need to make temporary arrangements for someone to care for your children until your designated caregiver arrives or until your children can be sent to the caregiver? Will your children be cared for in your home? Your family deployment guide should include the following information for the person who cares for your children in your absence:

- Names, phone numbers, and addresses of your extended family members.
- Name of your duty station or ship and duty mailing address.
- Does your unit know where your children will be? Give your unit the name, address, and phone number of your caregiver.
- Name and phone number of your Commanding Officer and First Sergeant (and Ombudsman, if applicable).
- Detailed information about each child, including full name, birth date, birthplace, favorite toys and foods, special comforts (pacifier or blanket), fears, and habits.
- For school-aged children: name of teachers, grade, school, and phone numbers. (Remember to update this every year.)
- Religious preference and place of worship. What are your desires for church attendance and the children's religious instruction in your absence?
- Note where your child's medical records are kept and list any medication that your child may be on, along with instructions about why the child needs it, how much the child needs, and for how long it is to be taken. List your pediatrician's name and telephone number. Make sure that your caregiver has a POA for your child's medical care.
- Make sure that each child has a valid military dependent ID card. If the

cards expire and you are absent, how will they be renewed? Your caregiver should also have access to copies of your children's birth certificates and a record or photocopy of their ID cards. If your children lost their ID cards while you were gone, how would they be replaced?

- Dentist's name, address, and phone number; frequency of visits, and when the next appointment is due to be scheduled (also for orthodontist if applicable).

- Your expectations and standards for discipline. You might want to make a note of specific methods of discipline you use or what works best for a particular child.

- Who to contact in case of an emergency. Be sure that your caregiver knows how to get assistance through the Red Cross, Family Support or Family Services, Accounting and Finance, the legal office, chaplains, Personal Affairs, and military aid societies. (See chapter V/2 for a description of relief societies, and chapter V/5 for the contact information of each agency.)

- Names and phone numbers of friends who might be resources for the caregiver.

- Do you expect the caregiver to attend parent conferences at school? If not, who will? You may want to give your children's teachers self-addressed and stamped envelopes and ask them to keep you informed of your children's school progress.

- Ask your caregiver for a regular description of your children's growth and development. Knowing what they are doing at each stage of growth will help you feel included in their care.

- Make sure that there is a clear understanding of who possesses legal custody of your children. If you have custody as a result of divorce, give the caregiver a copy of the divorce document. The caregiver also needs a POA to act *in loco parentis* (as parent). General information about legal issues that may affect you can be found at www.nolo.com.

- Will the deployment affect child support payments?

- If your family includes stepparents and stepchildren, custody is an important issue. Authority over children may not be a simple matter for a stepparent, both legally and emotionally. Laws regulating stepfamilies differ from state to state, so be sure to find out what laws apply to your family. Be sure that there is a clear understanding about what authority each biological parent has and also how much authority a stepparent may need.

- If the stepparent is married to a custodial parent, what will happen if the non-custodial parent wants custody during the deployment?

- Do you need these documents: special power of attorney, custody agreement, hold harmless agreement (if the caregiver lives in military housing)?

- Will your house be occupied while you're away? If not, you may want to ask the housing office, a friend, or your landlord to look in on it from time to time. Notify the police that your house will be empty so they can check it periodically. Perhaps you should leave a key with someone you trust.

- How will you arrange your finances to enable your caregiver to support your dependents?

- Do you need to get your caregiver access to the military installation? Do you need to get your caregiver access to the commissary and exchange? Even if the caregiver is not eligible for these benefits, he or she can purchase items for your dependents' use.

- Is there a pre-deployment briefing that you can ask your caregiver to attend with you? Is your caregiver interested in being included in any family support groups that may be available while you're gone?

- What documents do you have to get notarized?

- Be sure that your will has guardianship provisions.

- Review all of the above every year to be sure that it is still effective.

How to Get the Forms and Documents You Need

- Dependent care certification: See your unit orderly room. If you have questions, ask the orderly room clerk, First Sergeant, or Commander.

- Birth certificate copies: Request copies from the state of birth. You can call your military personnel customer service for each state's vital statistics office.

- Social Security number: Ask your military personnel customer service for information.

- Special ID cards for children under age ten: Ask your military personnel customer service for information. The most common reason a child under age ten would need an ID card is that the dependent is leaving the area to live with a caregiver during the sponsor's absence. In that case, the ID would be necessary to use CHAMPUS or TRICARE. This type of ID is limited to the time you are absent, and you need orders to process the card.

- Paperwork to make the caregiver a commissary agent: Obtain a commissary agent letter from your military personnel customer services. The letter can be drafted close to the time you leave. It requires the name and address of the caregiver of your dependent and the dates the caregiver will need commissary access. Proof of dependency and inclusive dates of the sponsor's absence are also required. The caregiver, as your agent, is permitted to purchase items at the exchange and the commissary only for the dependent, not for himself. You may want to ask whether unexpected delays in your return will affect your caregiver's access after your projected return date.

■ Paperwork to give the caregiver access to the installation: Your caregiver should be allowed on the military installation with a POA for that purpose. File a copy of the POA requesting installation access with the Security Forces (SF) or Military Police (MP), and your caregiver should always carry a copy. If the caregiver drives his or her own vehicle on the installation, it will have to be registered with Pass and ID.

■ Powers of attorney: Any POAs that you need may be obtained at your military legal office. You may need several specific POAs, and it is better to request several specific documents than one sweeping, general POA.

■ Paperwork to establish an allotment for the care of your dependents: Obtain paperwork from your military accounting and finance office. Make sure that the allotment goes where you want it to (possibly to a new account opened for that purpose) and that your caregiver's name is also on the account (you can also make your dependent secondary to the caregiver).

Start all of the paperwork early or have it in place before you are notified of your next deployment so that you don't have to rush to try to get it all done at the last minute. Ask your military legal office which documents need to be notarized.

Whether you entrust your children to a caregiver or to the parent who is not deploying, you must be sure that the appropriate person knows how to get medical care as it is needed. Because you are in the military, your dependents should have access to the nearest military medical facility. If care is not available there, or if you are too far away from a military facility to use one, do your dependents know how to use CHAMPUS and the TRI-CARE health-care system? Ask your health benefits advisor if you need more information.

I/7: DEPLOYMENT AND PETS

◩

Military members often enjoy having pets, but what happens to the pets when their owners are deployed? Sometimes, sadly, pets are abandoned—left to fend for themselves because there wasn't time to figure out how to provide for them when their owners deployed.

You can avoid leaving your pet on the side of a road somewhere if you plan ahead. You probably wouldn't think of doing anything that drastic, especially if your pet is like family to you. If you have a pet, you probably care about it enough that you want to provide for its care. There are a lot of organizations that are ready and willing to help if you don't have a friend or relative who is available to care for your pet.

Before we talk about who will care for your pet, though, let's discuss some of the things that you'll need to consider as you think about your pet's care during deployment.

- Would your pet be better cared for in a home with children or without children?
- Does your pet get along well with other animals? What if your caregiver has other pets?
- Do you want a caregiver with a large yard?
- Will you bring your pet's bed, cage, or kennel, as well as favorite toys, to the caregiver?
- Does your caregiver know how your pet likes to play? Will he play with your pet while you're away?
- Does your pet need exercise or special care? Be sure that your caregiver has all the details.
- Friends or family members who already know your pet can offer the pet more security than someone new. They also give you the security of knowing that your pet is lovingly cared for.
- Be sure your caregiver has access to the veterinarian of your choice.

- Be sure that your caregiver and the veterinarian have your pet's medical history, a record of any surgery the pet has had, the pet's vaccination record, and any medications the pet may need. Be sure that the caregiver can get any additional medications or medical care that may be needed in your absence. You'll want to be sure that your pet's immunizations stay current while you're away.

- Will you need to get a power of attorney for any care or provision related to your pet?

- Be sure to discuss how the expenses of caring for your pet will be taken care of. It's a good idea to write a contract that defines financial responsibilities. Remember, as the pet's owner, you are responsible for the veterinary expenses and the feeding of your pet, even when you're deployed. (For information about contracts, see the Web site listings later in this chapter.)

- Your caregiver should know how to care for a pet. You can better enable him to care for your particular pet by writing a personality profile of the pet. In the profile, include information about the animal's temperament, what it eats, how much it eats at a time and how often to feed it, habits, things the pet does and doesn't like, how it relates to children, how it relates to other pets, and anything else that would be helpful. You may want to ask the Humane Society whether they can provide you with a sample pet profile.

- Do you have any insurance policies that relate to your pet? If so, give information about the insurance to your caregiver.

- Be sure your caregiver knows how to contact you while you're deployed and also has contact information for someone in your family or a local point of contact. If you aren't available and a decision has to be made about the pet's care, the caregiver may want to discuss it with your family or other point of contact before making a decision.

- If your pet becomes sick while you're gone, be sure that the caregiver knows what you'd want him to do.

- What if your pet dies while you're deployed? You'll want to be sure that the caregiver knows how to notify your family. What do you want the caregiver to do if the pet dies? Have a plan made in case it's needed.

Once you've thought about all of the details involved in having your pet cared for during a deployment, you may have an idea about who to ask to care for the animal. Usually, a friend or relative is a logical choice if they're available and willing to help. You'll want to be sure that whoever cares for your pet and the pet are comfortable with each other. If the potential care-giver isn't already acquainted with your pet or has a pet that your pet hasn't interacted with before, you'll probably want to arrange an introductory meeting to see whether they fit together.

Military members don't always know someone who can care for their pets during deployments. If you don't know someone personally, you can still arrange good care for your pet. If there is a veterinarian that provides care for your pet, you may want to ask if she knows of a reputable foster service in your area. You can also ask local breeders or the Humane Society for recommendations. There are a number of Internet sites that bring pet owners and foster caregivers together.

- Net Pets

www.netpets.org

This Web site has a link on the home page to "Military Pets Foster Project." They provide references for the caregivers they recommend and also information about veterinarians. You can fill in an online form describing your pet, and then, at no cost to service members, they will match each pet with a suitable foster home. Of course, they'll also accept volunteers to be caregivers.

- 4 Military Families

www.4militaryfamilies.com

This Web site offers a lot of practical information for military families. Click on their "Pets" section for tips.

- The Humane Society

www.hsus.org

The Humane Society doesn't offer foster care services, but they're still a good resource for military pet owners. They may have foster program referral information, and they also provide checklists and a sample pet contract form.

- Feline Rescue

www.felinerescue.net

On the Feline Rescue home page, you'll see a link to "Operation Noble Foster" to help you with foster care. They maintain a database that you can use to search for a caregiver. They ask pet owners to submit a "pet résumé" to help with placement. You can also download a sample contract form at this Web site.

- **Foster Pets**

www.fosterpets.com

This Web site offers specific areas for different types of pets. It also deals with the death of a pet and pet monuments.

Hopefully, with all of the resources available, you can find a suitable caregiver for your pet. Unfortunately, your pet cannot deploy with you. There are good reasons why they can't come along. Obviously, veterinary care in a deployed location would be a problem, as would availability of pet food. But, the most important reason your pet can't deploy with you may be its own safety.

On one of my husband's deployments, even though pets weren't allowed, an Airman sneaked his cat along. He kept the pet in his room, until one day it got out. Large coconut crabs, so called because they could crack a coconut open, roamed freely in the area. Well, everyone surmised that the Airman's cat met up with a crab when they found the cat with one of its legs completely missing one afternoon. The Airman nursed the pet back to health, but he felt bad that the cat was permanently maimed.

Don't take an animal with you on a deployment. If you absolutely cannot find a caregiver for your pet, don't just turn it loose with the hope that it will find a home. It's cruel to do that, and the animal will surely suffer if it's abandoned. Domesticated animals are used to being cared for and won't know how to survive on their own. Give your pet away, or bring it to the Humane Society to be adopted if you deploy and cannot provide for its care.

I/8: PARENTS OF MILITARY MEMBERS

◩

We may think about the needs of spouses and children when military members deploy, but not all service personnel are married. Whether military members are married or single, they have parents, and parents are also affected when they deploy.

BEFORE YOU GO

by Bob Hefner

Dear child I'm proud to see you go,
Although your leaving hurts me so.
My mother's heart is full of pride,
Even though a million teardrops I've cried.
As you go forth answering your country's call,
Your uniform makes you look so tall.
I'm not alone in the way I feel,
Thousands of mothers are facing the same ordeal.
Before you go please hold me tight.
I'll pray for you both day and night.
Give me a smile as you walk away.
Stay safe and come back to me someday.[1]

Parents are concerned about the safety and welfare of their grown children and like to be included in their lives. Young military members may not communicate as frequently as their parents would like to hear from them. When they deploy, their parents may worry. During deployments, parents may need reassurance and support. They may not know others who have children in the military.

Dover AFB held a "take your parents to work day" to provide a connection between military members and their parents. A Commander expressed appreciation to the parents of the military members, and he acknowledged the role that the parents play in support of the military. He also gave the parents an overview of their military sons' or daughters' lifestyles. The parents were given tours of the base and the aircraft and observed a military dog handler demonstration. Of course, the day also provided time for families to enjoy being together.

Parents learned a lot about what their sons and daughters do in the military and gained appreciation for their hard work and sacrifices. Military members discovered that it meant a lot to show their parents what they do at work, to see their interest, and to feel their pride and support. Parents are often proud of the accomplishments of their children. Seeing them in their work environment may help parents become more comfortable during deployments and confident that their children are now well-trained adults.

A schoolteacher whose son was in Iraq turned her concern for him into a teachable moment for her class. She had a computer in her classroom and shared messages from her son with the children. They saw him on her computer screen, dressed in his BDUs, and they learned about the war in Iraq. After her son's tour was finished, he came to the classroom to meet the children who had become his pen pals.[2]

There are many similar stories that could be told. Each of them illustrates that both the parent and the military member are encouraged and feel support when they can connect from a distance. If you are the parent of a military member, think of ways that you can connect with your military offspring from a distance, as well as when you're together. Just remember that you aren't the center of their lives like you were when they were children. If you are a military member, try to keep in touch with your parents on a regular basis. They want to feel included in your life and hear about how you spend your days, and your communication is a great way to show them that you love them.

It can be hard for parents to make the transition as children grow up and move out of the home. The parental roles evolve from caregiver to nurturer to teacher to advisor and eventually to mentor and friend. Many young people join the military during transitions in their parents' roles. That can create emotional confusion for the parents, who are proud to see their children go off on their own but who still may feel protective and concerned about whether their children are ready for the increased responsibility.

Letting go of children is different for each of us. For some parents it may not be traumatic, but for others it may be. If our children are in the military, they face potential danger. A mother named Anne expressed her ideas about letting go on the Military Wives and Moms Web site:

> We need never "let go" of love, concern, support and prayers for them. But we must "let go" in a way that does not cause them to worry about us. We must "let go" with pride in them and what they are doing.... We must "let go" with our blessing. This is our role here on "the home front."[3]

Parents do adjust to the fact that their children are grown. Some parents' roles on the home front are impacted and adjusted in unexpected ways when their children serve in the military. Sometimes, parents of military children are asked to take care of grandchildren during deployments. Caring for children can be quite an adjustment for empty nesters—but also very rewarding. They provide more love and security for grandchildren whose parents are deployed than other caregivers may. Although parents of deployed military members may have concern for their absent sons and daughters, the contribution that they make in grandchildren's lives can give them a feeling of fulfillment. The children and the grandparents are drawn together in mutual support for the deployed loved one and for one another. The deployed military members are relieved to know that the children are in a loving and nurturing environment.

When some military members deploy, someone in their unit contacts their parents periodically to offer support and encouragement. Parents can also call people in the unit for information. Parents may find support in a number of ways.

In San Antonio, Texas, there is an active chapter of Mothers of Military (MOM). Mothers who attend the monthly meetings receive a lot of support from one another as they talk about their children and experiences. They all have a loved one serving in the military and experience the same feelings and uncertainties. MOM is a national organization that was formed after the September 11, 2001, terror attacks. It's growing as it meets needs.[4]

If you're the parent of a military member, I encourage you to adapt ideas throughout this book to fit your needs. There are a number of Internet resources that you may want to investigate. See "Resources for Parents of Military Members" in chapter V/5 for a list of Web sites.

If you're a military member, try to communicate regularly with your parents. Your military service affects them, even if you don't realize it. Remember that they love you and are concerned about you. Good communication will help to ease their concern about you and will help to build an even better relationship with them.

I/9: MOBILIZATION OF GUARDS AND RESERVES

W hat if your Commander called your unit together and said, "You are going to be participating in the hardest thing we, the Army, ask you to do. Drop what you are doing, say good-bye to your family, put your career on hold, and put yourself in harm's way. For every minute you are there, we will be behind you. You will not be forgotten."[1] That's exactly what Brig. Gen. Christopher Powers, Deputy Commander of the Texas State Guard, told his deploying soldiers who had answered the call to volunteer for a tour of duty in Iraq at their send-off ceremony.

The Guards and Reserves are called to Active Duty more often now than they were in the past. They're no longer seen as weekend warriors but as vital elements of the total military force. The Chief of the Army Reserve emphasized that when he said, "We're changing from a force in reserve in which people believe they will never get mobilized to telling them up-front: The intent is to prepare you and your unit for mobilization, and the likelihood is you will be mobilized."[2]

When Jacob Young told his wife, Jamie, that he wanted to volunteer to deploy because of his patriotism and a desire to do something for his country, she was shocked but promised him that she could handle caring for their children alone.[3] As he and the other Texas Guardsmen prepared to go to Iraq, their families joined them at a barbecue dinner where children were given Future Soldiers Foot Locker Kits. The send-off helped prepare the families for the separation.

When Guard or Reserve members go to do their periodic duty, their families may not know much about what they do while serving. If at all possible, take your family to your Reserve or Guard center and show them what you do there so that a mobilization or send-off ceremony isn't the first time they have a connection to your military duty. Help them to understand that whether part-time or full-time, your family is a military family. Being a military family means that sometimes your life will be different than that of those around you. Help them to embrace those differences.

Your unit may offer opportunities to introduce families to what Reserve or Guard members do on their duty days or when they mobilize or deploy. The Maryland Air National Guard's 175th Wing held a Family Deployment Day. Guard members showed their families the airplanes and work centers and took them to visit booths that explained the role of legal, pay, insurance, and family readiness.

The 176th Wing at Kulis Air National Guard Base, in Anchorage, Alaska, held a weekend readiness conference to introduce family members to their mission and to teach them how to prepare for deployments. While the military members performed their drill weekend, family members saw the aircraft, had lunch in the chow hall, and learned about the military structure and benefits. Their briefings included presentations about the commissary, the First Sergeant's role, OPSEC, COMSEC, military pay, family programs, and legal and other military benefits and services, in addition to presentations that addressed preparing for deployments, getting through family separations, and reunion.

If your unit doesn't have an event to help family members understand your role in the military and its mission, you may want to suggest beginning one. As you consider helping family members understand your military service, you may want to think about whether your employer understands it as well. The National Guard Chief compared the National Guard to a stool with three legs: "One leg is the service members. The second leg is their families. The third leg for the traditional soldiers and airmen is the employers. Those legs must be in balance if we're going to have a solid, strong stool," he said.[4] You may want to consider the Chief's comments and include both your family members and employers in events held to increase their understanding of your role in the military mission. Do all you can to help those nearest to you to understand your military involvement.

The more you can communicate to your family about what you do in the Reserves or Guard and make them familiar with the military system, the better equipped they will be to deal with the call to Active Duty and family separation. Try to visit with the families of others with whom you serve. Tell your family that it's likely that you will be called to Active Duty for a period of time, possibly without a lot of notice. Tell them what benefits they'll be eligible for if you're activated. If you aren't sure what those benefits are, ask the Family Service Center, someone in your chain of command, or your unit chaplain. Many families of Reservists haven't taken advantage of the support systems or benefits that the military provides because they didn't know about them. Don't let that happen to your family.

As you consider how to care for your family as you prepare for mobilization or deployment, remember to fill out a Dependent Care Certification/Family Care Certification form. This form relates your temporary and permanent care arrangements for your family in your absence. If you are a single parent, you must have someone designated as a legal guardian in case you are activated (see chapter I/6). Lack of preparation for your family will not prevent you from leaving, but it will make your departure more difficult for your family members when you go.

If you live near an Active Duty installation, help prepare your family for the possibility that you may be activated by taking your family to the installation to see where things are located. Then if you are mobilized, going to the installation for benefits or help will not be as difficult for or overwhelming to them. Give them the name and phone number of someone at the installation whom they can call for help if you are activated. The branch of service of the installation nearest your family does not make a difference; military benefits are the same for everyone and available to anyone with a valid ID card. If you are not near an installation, there are Web sites that you can access to get assistance—for example, www.defenselink.mil/ra and www.guardfamily.org. More are listed in chapter V/5.

ID CARDS AND ACTIVE DUTY BENEFITS

In most cases, Reservists or Guard members will have enough notification of being called to Active Duty that they can bring their families to installations to get military dependent ID cards. If your spouse is activated or mobilized, he or she should get your family ID cards before he leaves. If that isn't possible, be sure that he gives you copies of his official orders so that you are able to use your military entitlements. The family also needs copies of the sponsor's orders after they have ID cards. Along with the ID cards, the orders are the legal document that verifies the family's eligibility for benefits on the installation.

Guard and Reserve members must enroll each family member in DEERS (Defense Enrollment Eligibility Reporting System). Enrollment in

DEERS allows your family access to military installations, commissary and exchange facilities, medical care, and other benefits. Even if you live too far from an Active Duty installation to use some of your other benefits, your family must be enrolled in DEERS to use medical benefits and TRICARE in civilian communities. Before the deployment, be sure that both spouses know the status of any civilian health or dental insurance that you may have and whether your deployment will have any effect on your coverage. Will you be entitled to any military health or dental benefits?

A Guide to Reserve Family Benefits, a booklet written to help family members understand their entitlements (some of which have been recently enhanced) is available from the family support organizations. You'll also find a lot of family deployment readiness information on the Reserve Affairs home page: www.defenselink.mil/ra. During deployments, many units and installations have meetings for spouses or families to help them understand their benefits, to identify needs, and to provide support. Chaplains know what their installations offer to families.

FAMILY SUPPORT PROGRAMS

Families may not feel the need for military support groups unless they develop a military-related need that the civilian community can't meet, such as problems with CHAMPUS or TRICARE. It is important for families to have connections to the military so that military needs can be met, even if these families don't live near installations.

If you are a Reserve or Guard member and are called to Active Duty but don't live near an installation, a support network still may be available to your family. Ask what family programs are available before you deploy. Even if he or she is also being called to Active Duty, the chaplain is likely to be one of the first to know about family programs, since he or she is there to serve the needs of the people. (Refer to chapter II/9 for more information about support groups.)

There are a number of Web sites that are very helpful to families who do not live near installations. Look for them in chapter V/5. Preparation for how Reserve and Guard families will meet their needs and find support is an integral part of getting ready for the possibility of mobilization.

Many Commands have family days and programs like the ones in Maryland and Alaska that include family briefings as part of mobilization exercises. Family briefings teach families about the roles of the Reserves and

Guards, the benefits that are available, and how to use the benefits. Family Program Coordinators provide assistance to Reserve and Guard families when service members deploy and work to help family support groups. National Guard families should ask for their state's Family Program Coordinator or the local contact for that person. Army Reserve families can find help with their family support group, family support liaison officer, or unit administrator. The Air Force Reserve has civilian employees who work at the Family Readiness Centers to meet family needs. They also have a Reservist on staff who is a trained family readiness technician and is available when the unit is on an active-duty base. Many Air Force Reserve centers even have videophones for families to use when members are deployed. Naval Reserve, Marine Corps Reserve, and Coast Guard Reserve centers all have Ombudsmen to help with family needs. Many Ombudsmen are married to Reservists and have firsthand experience in family separation issues. Ombudsmen can be found at the training centers.

In 1998 the first Joint Service Readiness Center opened in Minneapolis. The Air Force Reserve is the host unit, but other Reserve components are also involved. More Joint Service Readiness Centers will probably be opening as the military components work together rather than independently. Because the Reserve emphasis on family support is still emerging, military members should be attentive to what is available for families in their Command.

BENEFITS/ENTITLEMENTS

When Reservists are on Active Duty, their benefits normally include access to most military facilities, use of the exchange and commissary, use of dining facilities, limited medical and dental care, and access to most military recreational and entertainment facilities.[5] There are also some death benefits available to Reservists who die in connection with their military service.

Many states offer Reserve and Guard members benefits because of their military service. They may include exempting military pay from taxes, special license plates, and other leave and educational benefits. Check with your Command or state to see what benefits may be available in your area.

When Reserve or Guard members are mobilized, their families are eligible to use certain military facilities, such as the commissary (a nonprofit grocery store on the installation) and the Post Exchange (PX) or Base

Exchange (BX) (a nonprofit department store on the military installation). You need a valid military ID card to use these facilities. If you haven't used military facilities before and are unsure about how to use them, find someone who knows the system to take you to the installation, show you around, and review the rules for using the facilities with you. At first it may seem overwhelming if you haven't used military facilities before, especially because you may be upset because of the mobilization. But it's worth the effort to become familiar with the system and use your benefits.

Guard and Reserve families who understand the military entitlements that they have and who support the duty of service members find that they can adjust to mobilization or deployment better when they are prepared. One wife who knew and used her entitlements said that she saved money shopping at the exchange and the commissary and that "being in the Reserve has helped me become more self-sufficient.... I've surprised myself by learning to take care of these crises on my own. I guess that's what they mean by family readiness."[6]

Depending on the amount of time your spouse serves on Active Duty, you may be entitled to health or other benefits. To help you learn what they are, get a copy of *Ordered to Active Duty—What Now? A Guide for Reserve Component Families,* which is available from most Reserve or Guard units. Call your local unit to request a copy of this helpful publication if you don't have one. You can find telephone numbers for local Reserve or Guard units in the federal section of your telephone book. Your family will also benefit from making your own family deployment guide as described in chapter I/5. The drastic change that mobilization may create for your family will be minimized if you have plans made and resources available to turn to during the deployment.

If you are not familiar with the military system, find out what is available to you while your spouse is activated. That can be discouraging if you don't know where to start. However, the military system is not that difficult to approach and is ready to answer your questions and help you use your benefits. If you don't know where to start, call the unit chaplain or your spouse's supervisor or Commander. If you don't know these people, your spouse has not given you the preparation for Active Duty that you need, but you can still find the answers. Look in your local telephone book's federal section for the military branch that is nearest you and tell them that your spouse has been activated and you do not know what benefits you are entitled to or how to go about using them. Also ask whether spouse or family support meetings are held in your area. If they cannot help you, they will refer you to the right office. It will be worth the effort.

CIVILIAN SUPPORT FOR FAMILIES

There may not be other military families available to identify with if the Guard or Reserve member deploys individually or his whole unit does not go together. In some cases, the unit may deploy as a whole, but since Reserve and Guard members often commute some distance to maintain their military commitment, there may not be families of the unit in your area. The potential for insufficient support during family separations is one of the most critical issues that Reserve and Guard families face. However, many Reserve and Guard families do have established support systems in their civilian communities. They may have relatives or close friends, churches, or community involvements that provide stability and care for them during military separations. These relationships can provide a great deal of encouragement for families of deployed personnel.

DISRUPTION IN CIVILIAN EMPLOYMENT

Another important issue that Reserve and Guard members have to address is the disruption in their civilian employment. When they are activated, Reserve and Guard members may experience financial strain because their military pay is not on the same scale as their civilian pay. People who are self-employed may wonder whether they will be able to keep up with their expenses and whether their businesses will continue in their absence. The Soldiers' and Sailors' Civil Relief Act is designed to assist those with needs beyond their control (see the current year's *Reserve Forces Almanac* or *National Guard Almanac* or ask your legal office for more information).

If you're in the Reserves or National Guard and are self-employed, plan ahead for what will happen in your business if you deploy. If you have a plan ready, you will have less stress when you're mobilized. Perhaps you have an employee you could train to take over as necessary or an associate with another business similar to yours who will partner with you during your duty.

When Reserve and Guard members return from deployments, their employers may give them different jobs than the ones they had before they were mobilized. The pay may be the same, but the positions may be less career-enhancing. There is a law to help employers and employees coordinate civilian work with Reserve and Guard responsibilities. The Uniformed Services Employment and Reemployment Rights Act (USERRA) was signed into law in October 1994. It outlines the rights and responsibilities of Reserve and Guard members and of their civilian employers. USERRA requires Reserve and Guard members to give advance notice of upcoming military duty in order to retain eligibility for reemployment afterward (unless that is not possible because of the military mission). The employer is expected to give the member time off for duty and return the employee to his previous position afterward. Some Reserve and Guard members and employers may not be aware of all of the revisions in USERRA and may want to review them. They are outlined in the *Reserve Forces Almanac* and *National Guard Almanac.*

As a Reserve or Guard member, you may have to negotiate with your civilian employer because of your military duty. Plan to keep your employer informed of your military duty as far in advance as possible, both verbally and by written memo. When you inform your employer, remember to talk about any insurance that may be part of your benefits package and how your deployment will affect your coverage. If you are activated for more than thirty days, your health benefits may be impacted. Be sure that you know what your options are and have a clear plan to be sure that your insurance coverage continues. TRICARE may be a part of your answer. Learn how to coordinate health care provided by the military and by your employer.

Maintaining good communication with civilian employers should keep military duty from becoming a problem. Most civilian employers are supportive of Reserve and Guard member employees. If you have a problem with your civilian employer that you can't resolve, you may want to ask your Unit Commander for advice. If the Unit Commander isn't able to help, you can call the National Committee for Employer Support of the Guard and Reserve (NCESGR) at (800) 336-4590 and ask for Ombudsmen services, or find them online at www.esgr.org. NCESGR also has state chairmen in every state. (Their names and addresses are listed in the *Reserve Forces Almanac* and the *National Guard Almanac.* Information about how to obtain these books is found in the "Reserve and Guard Resources" section in chapter V/5.)

Although Reserve and Guard members and their families have some concerns that are different than those of Active Duty military personnel, the needs of all military component families are similar. Reserve and Guard members are part of the Total Force and are important to the military mission. Reserve and Guard families benefit from seeing themselves as military families, whether in part-time or full-time service.

I/10: THE ROLE OF FAITH IN YOUR PREPARATION

◪

The Bible, in Deuteronomy 24:5, says, "When a man has just taken a wife, he shall not go out with the army to war, nor shall any active service be required of him; he shall be free at home one year to enjoy happiness with the wife he has chosen."[1] Many military members have discovered that Uncle Sam doesn't follow the directive in that Scripture. In reality, too many newly married couples find themselves parted as early as during the first year of their marriages.

Whether Uncle Sam gets directives from the Bible or not, it is still a good place for us to turn to prepare for deployments—whether we have been married for a short time or a long time. We who base our faith on the Bible find strength there to face challenges. The Bible draws us into a closer relationship with God, who gives us strength to face the circumstances of life.

If you share your relationship with the Lord with those you love, you'll find that one element of family life that gives security to families is the nurturing of your religious faith. Establishing a routine of attending your place of worship, Sunday school or other religious education, and holding devotional time or Bible study helps in that nurturing process. If the family does these things regularly, when Dad has to leave for a deployment, the church community will still be a part of the family's life and is likely to provide comfort and support in his absence. That's the experience of a dual-military couple who prayed for protection, wisdom, and God's will as they prepared for an upcoming deployment.[2]

Many military families say that religious faith enables them to keep a more positive attitude and that military separations become opportunities for growth and experiencing God's care in a more intimate way. Some people find themselves moving toward faith for the first time when deployment affects their lives. For me, preparation for deployment would not be complete without prayer.

Some of us may wonder how to begin to pray or even what to pray for at a time like that. Dr. Charles Stanley came up with a very helpful tool called "31 Ways to Pray for the Military." He gives one topic, or focus, for prayer and a related Scripture for each day of the month. You can request a copy on the Internet at www.prayeroutreach.com. On the home page, click on "Military Prayer Page" and scroll about halfway down to find "31 Ways to Pray for the Military." You may want to look at that Web site for other prayers and encouraging articles too.

Individuals may find reassurance in their faith when they face the challenges of the military lifestyle. "I often wrestle with the natural conflict between my calling to be a military man and my calling to be a Christian husband and father. Yet I continue to see that the Lord has given me a calling to do both well. I have decided that the best thing I can do as a military man who feels called by God to 'stay with it,' is to look for other ways in which I can minister to my wife and family rather than to be frustrated by the ways in which I can't."[3] Some couples prepare for deployments by purchasing two identical Bibles and developing a reading plan that they will follow together so that both spouses can read the same Scriptures at the same time while they're apart. You can look to your faith for strength and decide that you will have the same positive outlook.

If you have questions about faith or God, go to your chaplain or spiritual leader and look for answers. The more answers you can find to your questions before you face trials, the stronger you will be when you find yourself tried. When you face hardship, you may still find yourself asking why, but you'll have the security of your faith in God and the knowledge that he is with you through it.

Many Active Duty military members and their families worship at military chapels. You may decide to turn to your chapel community for support and to the chaplains for help during family separations. Most chaplains would be happy to counsel with you and help you with spiritual needs as well as other difficulties. Remember that your chaplain can help you even if he or she isn't the individual you want to counsel with. He or she understands the military system and knows what it has to offer to solve your problems or meet your needs. In addition, chaplains are always ready to refer you to competent civilians in whom they have confidence. During times of mass deployment of personnel, there may not be enough chaplains or military professionals available to meet the needs of all of the families who are affected. Civilian churches, hospitals, counseling centers, and service organizations work hard to provide care to military families during times like this. Be aware of the support networks available to you during the separations that you face and take full advantage of them for your family.

I/11: CASUALTY PLANNING

◩

If an Active Duty, National Guard, or Reserve family member doesn't return from deployment, the difficult decisions that the family will be faced with will be easier to make if there is a plan in place before the deployment occurs. The military helps you begin the process by urging every service member to have an updated will before deployment. You can also make plans to enable your wishes to be carried out and ease responsibilities for your survivors. Discuss your ideas with your family and consult your legal office for information about how to make your plan most effective. You may want to consider the following:

- Where do you want to be buried? Are you eligible for burial in a national military cemetery and, if you are, do you want to be buried there?

- Do you own a cemetery plot? Where is it located? Where do you keep the deed?

- Where do you keep your will? The original should be located in a place where it would be easily found if you died and someone had to look for it. You may want to give a copy of your will to the person you name as your executor and to your closest relatives, who would likely be notified first if you died.

- Where do you keep guardianship papers or instructions for the care of your dependent children, if that isn't included in your will?

- Where would your family choose to live if you were killed? If you live in military housing, they would have limited time to make that decision.

- Where do you keep life insurance policies and other documents that need to be available in the event of your death? Does your family know what insurance policies you have?

As you plan for the possibility of a casualty, refer to section 4 of this book, "Some Don't Return," for ideas to help you understand what is involved in dealing with grief and funeral planning and how death notification is made. You can also ask your military casualty assistance office how you can prepare for the possibility of your death in order to assist your family's decision-making process during the shock of death notification and funeral preparations.

I/12: RESOURCES TO HELP YOU PREPARE FOR SEPARATION

RESOURCES FOR SINGLE MILITARY MEMBERS

Please see chapter V/5, "Resources for Single Military Members," for a more complete description and contact information for the following resources:

❖ *The Savvy Sailor, The Savvy Naval Officer,* **and** *The Savvy Marine Officer*
   by Ralph F. Nelson

❖ *Starting Your Military Career: A Guide for Single Service Members*
   A Scriptographic resource published by Channing L. Bete Company

RESOURCES FOR SPOUSES AT HOME

Please see chapter V/5, "Resources for All Military Personnel and Their Families," for a more complete description and contact information for the following resources:

❖ *Service Separations: A Wife's Perspective*
   by Beverly Moritz
   Available from Focus on the Family or Officers' Christian Fellowship

❖ *The Woman's Guide to Staying Safe*
   by Cheryl Reimold

❖ *Keeping Your Family Close When Frequent Travel Pulls You Apart*
   by Elizabeth Hoekstra

❖ *Footsteps of the Faithful*
   by Denise McColl

❖ *Married to the Military: A Survival Guide for Military Wives, Girlfriends, and Women in Uniform*
   by Meredith Leyva

❖ *Holding Down the Fort*
   by Peggy Sue Wells and Mary Ann Froelich

❖ *The Sailor's Savvy Spouse*
   by Ralph F. Nelson

❖ *Scriptographic Resources Published by Channing L. Bete Co.*
   Make the Most of Family Readiness Groups
   Family Readiness Groups: Caring for Military Families
   Family Preparation = Family Readiness; a Deployment Planning Kit
   Deployment Planner: A Guide for Military Families

❖ *Today's Military Wife: Meeting the Challenges of Service Life*
   by Lydia Sloan Cline

❖ *Heroes at Home: Help & Hope for America's Military Families*
   by Ellie Kay, www.elliekay.com

❖ **Military Wives Web Sites (also includes a site for military husbands)**
www.militarywives.com is the home of many great Web sites. For a complete listing see chapter V/5.

RESOURCES FOR FAMILIES

Please see chapter V/5, "Resources for All Military Personnel and Their Families," for a more complete description and contact information for the following resources:

❖ **Military HOMEFRONT**
www.militaryhomefront.dod.mil

❖ **Web Sites operated by the National Institute for Building Long Distance Relationships. Each Web site has great links, ideas, and information.**
Dads at a Distance: www.daads.com
Moms Over Miles:
   www.momsovermiles.com
Long Distance Couples:
   www.longdistancecouples.com
Grandparenting from a Distance:
   www.longdistancegrandparenting.com

❖ *The Savvy Sailor, The Savvy Naval Officer,* **and** *The Savvy Marine Officer*
by Ralph F. Nelson

❖ **Parent Center: www.parentcenter.com or www.babycenter.com**

❖ **National Military Family Association: www.nmfa.org**

❖ **Fatherhood Online: www.fatherhood.org**

❖ **Children's Booklets from Army Community Service (ACS)**
www.armycommunityservice.org (Virtual ACS)
   When you go to this Web site, on the left side of the home page, click on "Deployment Readiness" then "Deployment Tools" then "Download Center." When the page comes up, click on "Children's Workbooks." You'll see the titles of children's booklets.
   Print any that you are interested in, and remember that these are for everyone, not just Army families!

❖ **Booklets to Help Children of Deploying Parents: www. dma.state.mn.us**
The Minnesota National Guard has some great resources for families of any military component, whether they are Active Duty, Reserve, Guard, full-time, or part-time. Go to the Minnesota National Guard home page, click on FamilyPrograms. Then click on "Soldiers & Families." Then click on "Youth & Development" and then on "Youth & Deployment." As you scroll down, you'll see the booklet titles. Print them out for your family's use.

❖ **Publications by The Bureau For At-Risk Youth**
Military Family Forum Booklets:
   Deployment and Reunion
   Stress and the Military Family
   Loss and Change in the Military Family
   Family Communication
   The Military Lifestyle and Children
   Family Readiness
   The Single Military Parent
Other Products:
   Military Family Writing Kit
   Inspirational Magnets for Military Families
   Our Military Family Scrapbook
Coloring Books:
   I'm Proud to be a Military Kid
   I'll Miss You (military deployment)

Welcome Home (military reunion)

❖ **Scriptographic Resources Published by Channing L. Bete Company**

Know What? My Parent Is Being Deployed! for ages 6–8

Let's Talk About Deployment: An Information & Activities Book, for ages 9–12

My Book About When My Parent Has to Go Away; for preschoolers

Until Your Parent Comes Home Again, a coloring and activities book about deployment for ages 6–9

Who Knew? The Deployment Issue, for ages 9–11

Deployment Days, a coloring calendar for military families

Military Families Are Special, a coloring and activities book

Preparing for Mobilization

Write from the Heart stationery kits for children

Mission: Readiness: A Personal and Family Guide, Active Duty Edition

Mission: Readiness: A Personal and Family Guide for National Guard and Reserve Members, Reserve Duty Edition

Deployment Planner, A Guide for Military Families

❖ *Dare to Discipline* **and** *Bringing Up Boys* by Dr. James Dobson

❖ *Withhold Not Correction* by Bruce Ray

❖ *Daddy, You're My Hero* **and** *Mommy, You're My Hero* by Michelle Ferguson-Cohen at www.booksforbrats.net

❖ *101 Ways to Be a Long-Distance Super Dad ... or Mom, Too!* by George Newman
Available from:
  Blossom Valley Press
  5141 E. Woodgate
  PO Box 13378
  Tucson, AZ 85732-3378
  Phone: (520) 325-1224

RESOURCES FOR SINGLE PARENTS

Please see chapter V/5, "Resources for All Military Personnel and Their Families," for a more complete description and contact information for the following resources:

❖ **Parent Center: www.parentcenter.com**

❖ **Publications by The Bureau For At-Risk Youth**
Military Family Forum Booklet:
  The Single Military Parent

❖ **Scriptographic Resources Published by Channing L. Bete Company**

Until Your Parent Comes Home Again, a coloring and activities book about deployment for ages 6–9

About Family Care Plans

Making a Family Care Plan

Protect Your Family with a Family Care Plan

Let's Talk About Deployment: An Information & Activities Book

Guardians for Military Family Members: Their Special Role

❖ *Single-Parent Family* **edition of** *Focus on the Family Magazine*
8605 Explorer Drive
Colorado Springs, CO 80995
Phone: (800) 232-6459
www.family.org

❖ **Parents Without Partners**

1650 South Dixie Highway, Suite 510
Boca Raton, FL 33432
Phone: (561) 391-8833

This organization is international and offers discussion groups, workshops, and publications. They teach practical parenting and help single parents learn how to be alone without being lonely, how to communicate more effectively, and how to enjoy life as a single parent.

RESOURCES TO HELP CHILDREN

Please see chapter V/5, "Resources for All Military Personnel and Their Families," for a more complete description and contact information for the following resources:

❖ *When Dad's at Sea*

by Mindy L. Pelton

The author offers free personalized and autographed messages to children on adhesive bookplates. Contact her at peltonm@earthlink.net.

❖ *Uncle Sam's Kids: When Duty Calls*

by Angela Sportelli-Rehak

❖ *Saying Goodbye When You Don't Want To: Teens Dealing with Loss*

by Martha Bolton

❖ **Military Kidz Web site**

Military Kidz Web site is a sister site of www.militarywives.com. Access Military Kidz through of the link provided at www.militarywives.com or directly at www.militarykidz.com.

❖ **New York University Child Study Center:**

www.aboutourkids.org/articles/war

This Web site offers articles about talking with kids about terrorism and war.

❖ **American Academy of Child & Adolescent Psychiatry:**

www.aacap.org/publications/factsfam

This Web site provides practical articles to help children of any age group deal with trauma and war.

❖ **Military Student:**

www.militarystudent.org

❖ **Children's Booklets from Army Community Service (ACS):**

www.armycommunityservice.org (Virtual ACS)

When you go to this Web site, on the left side of the home page, click on "Deployment Readiness" then "Deployment Tools" then "Download Center." When the page comes up, click on "Children's Workbooks." You'll see titles of booklets that talk about military separations.

Print any that you are interested in, and remember that these are for everyone, not just Army families!

❖ **Booklets to Help Children of Deploying Parents: www.dma.state.mn.us**

The Minnesota National Guard has some great resources for families of any military component, whether they are Active Duty, Reserve, Guard, full-time, or part-time. To find the resources, go to the Minnesota National Guard Web site and click on Family Programs, and then "Soldiers & Families." Then click on "Youth & Development" and then on "Youth & Deployment." As you scroll down, you'll see the booklet titles. They will take time to download, as the note on the Web site says, but they are worth the effort. Print them out for your family's use.

❖ **Publications by The Bureau For At-Risk Youth**

Coloring Books:
  I'll Miss You (military deployment)
  I'm Proud to be a Military Kid

❖ *The Business Traveling Parent: How to Stay Close to Your Kids When You're Far Away*
  by Dan Verdick

❖ **Scriptographic Resources Published by Channing L. Bete Company**

Until Your Parent Comes Home Again, a coloring and activities book about deployment for ages 6–9
Let's Talk About Deployment, an information and activities book for ages 6–9
Deployment Days, a coloring calendar for military families
My Book About When My Parent Has to Go Away, for preschoolers
Know What? My Parent Is Being Deployed! for ages 6–8
Who Knew? The Deployment Issue, for ages 9–11

HELP FOR CHILDREN FROM LIBRARIES

Any library has books to help children understand family separation. Ask your librarian to help you find them. The following list is a few titles to get you started:

❖ **Books at the Juvenile Level:**

Surviving Your Parents' Divorce
  by Charles Boeckman (see chapter 3, "What to Do About Your Own Feelings")
Coping When Your Family Falls Apart
  by Dianna Daniels Booher (see chapter 7, "How to Cope")
Everything You Need to Know About Living

With a Single Parent
  by Richard E. Mancini

❖ **For Younger Children:**

Don't You Know There's a War On?
  by James Stevenson
I Love My Mother
  by Paul Zindel
Will You Count the Stars Without Me?
  by Jane Breskin Zalben
The Terrible Thing That Happened at Our House
  by Marge Blaine
Will Dad Ever Move Back Home?
  by Paula Hogan
The Giving Tree
  by Shel Silverstein
The Goodbye Painting
  by Linda Berman

ARMY RESOURCES

Please see chapter V/5, "Army Resources," for a more complete description and contact information for the following resources:

❖ **Army Wives Web site**

Army Wives Web site is a sister site of www.militarywives.com.

❖ **Army Family Team Building**

Army Family Team Building (AFTB) is a comprehensive training resource to help families understand and become comfortable with Army life.

AIR FORCE RESOURCES

Please see chapter V/5, "Air Force Resources," for a more complete description and contact information for the following resources:

❖ **Ombudsmen**

The Air Force has an Ombudsman program to help families with deployments.

❖ **Family Readiness NCO**

The Air Force has appointed and trained Active Duty NCOs (non-commissioned officer) to work at the Family Support Centers to meet the needs of the families of deployed personnel.

❖ **Air Force Crossroads: www.afcrossroads.com**

This site gives information about all Department of Defense installations and also has an Air Force Spouse Forum. The forum is designed for spouses and provides communication on Air Force issues to assists spouses during family separation.

❖ **Air Force Wives Web site**

Air Force Wives Web site is a sister site of www.militarywives.com.

Navy Resources

Please see chapter V/5, "Navy Resources," for a more complete description and contact information for the following resources:

❖ *When Dad's at Sea*

by Mindy L. Pelton

The author offers free personalized and autographed messages to children on adhesive bookplates. Contact her at peltonm@earthlink.net.

❖ *Uncle Sam's Kids: When Duty Calls*
by Angela Sportelli-Rehak

❖ *Footsteps of the Faithful*
by Denise McColl

❖ *Daddy's Days Away* **(a deployment activity book for parents and children) and** *Navy Family Deployment Guide*

Phone: (800) FSC-LINE or (757) 444-6289
Ask your Navy Family Services Center for these resources.

❖ **Navy Wives Web site**

Navy Wives Web site is a sister site of www.militarywives.com.

❖ **Naval Services FamilyLine/LIFELines Network:**

www.lifelines.navy.mil/familyline
From the home page you may want to begin by clicking on "Welcome Aboard." There are links to several topics.

Navy Programs and Workshops

❖ **Couples Pre-Deployment**

Couples Pre-Deployment prepares couples for the emotional cycles of deployment. Suggestions are given for ways to cope, communicate, and keep connected while apart. It's usually presented two months to one week before departure.

❖ **Singles at Sea**

Single sailors are informed about financial issues, maintaining communication with family and friends, planning for reunion, and learning how to make the most of the deployment. This program is usually presented two months to one week before departure.

❖ **Financial Planning for Deployment**

Financial issues, including budgets, allotments, savings, bills, powers of attorney, and wills are examined. This program is sometimes presented with the Couples

Pre-Deployment Program or Singles at Sea Program and sometimes as early as five months before the deployment.

❖ **Parent/Child Pre-Deployment**

Parent/Child Pre-Deployment prepares parents and children to cope with confusion and anxiety related to the deployment. During the parents' meeting, the children participate in age-specific planned activities that are supervised by trained Navy Family Support Center staff members. The program sometimes includes a puppet show to help children learn how to deal with their worry about the deployment and is presented during the two months to one week leading up to departure.

MARINE CORPS RESOURCES

Please see chapter V/5, "Marine Corps Resources," for a more complete description and contact information for the following resources:

❖ *What's Next? A Guide to Family Readiness for the U.S. Marine Corps*
(includes helpful checklists and forms)
    Available from your Family Services Center

❖ **Marine Corps Wives Web site**
Marine Corps Wives Web site is a sister site of www.militarywives.com.

COAST GUARD RESOURCES

Please see chapter V/5, "Coast Guard Resources" for a more complete description and contact information for the following resources:

❖ **Coast Guard Wives Web site**
Coast Guard Wives Web site is a sister site of www.militarywives.com.

RESERVE AND GUARD RESOURCES

Please see chapter V/5, "Resources for Reserve and Guard Personnel and Their Families," for a more complete description and contact information for the following resources:

❖ **Guide to Reserve Family Member Benefits**
Available from your Family Support Center or on the Reserve Affairs home page at www.defenselink.mil/ra.

❖ **Handbook for the Guard & Reserve**
Annual insert to the *Military Times* newspaper, available every August. Available by subscription, in military exchanges, or in libraries.

❖ **Reserve Wives Web site**
Reserve Wives Web site is a sister site of www.militarywives.com.

❖ **National Committee for Employer Support of the Guard and Reserve**
Phone: (800) 336-4590

❖ **Scriptographic Resources Published by Channing L. Bete Company**
Preparing for Mobilization
Annual Training
A Family Guide to Annual Training
About Family Care Plans
Protect Your Family with a Family Care Plan
Mission: Readiness: A Personal and Family
    Guide for National Guard and Reserve
    Members, Reserve Duty Edition

ARMY RESERVE RESOURCES

❖ *What's Next? A Guide to Family Readiness for the Army Reserve*
(includes helpful checklists and forms)

❖ **Family Readiness Online**

The Army Reserve offers Family Support Programs to help families prepare for deployments. Many of these programs are part of the Army Family Team Building (AFTB) program. Operation Ready specifically addresses readiness for families. To access information online, look at the list of Web sites available in "Resources for Reserve and Guard Personnel and Their Families" in chapter V/5.

AIR FORCE RESERVE RESOURCES

❖ **Air Reserve Headquarters Hotline**
Phone: (800) 223-1784, ext. 71294

COAST GUARD RESERVE RESOURCES

❖ **Coast Guard Reserve Web Site: www.uscg.mil**
Look at the right side of the Coast Guard home page under "Our People" and click on "Reserve." There you'll find a lot of great information about deployment/mobilization and many other topics.

RESOURCES FOR PEOPLE SUPPORTING AND SERVING MILITARY FAMILIES

❖ **Patriot Greeting Cards: www.patriotgreetings.com**
Patriot Greetings is an online store that was founded by two veterans. They have cards for each military branch, as well as cards that are appropriate for all branches.

❖ *Caring for Military Families: Facing Separation, War, and Homecoming*
by David A. Paap

Available from
Stephen Ministries
2045 Innerbelt Business Center Drive
St. Louis, MO 63114-5765
Phone: (314) 428-2600

❖ **Parents Away Group**
Laurel Bay Schools in Laurel Bay, South Carolina, have a program called Parents Away Group. The school counselors present the idea to children at the beginning of each school year, asking how many parents are deployed or away from their families. They send a letter home with the children, explaining the support group and giving the parents or caregivers the opportunity to allow the children to participate.

At the support group meetings, children are encouraged to bring family pictures and postcards or presents from the absent parent, or to talk about special activities that the family is involved in. The structure of the group varies, but the objectives are to help the children realize that they are important members of their families, to promote sharing and expressing their feelings, and to provide activities that will help children communicate with the absent parent. Counselors may use world maps or globes to show each child where his parent is in relationship to where he is. They may even take group pictures to send to parents. You may want to begin a group similar to Parents Away Group in your community if there is no support group for children in your area.

❖ *While You Are Away*
by Norma Kimrey Colwell
Illustrated by Gloria Sallings
Available from
    MAR*CO Products, Inc.

Department S97
1443 Old York Road
Warminster, PA 18974
Phone: (800) 448-2197 (Monday-
Friday)

While You Are Away (order # WA910) can be used to help pre-kindergarten through sixth-grade students with family separation. The program contains plans and activities that can be used with individuals or small groups. (It is used by Parents Away Group, listed above.)

❖ **National Military Family Association: www.nmfa.org**
2500 North Van Dorn Street, Suite 102
Alexandria, VA 22302-1601
Phone: (701) 931-6632

This is a national organization whose sole focus is the military family. One notable project that they offer is Operation Purple, a summer camp for children.

❖ **Military Family Resource Center**
CS4, Suite 302, Room 309
241 18th Street
Arlington, VA 22202-3424
Phone: (703) 602-4964; DSN: 332-4964

The Military Family Resource Center has a wide variety of Web sites and programs to provide help, referrals, and information. The Web sites that they run include Military Children and Youth, Military Family Week, Parenting Initiatives, Child Abuse Prevention, and many more. Visit their Web sites for topics of interest to you or your organization.

❖ *Working with Military Children: A Primer for School Personnel*
by the Virginia Joint Military Family Services Board
Available from
    Military Family Clearinghouse
    4015 Wilson Boulevard, Suite 903
    Arlington, VA 22203-5190
    Phone: (703) 696-5806; DSN: 426-5806

This publication is targeted for school staff and guidance counselors in particular. It addresses the role that schools play in supporting the children of military service members. It includes an activities section for teachers to use with individual children or in groups.

❖ *Keeping Your Family Close When Frequent Travel Pulls You Apart*
by Elizabeth Hoekstra

This book provides an honest and practical view of family separation. There are questions for discussion and family-building resources after each chapter, making it an excellent tool on which to base a family-separation workshop or conference.

II

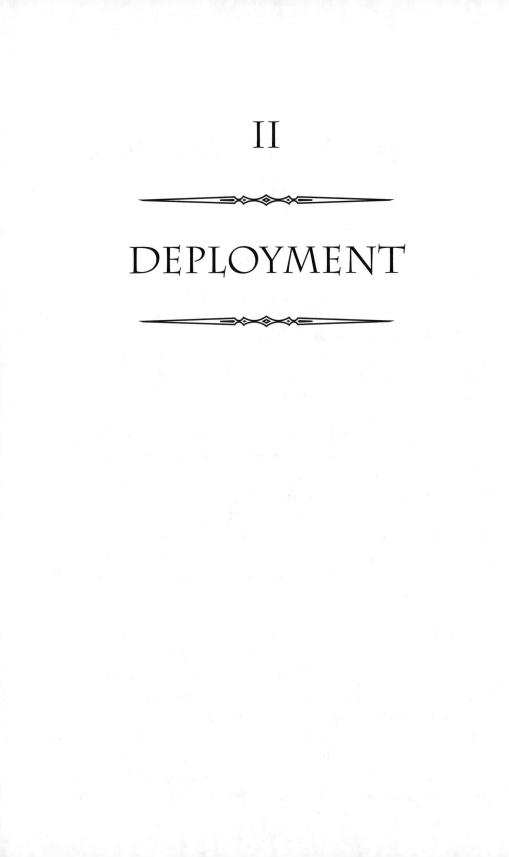

DEPLOYMENT

II/1: SURVIVING SHOCK

◨

It was a warm August afternoon, and I was still in shock emotionally. I wanted to write Ren a letter but wasn't sure where to begin. How do you start a letter to your husband when he was jerked away from you with only two hours' notice, without warning? He left for a classified location and didn't even have an address to give me.

As I sat and thought about what to write, I wanted to tell him how upset I was that he was sent away so suddenly and unmercifully. If only we had been warned about what to expect. My mind wandered through a lot of "what if's" and "if only's."

Ren had been gone for two weeks and finally called me to give me an address. The phone call was so short that I'll always remember every word:

"Let me quick give you this address so you know where to send mail, and then if we're cut off, you'll have it."

I scribbled it down as fast as he could dictate it to me, and then the phone line went dead. The ninety-second phone call was over.

At least now I have some connection to him, I thought. I decided that I'd write to him every day until he was on his way home. I didn't dare to think about how long that would be.

I began the letter by telling him how glad I was to hear his voice on the phone and to know that he had arrived safely at his destination. I told him all I could remember about what we did during the past two weeks. Dan and I had just returned from Michigan. I had mixed feelings about writing about our visit with the Dutch relatives, because Ren looked forward to seeing them, and I knew he felt bad about missing their visit. But I was determined to include him in all we did, so I told him all about the visit. He missed enough by not being there in person, I reasoned; I'd do whatever I could to help him visualize it. (He later told me that it meant a lot to him to hear about our trip.)

My emotions were on a roller coaster as I wrote that first letter. I had so many questions that couldn't be answered: "Will there be a war?" "How long will Ren be gone?" "Will he stay where he is or be moved to another location?" "If this is military life, do we still want to make it a career?"

The last question was the only one I could answer with certainty: Yes! We loved the military lifestyle and knew that separations could come. I dreaded the prospect of being separated, but now that Ren was deployed I knew that there would be faith and strength to endure. God called Ren to be a military chaplain, and I knew he would take care of our family, each in our separate locations.

All of the local radio and TV stations wanted to talk to Desert Shield families. A TV station called me to request an interview. I was repulsed by the negative attitudes being shown on TV interviews and said no. Many of the wives who were interviewed behaved as if they didn't realize their husbands could be called on for military action, and they were bitter about the deployment. As I wrote to tell Ren about it, I thought about the request that I had turned down and decided that I'd say yes if I was asked again. (I was.) Maybe I could show a healthy and positive attitude in spite of the uncertain circumstances. (I did.) I wrote everything that I was thinking.

After I finished the letter I walked to the post office to mail my ten-page first communication to my husband. I still didn't look forward to the separation, but I felt a change in my emotional response to it. Looking backward, I realize that I was coming out of my phase of shock and beginning to mentally plan how I would endure.

I would take one day at a time and keep a positive attitude. For mutual support, I decided to look for other wives whose husbands were gone. Shared time would be more pleasant and move faster than time alone. I'd go to the base support meetings every week too. The more I thought about it, the more I began to believe that Dan and I could make it through the separation.

PRAYER POEMS FROM A WIFE'S HEART

MOTHER'S VISIT

by Beth Blase

There she is, Lord,
Hallelujah!
You've brought her safely
Through ice and snow.
She looks terrific
At seventy-four.
She insists on relieving me
Of some of these responsibilities
For a spell.
She has a story
That outdoes any predicament
I've been in this year.
How she makes me laugh!
Lord, she has a great appreciation
For where I'm at.
She was thirty years a military wife.
She was often single-handed
"Holding down the fort."
Next to You, Lord,
She's the only one
Who understands me right now.
Thank You so much
For her friendship
And her rescue.[1]

FRUSTRATION

by Beth Blase

The car won't start
The dog won't wait
The baby won't stop
The phone keeps ringing
The toilet keeps running
The moths are everywhere
The toys are everywhere
The frig is empty
The dryer is full
The yard needs mowing
My hair needs washing
My daughter needs money
My purse is missing
My son is missing
Hold Everything!
Lord, I give my exasperation to You,
For you are sufficient
I will not give up,
I will give thanks!
Because for all of these situations
You, my God, are able
"to make all grace abound
Toward me,
Always having all sufficiency
In all things"
So that I might have
An abundance of Your grace
For every good work.

(Meditation verse: 2 Corinthians 9:8)

II/3: GOING, GONE

◩

Parting from a loved one is an emotional experience that we all handle in our own ways. One wife accurately expressed what many of us feel when our spouses deploy: "Deployment Day finally arrived. I am experiencing a myriad of emotions: sadness, fear, excitement. The excitement is not the happy type of anticipatory excitement, but more of getting ready to travel into unknown territory. I want to do a good job at this."[1]

Family separations are a fact of life in the military. Military families are likely to experience deployments more than once. Perhaps you'll be facing deployment soon. Whether it will be your first separation, or the second, third, or more, think about how you will respond to the notification and to subsequently sending your loved one off on a deployment or leaving your family to deploy. You may receive notification of your deployment months, weeks, or days ahead of your expected departure. On the other hand, you could have only hours or minutes to prepare.

Whatever amount of notification you receive, the effect is that the family is separated and must adjust to this change in their lives. "When that last olive-drab truck full of soldiers roars down the dirt road to an unnamed field site, or that Navy ship shoves out to sea for an extended deployment,"[2] or when the one you love boards the plane for other parts of the world, "many a military spouse left behind to juggle the household begins to wonder what malicious schemes Murphy's Law has in store for her."[3] Military wives know that whenever their husbands are gone repairs need to be made or children have accidents. But if the family prepares for separation, the wife will have no reason to fear even though she may still feel the shock of a sudden separation, because she knows what to do and where to find help.

The shock may take days or weeks to subside. Once your loved one is gone, you may feel like I did at first: You go through the motions, thinking that you'll wake up tomorrow to find out that it was a dream and that life is normal again. Expect to have mixed emotions. Maybe you'll be introspective or feel overwhelmed. Maybe you'll wonder why it seemed so easy for your loved one to go. You may feel anger. All of those responses are part of the shock of separating, and processing the change and emotion will take time. Shock at a time of change is not something that should be seen as weakness; instead, it should be viewed as a natural part of the body's emotional response to change. It enables wives whose husbands are deployed to adjust to the change and to "'catch up' emotionally with what they already understand intellectually."[4] Facing these feelings and recognizing them as understandable under the circumstances helps wives feel emotionally healthy instead of as if they are losing their faculties. Fears are minimized and they can carry on with life more effectively.

WHEN IT'S TIME TO SAY GOOD-BYE

When the day of departure comes, each family must decide who will go to see Dad leave. Some families say it's easier to watch him go together, even though the parting may be emotional. Whatever you decide, it's important for each family member to say good-bye individually.

Many wives feel a sense of relief once the good-byes are finished. That can be especially true for families who receive notification months or weeks before departure. They've anticipated the pain of separating, and waiting for it to happen can seem as unpleasant as the separation itself. Relief from the pain of saying good-bye is met with the challenge of going on with life at home without Dad.

Your family may find it easier to leave the departure location if you have an activity planned or something special to do. Depending on the ages of your children and their interests, you may want to go to the zoo or a park or go to the mall. When my husband left on short notice, our sixteen-year-old son and I went to McDonald's and then to register him for school, since it happened to be our assigned day to do that. It gave us an empty feeling to see my husband leave suddenly, but going to school cemented into our consciousness that we had to go on with life on our own. It was a good beginning for us because we were immediately brought into a routine that we would have followed even without the separation.

When you face family separation, think of routine things that have to be done as a way to help you get on track and survive the time apart.

Recognize that the separation demands some adjustment but that your family life can stay remarkably similar to your regular routine while you incorporate the necessary changes. Expect to miss your husband and have times of loneliness, but also expect that the time apart will be a time of growth and drawing closer to each other in new ways. Many women say that separations help them learn to be more independent and give them confidence that they can handle more at home than they thought they could.

11/4: TIPS FOR DEPLOYED PARENTS

◩

There are a number of things you can do to show love and care to your family while you're separated from them. Let them know that you've arrived at your location safely. Communicate often with them. Write your family letters and tell them as much as you can about where you're living and what you're doing. Give them an idea of what a day is usually like for you now. Any details you can share with them will help them visualize you in your surroundings and feel like they have a tangible connection with you. If there are brochures of sight-seeing attractions or literature about the area where you are deployed, send them to your family. If it's possible, take pictures to send home. You may find that keeping a calendar diary is a good way to communicate with your family. Each day, write on a calendar at least one thing you did that day, and at the end of the month send the page to your family.

COMMUNICATING WITH CHILDREN

Children enjoy receiving small souvenirs, patches, bumper stickers, buttons, stamps, shells, rocks, leaves, flowers, or pictures from the absent parent. You may want to make up games to mail to your children. For example, you could make a word search puzzle with a list of words and see how many your children can find. Maybe you'd like to play chess by mail with older children, each of you getting one move per letter. Games may stretch out over a long time, but they add anticipation to writing and receiving letters.

Children like to share special secrets with their parents, and you can incorporate a sense of personal connection to your children by finding unique ways to communicate with each of them. You may want to work out a special code, assigning a different letter to each letter of the alphabet so that when you write a message in code, only the child with the key can interpret the message. For example, *Q RQPP LAM* says *I MISS YOU*. If you keep a record of the key and send one to your child, you can use the same code throughout your deployment. You can develop a different code and key for each child.

Some children enjoy getting multiple-choice letters. For example, you could write the following:

> *Dear Bobby,*
>   *Today I was (a) thinking, (b) singing, (c) sulking, or (d) dreaming,*
> *about you. You were (a) in school, (b) at home, or (c) at the zoo with me,*
> *and we were looking at (a) pictures, (b) your math homework, (c) the rain,*
> *or (d) a zebra. Love, (a) Your Dad, (b) King Kong, or (c) Grandma.*

You could put the answers on the back of the page: *answers: a,c,d,a.*

Variations of the multiple-choice letters could be true/false test formats. Ask your children which of two foods is better or what activity is more fun to participate in or watch. Fill-in-the-blank questions could also be a fun way to get your children to tell you their favorite classes in school or their favorite television shows. Use your imagination to tailor ideas to each child.

You may already be close to your children, but as they grow, they change, and innovative letter-writing while you're away can help you keep up with subtle changes as they occur, as well as make letter writing fun. The way you choose to do that will depend on your children's preferences and your own. Try to think like each child does to help you decide what type of communication to use.

Children appreciate mail of their own from their missing parent; they love to see their names on an envelope or a postcard. Depending on your children's ages, you might want to use stickers, colored paper or pens, or different types of lettering when you write to them. You might want to share in your letters to your children that you miss them but that since you can't be there right now, you're glad that you can at least write to them. If you express some of your feelings to them, it will be easier for them to sort through and talk about their feelings. When you write to them, encourage your children to write back to you by telling them what you enjoyed from their last letters, and compliment them for writing good letters to you.

You may want to ask your children to tell you how your favorite sports teams are doing and make a game of guessing which teams will win certain games or championships. Don't forget to ask them to tell you about games that they may be playing too. Maybe your children aren't involved in sports, but they play the piano or another instrument or take art, ballet, or singing lessons. Ask them what they are involved in, what they enjoy about it, and how they're progressing.

If you have trouble coming up with ideas, *The Business Traveling Parent* by Dan Verdick suggests over one hundred ways for parents to stay close to their children when they're separated. Verdick includes activities to do with your children before you leave, while you're gone, and when you get back home. He also gives resources to expand on some of his ideas. His book is available at most bookstores and is worth asking for, even if the store has to order it for you.

II/5: COMMUNICATION FROM A DISTANCE

◩

An important way to nurture your marriage is to communicate freely and often. One of the best ways to do that from a distance is by letter. Some families find it helpful to date their letters or mark them with a small number somewhere on the envelope so that the person receiving it will know which letter was written first if they are received out of order, which you should expect during most deployments. Others like to communicate by telephone or e-mail.

We've become used to cell phones and instant messaging, so many of us have developed a mind set of expecting to talk to someone whenever we want to. We may become impatient if we have to wait even a short time to contact someone. During deployments we have to consciously change that way of thinking, or we will be frustrated and upset about long-distance communication.

We can't expect to be able to communicate with our loved ones whenever we get the urge to talk to them while we're separated because of duty. Cell phones may not be available, and even if they are, time zones and work schedules may interfere. Don't expect that you'll be able to use cell phones during deployments. Depending on the deployed location, telephone calls and the use of the Internet may or may not be possible. If telephones are available, remember that calls are likely to be very costly, so keep them within the budget of your family. Expect to rely on less technological and more old-fashioned means of communication.

PHONE

Phone calls can be disappointing because each spouse is so excited to hear the others' voice that they hardly know what to say. After the phone call they may spend the whole day thinking about everything that they wish they had said. So if you decide to communicate by phone, you may want to try to make a list of things to talk about before your call. As you go through each day and think of something to share with your spouse or to ask him, write it down. Then you can refer to your notes when the phone rings or when you write your next letter.

Keeping a list of things to communicate is a good way to remember to share details about the family's activities with your spouse and for your spouse to share his or her life with his family at home. Lists may seem cumbersome, but they will help you communicate more of yourself to your spouse while you are separated. If you can avoid writing to your spouse or speaking on the phone when you feel down or frustrated, you will also be able to communicate better. During those times you aren't your true self, and later you will probably regret something you said or the way you said it.

TAPE RECORDERS AND VIDEOTAPES

Exchanging tapes can be an inexpensive way to hear each others' voices without as much time-consciousness as may be necessary during phone calls. You may want to talk about the list of things that you want to communicate to your spouse that you have trouble knowing how to write and don't have time to talk about during phone calls. On tape you can take time to describe details and talk about how you feel. You may want to give each child an opportunity to talk to Dad or Mom, or tape school programs or sporting events that they are involved in for Dad or Mom. Of course, Dad or Mom must have a recorder or VCR available for his use.

E-MAIL

Computers are often available in deployed locations, so your family may have the option of communication by e-mail. Many people find it easier to send an e-mail than to write a letter, so they communicate more often by computer. Some family members send messages almost daily. That takes a lot of the pain out of the separation and keeps morale higher. Some units have computers that families of deployed individuals can use if they don't have one at home. Ask your unit whether e-mail will be available during your family's separation. Remember that e-mail is not a secure method of communication. Your message may be read by other people, so don't use it to talk about things that you want kept private.

If you know that your spouse will share the use of a computer with others, you may want to put his or her name and rank in the subject line so that your message is immediately identified as his or hers. Sometimes attachments cannot be transmitted to deployed personnel, so you may want to find out if your spouse can receive them before you send any. If you send pictures, also send your spouse printed photographs that he or she can put up in his or her living or work area.

VIDEO LINKS

Videophones allow families to see and talk to each other from a distance. They can be hooked up to any phone system and are used by military families when the components are available. This form of communication can be a mixed blessing, because some people say that they miss each other more when they can see their loved one but cannot touch him or be near him. However, there is comfort in seeing firsthand that family members in both locations are well, and the visual contact may help families envision the deployed member in his or her new surroundings. Ask your Unit Command or Family Support Center whether video links are available in your area.

MARS

An often unknown and less usual method of contact during deployments is MARS, the Military Affiliated Radio System. MARS operators are ham radio owners who are certified by the Federal Communications Commission and meet the qualifications to participate in the MARS program. They are volunteers who try to provide a point of personal contact for service members and their families. MARS operators have a strict code of confidentiality. The MARS operators will call you to verify that they've reached the correct person, give you their name and location, tell you they are MARS operators, and tell you who they are calling for. The operator will ask you whether you've talked on a patch phone. Be sure that you understand how to use it, because there is a delay between speaking and hearing, and you must say "over" when you want the other party to respond. The deployed person must initiate the call, and conditions must be just right for the calls to come through. These calls are billed as collect calls from wherever the MARS operator is located. So, while you can't rely on MARS calls for regular communication, they may provide a morale boost if they're available to you.

TELEGRAMS

Some families may want to send messages by Western Union during times of separation. Birthday, anniversary, or other special messages can be sent and received quickly. To ask for information or to send a message by Western Union, call (800) 325-6000.

LETTERS

When you write letters during deployments, remember mail delays often occur in correspondence with locations outside the continental United States. Mail from either direction may be delivered in three or four days, or it may take three or four weeks. So, if you don't receive mail from your spouse for a week or two, that is not necessarily a sign that your partner isn't writing to you. You may receive four or five letters at once and then have a week without mail. These delays can be frustrating, but if you expect them to occur you won't jump to the conclusion that your mate has forgotten you. In spite of mail delays, letters are a preferred way to communicate during separations.

You'll probably treasure letters from your loved one and feel a more tangible connection to your absent spouse as you read and hold the letters. Marshéle Carter Waddell, wife of a Navy SEAL (acronym for sea, air and land) and author of *Hope for the Home Front*, shared in her book why she prefers written letters to emails.

> I liked knowing *his* hands had held and folded the notepaper. I liked seeing and retracing the curves and angles of *his* handwriting. I liked the hearts and doodles *he* had lovingly sketched in the margins.... Every e-mail evaporated with one click, but a shoe-boxed record of Mark's handwritten devotion to me is neatly stored for my future reference and for our children to read and remember their father's love while he was away from them.[1]

I share her perspective. Letters are a good means of communication because they can be read over and over again. Knowing that your husband may read your letter several times, write him the details of home life that you know he misses and will enjoy hearing. Express appreciation for something he mentioned in the last letter or package you received. Without becoming overly nostalgic, you can mention something in each letter that will remind your spouse of a special memory you share, secrets between the two of you, or things that make you feel close to each other. It may help you write as if you are talking to your spouse if you have a picture of him in front of you while you write your letter.

Try to encourage, rather than criticize, in your letters. Let your husband or wife know that you appreciate the way extra challenges are being met, whether at home or for the military mission. Even though you may be miles apart, you can still have meaningful communication. Make communicating with each other a priority. Try to communicate that priority by telling each other as much about what is happening in your lives as possible.

Don't be afraid to share feelings with each other in letters; share them openly and specifically. Try not to leave your spouse wondering what you were trying to say. When you're sharing feelings in letters, don't assume that you know what your spouse means or try to read between the lines. If you aren't sure about what he's trying to say in his letter, ask questions or for more information in your next letter. Don't risk misunderstanding each other, but the fear of misunderstanding should not prevent you from sharing from your heart in your letters. Many people discover that it is easier to write about their deepest feelings and thoughts than it is to talk about them.

It can also be difficult to share household problems when your spouse is too far away to be able to help you. Try not to let your letters become negative when you write about family problems. If you prepared a family deployment guide (see chapter I/5) before the separation, you should have answers to most of the problems that could arise or at least know who to call for help. Then, instead of writing to your spouse about the problem when you feel helpless to deal with it, you may be able to write to him or her to share how you successfully solved it. You'll be able to tell him how happy you are to have the deployment guide that you made together before he left, and he will be able to tell you how proud he is of the way you took care of the problem. He will admire your ability to manage your household so well.

Our son Dan and I decided to help each other learn to drive my husband's stick-shift car after he deployed. We'd drive to a deserted area of the base in the evening as it was getting dark and take turns driving until we both felt comfortable shifting without killing the engine or jerking the car.

Then we decided it was test time, and one night we went to the commissary parking lot. The driveway to the parking lot was a steep hill, so we drove halfway up, stopped, and tried to continue up the hill without rolling backward or killing the engine. It was a comical sight, I'm sure, and it took more than one night of practice, but we finally mastered it. We both felt good about our accomplishment, and my husband enjoyed getting letters telling him about our little driving classes.

You may decide to get a job while your husband is deployed. When you write, tell him where you work, what your job is like, and what you do. Describe how you get there, what the building looks like, and what your work area is like. Then he can try to visualize you at work and will feel closer to you. You may enjoy keeping journals and sharing them with each other when he gets home. Maybe it would be fun to make up a questionnaire of thoughts you'd discuss if your husband was at home and send it to him. Send him cards or letters that you've received from friends who may not be writing to him at his deployed location.

INCLUDE THE CHILDREN

In addition to hearing from you, your husband wants to hear about and from your children. Pictures are a great way to show him your children's growth and interests. Encourage your children to write to Dad on a regular basis, maybe once a week or once every two weeks. Some families enjoy making a Sunday afternoon project out of writing to Dad, with everyone writing notes to put together in a family care package. If your family has a pet, Dad might enjoy hearing a story about the pet's activities that week. One of your children may want to write to Dad from the pet's point of view.

If you have small children or a baby born after Dad leaves home, he will want to keep up with each new stage the child grows through. In your letters, describe her looks, little things that she does (pulls on her toes, sucks her thumb, twirls a strand of hair, combs Mom's hair, tries on sunglasses, etc.) and her vocabulary development. Try to give Dad an idea of every child's growth, personality, and interests, regardless of his or her age level. If you have a new baby, you might want to send him the baby's footprint or handprint or a strand of hair periodically.

If you're expecting, you could include your unborn child by tracing a silhouette of your growing belly and mailing it to your husband. You may want to draw a hand on it to show him where you feel the baby kicking. Be creative. Your communication to your husband about your children can take the form of journal entries; you can add ideas or things that they've done as you think of them and mail an installment weekly.

MAKING TIME TO COMMUNICATE

The family at home and the deployed parent may each want to keep calendar diaries. The family can choose to keep one as a corporate project or each family member can keep a separate calendar. Use a calendar that has room to make a note each day or make your own calendars for each month. Each person can write at least one thing on his calendar before he goes to bed each night. At the end of each month everyone can mail his or her calendar pages to Dad.

Try to write more than once a week or once a month, though. Think of your letters as your time together if he were at home, and talk to him by writing as much as you would if you were talking to him in person. Even if you do this carefully and tell him everything, you will find later that there are things that you forgot to tell him and that he missed out on in your home life. We still discovered things that my husband missed a year after he returned from being deployed, and while he was gone I wrote daily to be sure he didn't miss anything. The more you share in letters about your daily lives, the easier it will be to understand each other when he gets back home.

Missing out on things that happen at home is inevitable because he is *not* there, but if you make a concentrated effort to communicate, often you can minimize the strain of what is missed and make him feel like he is still included in the family. Send your husband news about the relatives, neighbors, and friends. (Of course, he can return the favor by telling you about his friends, what he does when he is not on duty, and how he feels about his work—anything that is on his mind.) You may want to send him clippings from the newspaper or a copy of his favorite magazine.

CARE PACKAGES

A care package is a good way to let your deployed spouse know that he's loved and on your mind. Remember that his living space is probably limited, so it may be best to send him things that are disposable. Check with the post office to see whether there are any mailing restrictions before you prepare a package. There may be regulations about the size parcel you may send or about the contents you may include.

Once you know what mailing regulations allow, think about your spouse receiving your package. He or she will most likely open it in front of other people. Privacy is often hard to come by when you're deployed. Don't send something that is so private that your spouse would be embarrassed to have others see it. Before your spouse even receives the package, customs inspectors may open it. Care packages convey love, but they should not be expected to convey intimacy.

Care package items might include spiral notebooks, paper, envelopes, stamps, pens, gum, candy, trail mix, a favorite snack food, taped TV shows, puzzles, games, music tapes or CDs, videotapes or DVDs, magazines, newspapers, comics, your child's artwork, aspirin, Tylenol, shampoo, toothpaste, a toothbrush, soap, towels, new underwear or socks, family pictures, thumbtacks, tape, a few Christmas decorations, etc. Pack the box carefully, with enough paper that the contents don't shift when you tip the box, and use reinforced tape to seal the box. If you are sending a box for a special occasion, be sure to allow plenty of time for delivery if mail is slow.

If you send candy, cookies, or food that is not professionally sealed, ants may invade your package and enjoy your goodies before your husband gets it. I always wrap food in plastic wrap, then insert it into a sealed baggie. If I have metal tins available, I put baggies of food inside the tins before mailing. Before I learned to do this, one Christmas we received a luscious-looking box of homemade fudge from some relatives—that was full of red ants. Our family made a joke out of it, but we were sure disappointed to have to throw it away. Don't let that happen to any goodies you mail.

Be creative as you make care packages. You know what your husband enjoys. Let him know that you are thinking of him and waiting for his return. He wants to know that he's missed, just like you want to know that he misses you. Do all that you can to keep your husband involved in the family. Some families enjoy making a family newsletter to send to Dad. If there are grandparents, aunts, uncles, or cousins who are close, you may want to include them in your newsletter. Children may want to include news about school or other activities they participate in.

OTHERS CARE TOO!

Enlist the help of your children in your effort to keep your husband informed. If decisions that affect them can wait until you hear from him again, ask your children to write and discuss it with Dad before you make the decision. Children of all ages can sense your attitude and will imitate, to some degree, your response to the separation. Think about the fact that you set the tone for your family's response to the separation. If you have an attitude that honestly communicates that "it hurts to be apart, but if we all stay positive we'll get through this and be able to handle whatever comes our way," you'll probably be surprised at how much easier it is to handle the daily trials that you encounter.

It will also be easier to handle the separation and maintain a positive attitude if you know that others are contacting and encouraging your deployed loved one. One soldier in Iraq received monthly care packages from his home church. Someone at his church stuffed BDUs and sat the stuffed soldier on a chair, with a picture of the deployed soldier where the face would be. A backpack was placed on the floor between the feet so that people could bring goodies to include in the care packages. His family was happy to see others sharing their concern and love for him.

II/6: CARING FOR CHILDREN WHILE A PARENT IS AWAY

◣

Children don't have enough life experience to know how to react when a parent goes away for military duty. Research shows that the way children respond to family separation is probably connected to their sense of identity and how they relate to others instead of connection to the pain of saying good-bye to their parents. Children react to the stress at home caused by the separation and specifically reflect their mothers' reactions to their fathers' absence instead of their own grief that he's gone.

Many people say that children who have a strong bond with their father miss him more when he leaves but get used to his absence faster. Randall Lindsey, a professor at California State University at Los Angeles who specializes in education and outreach for at-risk youth, said, "Typically ... younger children fare best during deployments—and the shorter the deployment, the better for all."[1] Lindsey agrees with other researchers in his emphasis on meeting the needs of families, as well as the mission, in planning deployments. If the needs of families are considered and an effort is made to help meet the needs, both parents and children will be able to cope with the family separation more effectively.

Needs can be met on individual levels and also in groups. For example, the National Military Family Association (NMFA) sponsors summer camps called Operation Purple around the country to bring military children from all branches together and to help them deal with deployment-related stress. The NMFA is an organization dedicated to serving military families. They offer a number of wonderful services and resources, and I encourage you to look at their Web site, www.nmfa.org, to learn more about them. The Web site explains Operation Purple further.

One of the camp directors, Scott Cross, who is a veteran himself, is happy to work with the children of soldiers. "It makes it a whole lot easier to be over there doing what you need to do if you know your family is being taken care of," he said.[2] As he observed, it does make it easier for the deployed parent to know that his or her children are involved in programs like Operation Purple, but it also makes life easier for the parent who is at home with the children. The caregiving parent will feel relief that he or she doesn't have to carry the responsibility alone when there are others who are available to help with the children, and that makes the parent feel better equipped to deal with the children's stress.

Children usually look at their parents to learn how they should respond to the deployment. "Children will find their own way of coping.... The main influence on how well the children cope with the family separation is the attitude displayed both by the present parent and the absent one."[3] "If a separation is 'Mommy goes bonkers' time, the kids go bonkers too. But if Mommy remains cool, the kids remain cool."[4] How parents *act* during difficult times often teaches children more than what they *say*. If parents are positive and attentive to their children's responses to the changes, they can guide children through military separation with a minimum of difficulty.

A sensitive mother will tell her children's teachers that Dad just left so that the teachers will understand if there is a change in the children's behavior or performance at school. Then teachers can help evaluate the children's needs.

Junior high or high school children may be embarrassed to have Mom come to school but may appreciate the fact that you want to help them. You may want to inform their teachers with a phone call when the kids aren't around to avoid embarrassing them. Teachers at the higher grade levels are often role models for students, especially if they are involved in special activities like band, choir, sports, or plays. If those teachers know that a parent is gone, they may use the opportunity to show support for the young person without even specifically talking about the deployment.

Don't be afraid to let the adults in your teenagers' lives know that Dad is deployed. Your teenagers may be more open to talking to adults outside of the family. That's one reason it's important to know the people your youth relate to. They are learning to grow away from you as their parents and to make their own decisions, and you can help them go through that process by giving them the freedom to talk to responsible adult friends. Let your older children make the decisions that they are ready to make and maintain open communication with them without smothering them.

Even though her sons may seem to be very mature, a mother should not turn to them to take the place of her husband during deployments. Don't ask boys to "be the man of the house" while their father is away or girls to "fill in for Mom" while she's gone. They aren't ready for that kind of responsibility, and they take those requests very seriously. One soldier told his son to take care of Mom while he was gone. His wife later found out that wasn't a good idea. "On our way home from taking Red to the airport, my young son said, 'Mom, I can't do it! I can't be the Daddy.'"[5] When his mother tried to console him, he said that he thought he would let his dad down if he didn't carry out his responsibility.

Another young boy was told that he'd be the man of the house while his dad was away. After he thought about it, he wanted to know if that meant that he would have to take care of the TV remote and watch the news and sleep in bed with Mommy. He tried to process what it would mean to be the man of the house, but it was beyond his understanding. Don't confuse your children by asking them to take your place. Allow them to be the children or teenagers that they are. They don't have responsibility for your family and are not ready for that kind of burden. They know they can't live up to the task and feel inadequate because they can't.

However, children *are* ready to help with chores and some of the family's daily responsibilities, but don't make them feel like keeping the family together through the separation depends on them. They may be ready to take on the responsibility for keeping the car tires inflated or caring for the lawn, but they are *not* ready to take on the responsibility for keeping their mothers from feeling depressed or being their companions while their dads are gone. Be sure to assign household chores to children in a way that helps them understand that they are *contributing* to the family but not *responsible* for the family.

They will understand how they can contribute if you ask them to do things like obey Mommy while you're gone or to get along with their brothers and sisters instead of fighting or to do their chores without complaining. They need to know that their mother is in charge and that you expect them to do well at home and at school while you're away.

In addition to heightening your sensitivity to your children during the separation, there are more tangible things you can do to help them. Consider the following tips.

Relating to Dad

- Give each child a picture of himself or herself with Daddy.

- Every morning say, "Good morning," and at night say, "Good night" to Dad's picture with your child. You may want to add, "See you soon!"

- Encourage each child to write to Dad regularly. If it's hard for them to begin, The Military Family Writing Kit is a resource that you may want to consider. (Refer to "Resources for Families" published by the Bureau For At-Risk Youth in chapter II/11 for more information.)

- Help each child think of things to send with a letter to Dad—artwork, school papers, or maybe a copy of a book report or assignment that they did well on or are particularly proud of. Take a picture of your children with any special school projects that they may have to make or at programs that they may have a part in. Maybe they'd like to record a tape to send (if Dad has the equipment to play it on). They may want to send a puzzle message (a letter cut into parts that needs to be assembled in order to read it).

- You may want to suggest that your child make an adventure out of writing to Dad. Liz Harte, a third grade teacher at a Department of Defense (DOD) Dependent School in Germany, had her class send foot-tall paper dolls to deployed parents. The class named the dolls Flat Stanleys, taken from a book by Jeff Brown (published in 1963). They sent their Stanleys on a mission to have an adventure and come back with a report. One Stanley came back with a journal: "Master Sergeant Jose Fontanez sent [Stanley back to his son Marcus with] a journal with photos.... First he and Stanley ate lunch. Then they visited the watchtower and motor pool. Stanley was photographed helping one of the soldiers install a part on a vehicle."[6] Major Tom O'Donovan wrote a letter to his daughter Meghan to tell her that he and Stanley shared a Meal, Ready to Eat (MRE).[7] When Chief Warrant Officer 2 Samuel Johnson received Stanley from his daughter Latreace, he showed Stanley to his coworkers and then showed Stanley around his work area, telling him what his work was like.[8] The class project helped the children feel closer to their absent parents. You can use the same idea at home. Get imaginative and have fun with it.

- Suggest that your children write multiple-choice letters to Dad. They could write parts of sentences, along with three or four options of endings, and ask Dad to mark the ones that are correct. For example, they might write the following:

Dear Dad,

    This week my (a) teacher, (b) mother, (c) sister, or (d) brother, was (a) nice, (b) naughty, or (c) beautiful. I saw her in (a) math class, (b) reading class, (c) the principal's office, or (d) the mall. I've been (a) good, (b) doing my homework, or (c) making the dog do my homework.

    Love, (a) Susie, (b) Jane, or (c) Bob

On the back of the page they would give the answers: *a,c,d,b,a.*

- Suggest that the children draw a maze puzzle showing Dad where he is and your house as his destination, with only one path that leads home. Send it to Dad and see if he can find his way home.

- Children may want to make a silhouette drawing of themselves to send Dad. They could have someone trace their bodies on butcher paper while they stand against the wall or lie on the floor. Or, they may want to send Dad one traced arm, hand, head, foot, or leg. They can draw pictures or write messages on the silhouette drawings to show Dad how they've grown or what they like to do.

- Your child may want to write a letter to Dad in code. The child could draw up a code by assigning a different letter or symbol to each letter of the alphabet. For example, ^ L^TT B<O says *I MISS YOU.*

- Even if your children do not write to Dad regularly, they need to hear some kind of message from him on a regular basis. Children need to know that their absent parents are thinking about them and still love them.

- You may want to give your children a calendar that has some room to write a message on each date and ask them to write one thing that they did each day on the calendar. At the end of each week or month they could send their page of the calendar to Dad to help him keep up with their activities.

- Give your children's teachers stamped envelopes so they can send samples of your children's work to their dad and tell him about their progress.

- Keep family pictures that include your husband out where your children will see them often.

- Make a map that shows Dad's deployed location and your home, and draw a line to connect the two locations. Hang it in a place where your children will see it often. You may want to attach pictures of your family at home and of Dad where he is.

- You may want to put together a footlocker or deployment bag for your children to play with. It could contain a mess kit, canteen, dog tags, boots, uniforms, or anything that might be in their deployed parent's gear.

- Give the children tangible ways to feel connected to Dad on their own, like suggesting that when they look at the stars, Dad is probably looking at them too. When her husband was deployed, Joey Diaz told her children that Daddy was away working on an airplane. "Whenever we saw an airplane go by, we talked about Daddy being on the airplane. Just kept telling them he was working and that he'd be home as soon as he could."[9]

- You may want to give your children toys that have a connection to what Dad's doing. Playing with airplanes, tanks, battleships, submarines, GI Joe, or other military-related toys may make them feel closer to Dad.

- Your children may enjoy wearing one of Dad's military shirts or hats to feel closer to him.

- You may want to start a "Things to Tell Daddy Jar." Family members can write notes that can be saved in a jar for his return or mailed to him periodically.

- If Dad recorded any bedtime stories, play them before the children go to bed if they are used to having a story read to them at night.

- One mother found that a doll, dubbed "Daddy Doll" by her daughter, enables her little girl to feel connected to her father when he is deployed. The doll has a plastic sleeve instead of a face so that Daddy's picture can be inserted. Daddy Doll is the girl's constant companion when her father is away and provides an emotional connection to him that is priceless.[10]

- Young children may get excited when they see someone wearing BDUs from a distance and think that it is their dad or mom coming home. You may have to remind them that BDUs are work clothes that lots of moms and dads wear. You may want to tell them that it makes us happy to see other moms and dads in their work clothes, because it makes us think about how much we love Dad. Always remind them that Dad loves them too and will be back as soon as his work is finished.

- You may want to stuff a set of BDUs and put your husband's picture on the head of the stuffed uniform. The stuffed soldier could sit on the floor or in Dad's chair, and your children could pretend that they're sitting on Daddy's lap. Perhaps they'd like to read or write letters there or listen to any recordings that Dad may have made for them.

- You may want to synchronize the child's alarm and Dad's watch or alarm so that both will ring at the same time every day. Both the children and their father will be reminded of the other when they know that they are hearing the alarm at the same time.

■ If you can, give your children a way to measure the time until Dad will come home, such as crossing off days on a calendar. To give this a positive spin, you may want to make a paper chain to decorate the house for the homecoming, adding one chain link every day. Then if Dad's time away is lengthened, you can make comments about what a nice big chain you are making, and won't that be a great surprise for Dad? Some families may use chains to count down, taking a link off every day, but that can be disappointing if the deployment is of uncertain length or the time is subject to change. Not many deployments are predictable, so I'd suggest finding some activity (that does not depend on the amount of time you are told your husband will be gone when he leaves) to help children count the days until Dad's return that counts upward.

SUPPORT AND ENCOURAGEMENT

Your children will probably have times during the deployment when they especially miss Daddy. During those times, a book like *When Dad's at Sea* by Mindy Pelton can be comforting for children ages four to ten. The story captures children's feelings about separation and offers ideas to maintain closeness in parent-child relationships at a distance. Admit to your children that sometimes while their daddy is away you get sad and miss him too. Tell them that when you feel sad you can help each other. Maybe you can write Dad a letter, sing songs together, tell each other jokes, draw pictures, say extra prayers for your family, or just tell each other that you love each other. Ask your children what you can do to cheer them up if they feel sad about Dad being away. Other ideas you may find helpful are:

■ Look for ways to compliment your children's abilities, efforts, persistence, or courage to try something new.

■ If the separation is due to war or if the absent parent is in danger, be open to talk to the children about it. Some children worry that they will also be in danger. Be honest with them as you reassure them; don't give them false hope or tell them things that may not be true (such as that no one will be hurt or die).

■ Don't feel like you must have answers for everything. It's OK to tell children that you don't know. You can give them the message that you'll do all that you can to help them and keep them safe even though you can't answer all of the questions that they may have.

- If your children aren't talking about how they feel, ask, and encourage them to ask you questions. Be honest with them and try to answer their questions in ways that they can understand.

- If there is a support group for children of deployed personnel available in your area, involve your children. They will both be helped and help other children as they talk about issues that matter to them at the meetings.

- Show them on a map or globe where Dad is.

- Find ways to say that you love them that are meaningful to each child.

- Give plenty of hugs.

- Reassure your children, in a way they can understand, that you'll take care of them and that they don't have to worry about you leaving them too. They need to know that your family won't fall apart even though Daddy is gone for a while. If you're a single parent, be sure that the caregiver you've chosen will nurture an extended family-type bond with your children to provide that same sense of security for them.

BEHAVIOR

- Regression in toilet training or thumb sucking may be a response to the separation.

- Children may cling to you or to a favorite toy or blanket.

- They may become more aggressive or have trouble getting along with their friends.

- Children may complain of stomachaches or headaches when nothing seems to be wrong.

- Try to keep them on the same schedule and same daily routines. They might need extra cuddling, hugging, or time with you, but continue your regular sleep and discipline practices. Try not to give in to the temptation to let children sleep with you instead of in their own beds.

- Don't forget that children need to exercise, to get enough rest, and to eat right, just like you do.

- Set and keep your regular boundaries and rules.

- Avoid telling your children that when their father comes home they will be punished—carry out the discipline when the behavior occurs.

- Expect your children to test your limits. Give them discipline that is appropriate without overreacting to their behavior.

- Remember to laugh with them.

■ Listen to your children and be available to talk when they want to talk. Observe their behavior and attitudes as well as what they say. Keep good eye contact. Acknowledge their feelings and reflect them back to the children without judging or interpreting the feelings. Keep your words to a minimum.

■ Encourage children to foster relationships with extended family members or friends who love them and express that they care.

■ Take time each day to read them a book or watch TV with them.

■ Read your children books that will help them understand the separation and reassure them that they will be OK. Children can usually relate better to a story in a book than to spoken concepts.

■ Make craft or science projects that illustrate the normal change in seasons (pumpkins, snowflakes, leaves, seeds). Noticing seasonal changes will help children understand the passing of time and may help them understand when their dad will come home.

■ Don't make unrealistic promises to your children to try to make them feel better. If you make a promise to them, be sure that you can keep it; don't forget about promises, because they won't forget and will be waiting for you to do what you said you would.

■ When you become frustrated or angry with them, choose your words carefully.

■ Don't neglect going on family outings just because Dad is gone. Take your children to the zoo, on picnics, or to the mall—whatever fits your family's interests and ages. Keep an atmosphere of fun alive in your family.

■ Give your children the opportunity to help solve some of the smaller household problems that come up. (Do you need to check the air in your car's tires? How do you change the furnace filters? How do you replace lost keys? Can you fix a flat tire on the bicycle?) If you made a family deployment guide (see chapter I/5) before Dad left, ask one of your children to find the reference to help with the problem.

TEENAGERS

Teenagers may have very confused emotions, especially if they think that the deploying parent will be in danger. Some of them may have difficulty controlling their emotions, while others may seem totally disinterested. Most teenagers need reassurance that mixed emotions are normal when a parent deploys. Here are some concepts to talk about with teenage children:

- It's normal to feel some kind of denial. The denial may be expressed by withdrawing, by refusing to discuss how they feel, or by avoiding activities that make them think of the absent parent. Remind them that they aren't alone and that one way to adjust to Dad's absence is to participate in school activities or to make friends with other teens who are going through deployments.

- Support groups with peers can be a great source of encouragement for teenagers and can help them express what they're feeling in a nonthreatening environment.

- Encourage your teenagers to be positive and to focus on the good things in life. Perhaps they could help encourage younger siblings or other children who have a parent deployed.

- They may have more stomachaches or headaches than normal or have trouble sleeping.

- Help them try to end the day with a relaxing and pleasant experience. Perhaps they'd like to read before going to bed. Many teenagers like to play video games that may include violence or listen to music that includes violence or that excites them. Electronic games and listening to music may be taking the place of reading for some young people, but often they don't have a calming effect. Try to help them realize that playing electronic games or listening to high-energy music before bedtime doesn't help them relax as they get ready to sleep for the night. Maybe they'd like to read before going to bed or listen to soothing music. If your teenager doesn't like to read, help him or her find other relaxing ways to unwind before bed. Perhaps your teenager would enjoy the old comedy routines of Abbott and Costello, the Marx brothers, or Sid Caesar and find that relaxing. Try to help them find relaxing activities that will leave them feeling happy.

- Make some of their favorite foods.

- They may have trouble concentrating in school. Getting more exercise and participating in activities they enjoy can help relieve some of the restlessness and help them concentrate better.

As I mentioned earlier, our son Dan was a teenager when his dad was deployed on two hours' notice. He later taught at the high school level, and I asked him what advice he would give to parents of teenagers who have a parent deployed. He said, "Get them to talk." He also gave me more insight into how teenagers may process a parent's deployment by sharing what he learned from his experience:

> I learned a lot from my dad's deployment, but not immediately. Some things didn't dawn on me until a couple of years later. For example, people were constantly asking me how I was doing and what they could do for me. I didn't have an answer, and it was kinda frustrating trying to figure out not only how to handle what I was feeling but also how to handle dealing with others on top of that. I later realized that they only meant to help and didn't realize that giving space would have been a help too. So, now I am grateful to know that people don't always know what to say but really want to do something to help, and that it's OK to tell them that I don't know how they can help me. It's OK that I didn't know what to tell people. Communication is a tricky thing, but better to err on the side of at least trying. It's fine for me to want to be who I am. I didn't, and still don't, show emotion outwardly, hardly at all—and that's fine. That is how God made me. I would rather be a strength for others in times of hardship or crisis. Others have to accept that. We are all unique individuals. I didn't let anyone force me to show emotion. That is an intimate thing, and they didn't have the right to ask that of me. As long as I was real before God, I had nothing to worry about.[11]

Whether the teens in your life express what they're feeling or hold it inside, be sure that they know they're loved, and respect the boundaries of sharing that they dictate. Like Dan, they may not talk much about how they feel emotionally, but they *will* talk when *they* are ready. As parents, we know how our teenagers typically respond to circumstances in life. During deployments, we have to be sensitive to any changes in their normal patterns of behavior and be ready to talk whenever they are.

If we think that they may be holding too much inside, we can respectfully ask them how they're feeling and whether they think it would be helpful to talk. If they tell us that they don't want to talk or aren't ready, we must accept that and let them know that we're available any time they need us. They need unconditional love, especially when they miss a parent who is away and when they are at a stage in life during which emotions are confusing even under normal conditions.

Even if they seem to handle deployments well, teens may be torn up inside and not sure how to express themselves. An extra amount of love and understanding can be exactly what helps them through the challenge. The parent who is at home with children during a deployment may be too emotionally affected by the separation to give as much support and understanding as he or she normally would. That's one reason it's important to have other adult role models in your teen's life, especially adult friends who will communicate friendship and care when they really need it.

Most of us know about the Big Brothers and Big Sisters and how adults step up to provide a positive adult role model when children have a lack in their lives. Teenagers who have a parent deployed need those types of relationships too.

Young Adults/Post-High School and Students in College

Young adults who are finished with high school may be helpful as Big Brothers or Big Sisters for younger children of deployed parents. However, we may be so concerned about children who are at home with the non-deploying parent that we forget that post-high school youth and college students may also need help when they have a deployed parent. Post-high school children may seem to be quite mature and unaffected by a parent's absence when in actuality they're not.

If your young adults are going to college and living on campus or in an apartment of their own as they join the work force, as a parent you adjust to their increased independence from the family home. As they grow into adulthood, they don't need Mom and Dad as much or in the same way as they did when they were younger. But *none* of us should ever totally outgrow having relationships with our parents or children. The relationships change, but they are still very important to each family member.

As our relationships with our young adults undergo changes, our offspring go to college or move into apartments and enter the work force. They prepare for and begin their adulthood, and our roles as parents may become more like that of mentor and friend. They may not even notice that there is less active parenting from us as they have fewer hours with us. Even though we miss having them at home, they enjoy their independence; they may not recognize the changes occurring in the relationships with their parents or how the changes are affecting their parents.

Even though they don't need us to parent them in the same way that we did when they were younger, I believe that these young adults may care more about Mom and Dad than they appear to or are willing to admit. They find security in knowing that their parents are available and love them, even though they may not say so.

When one of a young adult's parents is deployed, he may have more of an emotional response than we would expect. At this time in his life, he's probably also not as equipped to handle the emotion as he thinks he is. Without patronizing them, we can help young adults during deployments by sharing how we feel and by asking them specific questions. Perhaps we can find a non-threatening way to give them opportunities to share with us.

However, parents may not be the people young adults choose to share their hearts with. We must accept that and encourage them to find someone whom they admire to talk with when they need support. Our oldest son, Mike, was a young adult when his dad deployed on two hours' notice. At college that year, he talked with the campus chaplain, who became his mentor and friend. His perspective may help you as you relate to young adults during deployments.

MIKE'S PERSPECTIVE

Here's my perspective on deployment while away at college alone:

Being separated from family is very difficult in any situation. I believe that to be especially true for military families. There are so many unknowns that the civilian population simply does not have to consider when someone leaves for a few days on business. When my dad was deployed suddenly, at first, my personal feelings ran the gamut from scared to lonely to depressed to hopeful to confident. I'd say that my feelings each day depended on what I heard from various news sources and what I learned from family.

The next several months were tough for me at college. I didn't study well because I couldn't concentrate well, so I spent the vast majority of my time in the gym or playing sports. That was my outlet. Being away from home to begin with was hard enough, but I felt that since I was the oldest boy I needed to be home taking care of the family. Hearing things on the news was hard because I never knew exactly what I could believe and what wasn't all true. My dad wrote when he could, and I tried writing back. My mom wrote and called once or twice a week and did her best to be positive.

Did deployment have an effect on my studies? I would say yes. Not to hide behind that as an excuse for poor grades, but it was a contributing factor. It was hard to concentrate at times; I would much rather just sit and read the paper or watch the latest news to figure out how things were going. Until Desert Shield turned into Desert Storm, we were all very concerned because the reports were that Iraq's military was supposedly very strong and formidable. Once the war itself began, we began to see that their strength wasn't as advertised. This helped, but it was still difficult. My dad was at a classified location, so I wasn't sure about how much danger he was in.

Over the next passing months, and especially after the first week or so of the air and land war, I personally started to relax a little. I read everything I could get my hands on concerning what was going on over there and started to feel better for my dad's sake as I realized that we were accomplishing what we set out to do, and with far fewer casualties than expected.

These five things helped me get through Dad's Desert Shield/Storm deployment:

1. Faith: Shaky as it may have been, faith gave me an indescribable peace. That may not mean that everything made sense, just that there was comfort in knowing that things were out of my hands. I had no control over it, and that was OK.

2. Letters, phone calls, e-mail, care packages, etc. from home and from the deployed parent. That helps immensely, because even if a kid won't admit it, it helps him feel connected across the miles. I've never been the best communicator, but it is/was good to hear from my parents, whether I said that or not.

3. Community of friends and family. Both groups are important. Family, because they are involved as they are also related to the deployed family. Friends, because they helped me to stay busy. Going to someone's house for dinner or out to a movie really helped. As a subset of this, I thought it was invaluable to have two or three close friends who I could confide in, sort of spill my guts as needed, and have access to them whenever I needed them.

4. Activity: studying, reading, sports, etc. I probably spent most of my time with friends or playing sports when dad was deployed, more than I did at any other time. Those were my two main release mechanisms.

5. Connecting with other kids whose parents are in the military, whether they were deployed or not. It was always good to meet someone like that because they understood better than anyone else what I was going through.

Looking back on the many years that have passed since that time, I think I have learned much. My faith in God is much stronger (to say the least) than it was at that time. Although I may not have been very close to God at that time, in hindsight I can see that he was close to me even though I didn't realize it.

One other thing I learned is that it is absolutely crucial to let yourself, and those around you, deal with a deployment or separation in their own way. Let yourself be angry. Allow yourself to grieve. Let your emptiness show. Whatever shape it takes, work through it. Don't try to hide feelings or gloss over them; that only makes it worse.[12]

BABIES BORN DURING DEPLOYMENT

Sometimes military members must be away from their wives over holidays and important family events. The birth of a child may not wait for Dad's return, and he may have mixed feelings about that. His pride about the new child may be colored by apprehension about the responsibilities that he faces, guilt or anger about not being at his wife's side for the birth, and concern that his wife and child are safe and well cared for.

While Dad is sorting through his feelings and wondering what the baby looks like and how he or she acts, Mom has her own conglomeration of responses to the birth. She may feel fulfilled and excited as she enjoys the special bond with the new child. She may feel totally exhausted and overwhelmed with the responsibility of caring for the baby alone, especially if there are other children she has to care for at the same time. Some new mothers experience the blues or even depression after a baby's birth.

Technology is now available to give some dads who are away from home a chance to share a moment with their wives and new babies. Dalton Mills was on the aircraft carrier *Enterprise* in the Persian Gulf when his wife gave birth to their daughter in Chesapeake, Virginia. He was able to see his new baby through a video linkup between his ship and the Navy hospital in the States. "'I was fortunate to be one of the first,' Mills said. 'It's a big morale booster.' Not only for the guys at sea. Knowing that her husband has seen their new baby is making the rest of his deployment … easier for her to handle, Sherry Mills said. The mother of three no longer feels guilty that she alone has had the joy of seeing their daughter."[13]

However, the video linkup that the Millses experienced is not available to everyone in the military. Most men who become fathers while on duty away from their families have to wait until they return home to see their babies. Both the husband and the wife want to be together to support one another and enjoy the new family member but must find a way to do so from a distance. How is it possible to include the new father from a distance? Here are some ideas that mothers may want to consider:

- If you're pregnant while he's deployed, you may want to trace a silhouette of your growing belly and send it to your husband. You may want to draw a hand on it so that he can see where you feel the baby kicking.

- After your husband leaves on his deployment, you may want to do what one wife did: "I sent a balloon with a note, 'Blow this up to discover how I'm doing.' As he inflated the balloon, words grew, proclaiming, 'I'm expanding.'"[14]

- Write Dad a letter to tell him about the birth experience.

- Write letters that describe the baby's looks, likes, dislikes, personalities, abilities, and growth.

- Send videotapes of the baby and mother or audio cassettes of their voices, if Dad has the equipment to play tapes.

- If you talk to your husband on the phone periodically, hold the phone to your baby's ear so that he or she can begin to learn Daddy's voice.

- You may want to get him a copy of the National Fatherhood Initiative's brochure entitled "So You're a New Father, or Are About to Become One!" (Ordering information is available on their Web site, www.fatherhood.org, as listed in chapter V/5 under "Resources for All Military Personnel and Their Families," at the end of this book.)

- Send pictures of the baby to Dad on a regular (maybe weekly) basis so he can see the baby change and grow.

- Send Dad a footprint or handprint of the baby, some hair, a shirt or bootie (so he can picture the size of the child), a hat, or anything that belongs to the baby that will help him feel connected.

- Write letters to Dad as if the baby were talking to Daddy.

- Keep a diary and baby book to share with Dad when he gets home.

Children, War, and Terrorism

A child's response to knowing that a parent is deployed to war is likely to be more intense than other less-dramatic missions. Terrorism is the war of our time. Children hear about terrorism and war and may have trouble understanding what it all means. Of course, a child's age level affects her ability to understand.

Young children may have trouble distinguishing reality from fantasy. When they see events rebroadcast on the news, they may think that something is happening again. The tendency to interpret each broadcast as a new event gives young children the impression that tragedy is more widespread than it really is.

Children who are old enough to separate reality from fantasy may still blur that distinction when tragedies happen in the world. When they see news on television, they may think that everything they see is in their own neighborhoods. Older children may take an interest in the news with adult-like concern.

If you feel like you need advice about how to talk with children about these tough issues, I recommend a couple of resources. The first is the Child Study Center at New York University. You can download or print helpful articles from their Web site at www.aboutourkids.org. On the About Our Kids home page, click on "article archive." Then, toward the bottom of the page you'll find a search by keyword. Enter "war" and the list of articles will be available. Their articles give sample questions and suggestions about how to talk with children about war and terrorism. The American Academy of Child and Adolescent Psychiatry also has excellent articles available online. You can find them at www.aacap.org/publications/factsfam. They present practical information that is helpful for children of any age group.

Adults have to be sensitive to how children are feeling and whether they are worried about war or a parent's role in the war. It can be difficult to interpret how they feel. Parents need to use resources that are available to help them in this process, including the help of counselors when parents aren't sure of the right approach. A parent who is concerned about a deployed spouse may be under enough stress that he or she cannot care for children as effectively as he or she would under normal circumstances.

As parents talk to their children about war, it's best to ask questions that encourage children to tell them what they've heard. It may take several different discussions over many days for children to finally open up about what they're thinking and feeling. That's why discussions must be ongoing and continual. Watching news reports with children can encourage those kinds of discussions.

As you discuss something as serious as terrorism or war with your children, listen thoughtfully to their ideas. Help children feel good about their thoughts. If their ideas need to be influenced, gently show them why without making them think that they're wrong. They're learning as you discuss, and positive reinforcement encourages learning. Help them learn the difference between morality or ethics and politics. Protecting morality and ethical concerns are the underlying reasons for most conflicts. As children begin to understand that, they can begin to understand how those involved in the mission are protecting our freedoms as well as those of people in other countries. Talking about protection can include those doing the fighting as well as those who live in the battle zone or area where the terror takes place.

The talk of protection finally filters to our safety at home. As we discuss such intense subjects with our children, it's important that we give them plenty of assurance and as much security as possible. When a child's parent is involved in the conflict, it can be very difficult to make him feel secure. Limiting the amount of news that children are exposed to helps to keep the war or terrorist attacks in perspective in their minds. Limiting children's exposure is different than minimizing the truth or shielding them from the truth.

As we talk about the truth of war or terror, we need to be sure that it is in an atmosphere that provides a normal way of life and routine for our children. We need to be available whenever they decide that it's time to talk. They look to adults for leadership, and we must be ready to provide it. As adults lead children through the tough issues, we have to be sure that we don't give them the idea that the issues are easily and simply solved.

Children process information differently than adults do, so discussions must be in terms that they can understand and relate to. They may understand best if they can hear clear presentations and see word pictures that illustrate the points made. Children are also very aware of the mood or reaction of adults to the war, and their observations affect their responses. By their presentation of the discussion, parents can show children that we can be concerned and sad about the circumstances and that we can control our emotions and remain calm as we deal with the problem. Sometimes we may feel more sad than other times, for example, but we can remember that our sadness is a reaction that does not last and that it will change in time. During the sad times, we can talk about the fact that taking care of ourselves by getting enough rest, eating right, and exercising will help us feel less sad over time.

War and terrorism aren't easy for any of us to understand. Thinking seriously about it can be unsettling to adults and to children. Maintaining an environment in which we can discuss concerns and fears is important to our well-being during such troubling times.

II/7: TAKING CARE OF YOURSELF WHILE YOUR SPOUSE IS GONE

◪

One Squadron Commander's wife told me that while her Special Forces husband was deployed with his unit, she was running all over the base to help the families under his Command. One day she was called to her daughter's school, where the counselor told her that her daughter felt abandoned because her dad was away and her mom was always gone to help someone. The daughter was having problems with the deployment, and her mom didn't even notice it because she was so busy helping everyone else. That was a wake-up call for that mother.

Others of us are more inclined to take care of our own needs and those of our families first and closely guard our time before we reach out. If you're like that, remember to think about what other families are going through, and when you're ready, reach out to them. Offer specific assistance that you can see that they could use, such as meals, babysitting, social outings like picnics, or inviting them to events that they may not want to attend alone. Friends invited me to go with them to an art auction on base while my husband was deployed, and I know that I wouldn't have made the effort to get out if they hadn't invited me and offered to pick me up. During that deployment, I identified with the wife who said, "I feel like a twin-engine plane piloting on a single engine when he is away."[1]

Caring for each other helps make sure that our needs are met during deployments. One military wife came up with an excellent word picture that describes the needs that spouses feel during separations: "Realistically, holding down the fort is an exasperating and exhausting experience for the spouse who is frequently left solo to bear burdens meant for a duet.... She is required to scale mountains of unfamiliar territory, already strapped, cinched, and weighted down with a backpack full of normal everyday demands."[2] Wives have spiritual needs, emotional needs, and physical needs that have to be met when their husbands are gone, and often they are

What support do wives recognize as available to them during deployment?

94 percent of wives said there was someone they could contact who would listen to them.

88 percent said there was someone they could go to for advice.

86 percent said there was someone they could have fun with.

85 percent said there was someone who gave them emotional support.

83 percent said there was someone they could get information from.

80 percent said there was someone they could go to if they needed transportation.

61 percent said they had someone they could call to take care of their children if there was an emergency.

—AMY B. ALDER, PH.D., PAUL T. BARTONE, PH.D., AND MARK A. VAITKUS, PH.D. USAMRU-E TECHNICAL REPORT 95-1: FAMILY STRESS AND ADAPTATION DURING A U.S. ARMY EUROPE PEACEKEEPING DEPLOYMENT. U.S. ARMY MEDICAL RESEARCH UNIT-EUROPE. APRIL 1995: 21–24.

so interrelated that meeting one need will help relieve another. The following are some ideas to help you get through separation.

SPIRITUAL NEEDS

■ See separation as an opportunity to grow rather than focusing only on the fact that your husband is deployed.

■ Spend time daily in devotional reading, meditation, and prayer.

■ Every day that your husband is away, try to do something to improve yourself.

■ Count your blessings regularly. Think about the good things in your life.

■ Attend religious services and maintain your relationships with friends.

EMOTIONAL NEEDS

■ Keep your husband's picture out where you'll see it often. Don't let him be out of sight and out of mind. If you feel overwhelmed, don't be afraid to ask for help, but don't compromise your marriage relationship by developing a close kinship and sharing personal problems with someone of the opposite sex. Spend time with opposite-sex friends only in groups.

■ Try not to give in to the temptation to go live with parents or family members until your husband gets home. One wife said, "My first reaction was 'Oh my God, how will I cope? What will I do for six months? I'll pack up and go home.' Then, I thought about it and decided to stick it out since my home is here now. I'm glad I did."[3] Try to think of wherever you live as your home instead of where your relatives are, and reassure yourself that you can live at home for a while without your husband.

Myrna Borling went to stay with relatives when her husband went to Vietnam in 1965. She said, "It was a wrong decision. I didn't have the support of the military community because I wasn't there, and there was no support from the civilians."[4] It is especially significant that Myrna said this after her husband's plane had been shot down and he spent six and a half years as a POW while she was in the civilian community with their relatives.

Civilians may ask why you are there without your husband and comment that they could never live like you do. In a civilian community you also may not be near military health care, a commissary, or other military family activities. Why put yourself in that awkward position when you could be in a community that understands your lifestyle and has benefits for your use?

If you aren't sure about whether you should go to stay with relatives, make a list of pros and cons for each choice of where you might want to live. Making a list will help you sort it out and make a good decision.

- Some of you may find that your needs are met best if you do go stay with other family members while your spouse is away. If you go to be with relatives, you may want to ask the housing office, a friend, or your landlord to look in on your home from time to time while you're gone. Notify the police that your house will be empty so that they can check it periodically. Perhaps you should leave a key with someone you trust. Also, be sure that your unit knows where you are and can conveniently contact you wherever you stay.

- Don't turn to drugs, alcohol, smoking, or junk food when you feel down. Try to think of things to do that will make you laugh or lift your spirits instead. Maybe it would help to rent comedy videos or DVDs and have a friend over to watch them with you.

- Think about your body's cycles. Can you predict times when you might expect to feel moody, down, or tired? If you realize when those times are and expect them, it will be easier to separate them from your feelings of loneliness because of your husband's absence and to get through them without becoming depressed.

- Think about the good times you've shared with your husband and plan for more.

■ From the first day of your separation, know where to go for help if you begin to feel overwhelmed. Then if the time comes when you feel the need to seek counsel, you will have phone numbers and names ready and it won't be as difficult for you.

■ Some deployments are more stressful than others; don't compare yourself to other people. It's OK to feel like you don't understand everything. You don't have to be strong all of the time. Admit that you have emotional needs without dwelling on your problems. The more you think about problems, the larger they will seem.

■ Tell yourself that you're doing a good job of maintaining the home by yourself once in a while. You probably are!

■ Brainstorm ideas for leave time when your husband gets home.

■ Think about long-term goals for your family. What do you want out of life? Share your ideas with your husband in a letter.

■ Be flexible! See the unexpected and uncontrollable parts of life as adventures that you can get through, even if they make you feel like you're finding your way through a maze.

■ Initiate relationships with spouses of other deployed service members instead of waiting for someone to come to you. They are going through the same feelings and experiences that you are. Try to get together with them regularly during the deployment.

■ Attend spouse support activities offered at your military installation (or the one nearest you if your husband was not on Active Duty before the deployment). Depend on the military support network around you.

■ If there is no support group near you, try to start one. Whether you have a formal group or an informal home gathering, you need the support and encouragement of others who understand what you're going through.

■ Don't listen to gossip or rumors. If your husband is in a hostile or dangerous environment and the media is covering the action twenty-four hours a day, avoid the temptation to stay glued to your TV. Listen to enough news to know what is happening and then turn it off. If you watch too much coverage, you will find more reasons to fear and worry. *Depend on your husband's chain of command or the support groups at your installation for information about your husband's situation, not the TV.*

■ Remember that separations are often extended, so don't expect your husband's original return date to be reliable. Your husband wants to come home as soon as possible but has no control over his return date. Prepare yourself for the longest time period that you think the separation could last, then expect the worst and hope for the best. Break the time up into manageable sections: Get through one day or week or month at a time before you look ahead to the next day, week, or month. Find meaning in each day.

- If you begin to feel resentment that your husband is gone and you are left to handle everything, try to imagine how he feels about being away from the family. Knowing that he also feels the pain of separation can help you not blame him for it. *Remember that you have the comfort and familiar atmosphere of home to enjoy. He doesn't.*

- Keep a journal. On days that are especially difficult, you may find encouragement as you look at earlier entries. The journal will also be a great record of what happened for your husband to read when he gets home.

- Do fun things with your children. Maybe you'd like to make a "treat ourselves to fun jar." Put ideas for fun things to do with the children on paper, and when you or your children need a lift or want to do something special, draw a paper out of the jar and do what it suggests. Children can help with ideas. Include each person's ideas and interests in the jar, and feel free to add to it as you think of things to do.

- Keep busy. Instead of thinking about what you and your husband are missing because of the separation, find a goal that you can pursue that would be hard to accomplish if he was at home. Some ideas include going back to school, getting a part-time job, becoming more computer literate, doing volunteer work, losing weight, beginning a regular exercise program, growing a garden, cleaning out the closets, doing a special craft or sewing project, learning to make picture frames, learning a foreign language, painting, or learning to play an instrument. If you smoke, surprise your husband and quit!

- You may enjoy having the company of a pet. (If you didn't have a pet before the separation, be sure that your husband won't object to an addition to the household.)

- Emotional needs can be hard to recognize and hard to identify. Elizabeth Hoekstra wrote a book entitled *Keeping Your Family Close When Frequent Travel Pulls You Apart*. I highly recommend it as a resource to help sort through the emotional elements of separation.

PHYSICAL NEEDS

- Eat right. (Here's your chance to eat the meals that your husband doesn't like!)

- Get enough rest.
- Exercise regularly.
- Maintain your sense of humor.
- Relax your housekeeping standards. Pamper yourself once in a while. Give yourself private time as often as you need it.
- If you have a question about military benefits or need a repair made, don't ask a neighbor who you think had a similar need. Go directly to the office or serviceperson who can help you. Don't be afraid to ask for clarification if you aren't sure that you understand what they say. If you need to, use your husband's chain of command to get help.
- If you need to go to any military or government office, call first to ask what documents you will need to accomplish your errand.
- Keep doors locked, even when you're at home. Use light and radio timers. Don't overreact and become housebound or fearful; just use common sense.
- Don't tell strangers that your husband is gone. If telephone callers who you don't know ask to speak to him, take a message and tell them you'll be sure he gets it. Tell babysitters how you want them to answer calls that may come for your husband when you are away.
- Don't talk about your husband's absence in public where strangers will hear you.
- Don't go out at night alone. When you drive, always keep your car doors locked.
- Never let your car get below a quarter of a tank of gas.
- Yellow ribbons and similar decorations advertise that someone is away unless the whole neighborhood decorates the same way. Wait until the day he returns to put out the yellow ribbon to welcome your husband home.
- Depend on your family deployment guide (see chapter I/5) to help you run your household. If your family didn't prepare one before the deployment, you can start making one now. Your husband will probably be proud of your effort.
- Give yourself realistic goals and schedules. Take time to relax without guilt.
- If you take a trip or leave home for any length of time, be sure that your husband's Commander knows how to reach you and where you are. Then if there's any information that you need or an emergency that takes place, there will be no delay or problem locating you. Also, be sure to take security precautions for your home while you're away. Notify the housing office, your landlord, or a friend that you'll be gone, and ask them to check on things

while you're away. You may want to notify the police so that they can check your home periodically, or leave a key with a friend.

CHILDREN

- Make time to get out without your children. Spend time with positive, enthusiastic people. If you can't afford or find babysitters, ask a friend if she would be interested in trading babysitting with you.

- If you are a wife who works full-time outside of the home, you may need to cut back on some of your other activities in order to have time to take care of your family without your husband's help. Your children may already feel the loss of their father, and if you are too busy to notice their feelings or spend time with them, they may feel like they've lost *both* of their parents. For their stability and security and for your own peace of mind, think about whether you should give up some of your outside-of-the-home involvements while your husband is gone.

- Be aware of how you respond to your children while your husband is gone. It is easy to overreact to their childish behavior and to mistakes they make.

There are lots of things you can do to help yourself get through family separation. If you avoid the temptation to withdraw from others, you'll see that families and friends in the military community will gather together to care for each other during the hard times. Today, the military emphasizes morale and quality-of-life issues more than they have in the past. This emphasis includes programs to help families during separation; anyone who looks for help or information should be able to find it.

II/8: OPSEC/COMSEC

◩

We all know that for the military mission to succeed there has to be a certain amount of classified information. In military terms, OPSEC is Operations Security, and COMSEC is Communications Security. Do OPSEC and COMSEC affect military families? COMSEC definitely affected me when my husband was deployed to a classified location!

Soon after Ren left, I asked our Wing Chaplain for a list of other spouses whose husbands were gone so that I could connect with them. Because of privacy issues and COMSEC, he wouldn't share that list with me. He advised me to come to the support meeting, where I'd be able to meet other spouses. I didn't mean to ask him to compromise information, but naïvely, and out of curiosity, I had asked him for information that he couldn't give me. When I attended the meetings, I did meet other spouses, and we got together to do things after that.

From my perspective as a spouse, COMSEC can be thought of from an individual point of view as well as a social one. What I mean by an individual point of view is illustrated by my personal experience when my husband told me that he was going to a classified location and also when he called to give me his address. I had to resist the urge to ask questions that he couldn't answer, and that wasn't always easy. One thing that helped me refrain from asking him questions was knowing that his safety could be compromised. That meant I couldn't ask him questions but also that I shouldn't expect him to tell me, even in confidence, where he was. I didn't have a *need to know*. So, to exercise good COMSEC, I didn't talk about it.

The social aspect of COMSEC means that I didn't talk about location even with spouses whose husbands were at the same location as mine. If we had talked about where they were or what type of aircraft there were at their locations or even information as simple as what specific jobs some of our husbands did, that could have put them in danger. The more people know, the greater the possibility that they will talk about what they know in public: on telephones, in restaurants, at their churches, while they're shopping, or at places like night clubs and Officers' and Enlisted Clubs.

When we were stationed overseas, the Armed Forces TV Network had public service videos in place of stateside advertising. I remember one of the videos in Okinawa that showed two people talking in a restaurant and a spy listening to them. The spy was dressed in a trench coat, a hat, and gloves and was writing on a notepad as he listened, giving the visual image of the danger of sharing private information, and we laughed at that. But the message was real, and we need to remember it. Spies and terrorists may not look any different than the person who sits at the next table at the restaurant you go to or shops next to you in the store. Little bits of information that may not even be classified can help people with bad intentions fill out the picture. So, don't talk about details of your military life that don't need to be shared.

If you hear someone else talking, remind him that it's better not to talk about what your spouses do or where they are. It's our responsibility to remind each other that when we talk to one person, it's easier to talk to another later, so to prevent sharing potentially sensitive information, we shouldn't talk at all. It's better not to say anything to anyone. That includes your children. Children don't understand what they should or shouldn't talk about, so don't give them information that they shouldn't spread in public.

Talking publicly about your husband's absence could also potentially put *you* at risk. Whether it's politically correct to say so or not, women alone make good targets. That's one reason I recommend that you don't hang a yellow ribbon in your window unless everyone on your street does. Don't advertise that you're alone.

If you absolutely *can't* resist talking to someone, talk with your chaplain. Chaplains are the only military members with complete confidentiality, and they will not share what you talk with them about.

However, COMSEC doesn't mean that there is no communication. When my husband was deployed to a classified location, on a couple of occasions I received phone calls from air crew members from our base who told me that they were going to go to my husband's location and that if I had anything I'd like them to take to Ren, they'd take it for me. Without divulging any secrets, they gave me support and consideration through their availability and willingness to provide a link between my husband and me.

There were other wives whose husbands were deployed with mine, but when we visited with each other, we didn't talk about where they were. They were all away working for a common mission, and we were all at home having similar experiences. Instead of exercising our curiosity about things we can't know, let's be proud of our military spouses and support them.

II/9: SUPPORT GROUPS

Support groups can take a variety of forms of organization, from informational meetings with question-and-answer time to group therapeutic discussions. Don't be afraid to go to meetings to see what specific groups offer. Most groups welcome visitors, and you don't have to go back every time they meet if you don't want to. Deployment support groups on military installations are usually informal and informational. Whether they are organized by the Family Service Centers, the chapel, or military units, their purpose is the same: to make life better for the families of deployed personnel.

You may benefit from thinking about things that encourage and comfort you when your spouse is deployed, and you may feel overwhelmed. Everyone needs encouragement and support. You may experience encouragement and support by being creative during deployment. My Dining Out experience is an example of the kind of creativity that I'm thinking about.

When my husband was deployed, there was a formal Dining Out to celebrate the Air Force's birthday. Since I lived on base, I could see everyone in their mess dress uniforms and formal dresses leaving for the party. The wives of other deployed service members in one squadron on our base had adopted me into their group, and on the night of the Dining Out, we got dressed up and went to a nice restaurant for our own celebration. We gathered all of the children at one house, where the teenagers babysat the younger children. About twelve wives had a nice evening out, and about twenty-five kids had a pizza party with balloons and games. We ended the evening watching a video that some of the husbands had sent, showing their tent city and deployed location. Instead of feeling left out, we all felt encouraged.

COMMAND SUPPORT

When my husband was deployed, our base had weekly support meetings held at the base chapel. At every meeting there were representatives

◪ What are wives' biggest frustrations during deployment?

Wives in the Army study said their biggest frustrations were wondering what will happen to their husbands' units, not knowing when their husbands would be back, lack of sufficient information, lack of a good Family Support Group, divorce, no information at all, being jerked back and forth between delays and orders that the unit was leaving, no alternation of troops, child care, unsuccessful Family Support Group meetings, no Family Support, and no support from the chain of command. Alder, Bartone, and Viatkus, 19.

from the post office, the legal office, the Red Cross, family services, the chapel, public affairs, and the base exchange, along with the Base Commander and the Wing Commander. They gave us information about mail flow, how to deal with people who were reluctant to accept our powers of attorney, what services were available to our husbands, and much more.

When the media asked wives for interviews, the requests came through Public Affairs to protect our privacy. When a professional sports team in our area offered free tickets to families of deployed personnel, I heard about it (and got the information that I needed to get tickets) at the support meeting. Other businesses in the area donated T-shirts and food to deployed families, and we received information about that at the meetings too. We were even treated to meals after a couple of the meetings.

The Commanders helped us sort through rumors during question-and-answer sessions every week and told us what they knew was factual or exaggerated in the news. They reminded us that the media has a story to sell, which may result in broadcasts that are riddled with partial truth or conjecture. It's always best to get information from your command structure or command-sponsored support meetings.

Our support meetings offered practical help too. One wife had a problem with her quarters and needed help getting the housing office to take care of it. The Base Commander offered to talk to the housing office. Another wife had problems with her bank because their new checking account was opened in her husband's name and they hadn't had time to put her name on it before her husband deployed. The lawyer from the base legal office offered to go to the bank with her to try to straighten out the problem.

UNIT SUPPORT GROUPS

Many military units also organize support groups for families of those who are deployed. Unit Commanders and other leaders usually know the military members in their units and their families personally. When someone from a unit is deployed, there is often a network of familiar people ready to help the families who are left behind. They may help by holding group meetings and through personal contacts, or there may be a unit newsletter or telephone information chain to keep families informed.

When my husband was deployed, he was deployed individually, not with a unit. There was another squadron at our base with a number of people who were deployed to a different location than my husband, and in the spirit of military camaraderie, that squadron adopted me while my husband was away. The wives of those who were deployed in the squadron met for dinner, shopping, and picnics with their children, and they included me.

One Saturday, the men of the squadron held a car-care day for the spouses of those who were gone. We all brought our cars over to the auto hobby shop, and while our children played and were treated to pizza, they changed our oil and filters, checked hoses and tires, etc. I was thankful for that because their examination of my car revealed that I had a bad spot on one of my tires and the tire needed to be replaced. They were kind enough to tell me where to get one and saved me a blow-out. I appreciated their sensitivity and inclusion of me in their unit during that time.

SUPPORT IN THE MILITARY COMMUNITY

Unit support often extends beyond the confines of the unit that is sponsoring the activity, although the attention naturally is focused on unit needs. Unit Commanders and leaders provide encouragement to families just by showing interest in how they are doing during the separation and listening carefully to pick up on needs that they may be able to help meet. When personnel under his leadership are deployed, one Commander writes notes to the parents of his young troops to tell them that he knows that they probably feel a bit anxious about their sons or daughters but that as the Commander he will make sure that they are doing well. He also offers his phone number and that of his First Sergeant, encouraging parents to call if they have concerns or need assistance. In addition to caring

Commanders, your installation may have Ombudsman or Key Volunteers who are sensitive to the needs of families and ready to help when there is a need.

There are countless examples of how spouses and families have been supported. My husband told me that the morale of troops who knew that their wives or families attended support groups was higher than the morale of those whose wives did not attend. Troops who knew that their families had support back home didn't worry as much about them, which enabled them to concentrate on their mission. For me, the spouse support meetings were both a connection to the military while my husband was gone and a source of encouragement to help me through the separation. My relatives could not offer me the same kind of support and encouragement.

Most Active Duty military families don't live near their relatives, so they can't look to them for support. Even those with relatives nearby may find that relatives don't understand the military lifestyle and can't identify with their unique needs, even though they may sincerely love them and try to understand. If your relatives haven't lived the military lifestyle, they're limited in their ability to help meet your needs. The military is different from the civilian culture around it and has a reputation for caring for its own. "The military subculture, with its interpersonal relationships and its tradition of mutual help, plays a potentially significant and primary role in helping families cope with the stress of military separation."[1] Becoming involved in the military network and making use of its resources will be more satisfying and helpful to most military spouses and families than going back home to their relatives.

SUPPORT FOR RESERVE AND GUARD FAMILIES

The Reserve and Guard components have family support groups available as the need arises. Their families can also take part in support groups offered on Active Duty installations. Reserve and Guard family members may have to remind themselves that during mobilizations, when their loved ones serve full-time, they are, in fact, Active Duty service members. While they're serving, the mission will have to be their focus. So, think of yourselves as Active Duty families and take advantage of the support of the military community.

However, some of you who are Reserve and Guard families may not live near enough to an installation to benefit from the support that the

How do wives cope with problems when their husbands are deployed?

To cope with their most important problems, 93 percent of wives said they take one day at a time, 90 percent said they would talk with their husbands, 86 percent would try to find more information, 84 percent would talk with a friend, and 83 percent said they would write a letter to their husbands. Alder, Bartone, and Vaitkus, 19.

military community provides. Often, Reserve and Guard members drive a distance to their drill areas, so they are not close to the unit. You may not have an opportunity to meet or form friendships with families of those who serve with your spouse. However, you can access a lot of resources and support on the Internet, at a variety of Web sites. (Please see the resource listings in chapter II/11 and in chapter V/5.) Some of you who are Reserve and Guard families may receive the support that you need during mobilizations and deployments from your extended families and your churches. The relationships that you have in your civilian communities provide a sense of continuity and stability that helps you endure the family separation.

There are some needs that the civilian community cannot meet. Although Reserve and Guard families may not be near enough to an Active Duty installation or local unit to use many of their military benefits, you have access to some benefits wherever you live. One such benefit may be CHAMPUS or TRICARE. In order to use the medical benefits, Reserve and Guard families may need to call someone in the military system for help. Active Duty families also have to know who to call when they need help. The military tries to meet the needs of families of every component, but individual service members can help their families by telling them how to use their benefits and by providing them with the names and phone numbers of military personnel who can answer questions after they deploy.

WHY SUPPORT GROUPS ARE IMPORTANT/HOW TO HELP EACH OTHER

An Army study showed that many wives were either reluctant to use the resources that the military offered or did not know about them. These wives were mailed information about the resources that were available before their husbands were deployed. Some wives didn't know whether they should use the military resources because they were afraid that it would reflect negatively on their husbands' careers. The sad result was that the support and help that the military offered was underused.[2] The same study showed that wives who thought that the Army provided enough support for them had less depression than wives who were dissatisfied, verifying that Army support is important to a family's adjustment to separations.[3] This is true for any branch or component of the military. Knowing that someone cares and is available when you need help enables you to remain more calm and confident when you are separated from your spouse.

The primary purpose of support groups is sharing. Military organizations hold meetings to *help* families cope with the challenges of deployments. Spouses do not go to military support meetings to receive charity or pity. Attending a military spouse support group once may show you that it is a place to meet other families with whom you have much in common. Support groups provide help and enable you to help others. There may be someone who has a problem larger than yours who you are able to help or a need for volunteers that interests you may be presented. Someone may share what helps them, and you can do the same.

Whether your deployment is due to a war, a peacekeeping or humanitarian mission, or other duty, the separation may result in some form of fear or anxiety. Some issues that cause concern are the following: not knowing exactly where the service member is or whether he has arrived at the deployed site; wondering what danger the serviceman may face; media reports of fighting or unrest in your husband's location; not hearing from your husband for some time; not knowing how to contact him; communication from him that shows that he's afraid; uncertainty about the amount of time your husband will be gone; not knowing how to show your husband support; not knowing anything about

What do wives see as their biggest problems when their husbands are deployed?

The majority (76.7 percent) said missing their husband's companionship was the most difficult problem they had to cope with. After that they cited loneliness, having to make decisions alone, decrease in their social life, concern for their health, and guilt about taking the role of leadership at home.

"The major source of stress was deployment; factors such as uncertainty about the length of deployment, missing one's spouse, difficulties in communication, concern about spouse's safety and living conditions produced considerable distress among the respondents." Dahl, Hunter, and McCubbin, 119.

his situation; uncertainty about managing the home over an extended time without your husband; concern about the health and welfare of family members in both locations; concern about the family's finances; and concern about your husband's reintegration into the family.[4] Whether family stress is caused by these or other concerns, it can wear down your ability to resist depression, irritability, or feeling overwhelmed.

Many families experience distress because of repeated changes of the departure time or because the departure interferes with family vacation plans or visits to relatives before the family member deploys. My family had nonrefundable plane tickets that we tried to return. If you find yourself in that situation, call the airline or travel agent. Tell them that unexpected military duty has changed your plans, and ask whether they can refund your ticket or give you a credit voucher for later travel if you send them a copy of your husband's orders or a letter from his Commander on official letterhead. Most airlines are understanding and will accommodate your request.

In addition to feeling overwhelmed after your husband leaves, your family may have to deal with the disappointment of being unable to go on a family trip that you had been looking forward to. To prevent feelings of disappointment from taking over, the family must find a means of strength to cope with the extra demands that they face. "Family members need support, not smothering; they need to be reminded of their strengths, not their weaknesses; they need to be invited to do what they can for themselves, not to have others do more and more for them."[5]

If you've experienced family separation and you know someone who is going through one for the first time, you may want to help her find ways to help herself. Both spouses who are going through separation for the first time and those who have been through separations before need support when their families are affected by deployment. They can probably help and encourage each other.

If you've experienced family separation before, try to help someone who has not by inviting her to the spouse or family support meeting at your military installation. You may also want to invite her to church or community meetings that are meaningful to you. If you have not been separated from your spouse before, look for meetings that will help you learn more about how to get through deployment. Ask your chaplain or someone in your spouse's chain of command (for example, the First

Sergeant, Chief Petty Officer, Unit Commander, or Ombudsman) if you don't know whether there are meetings on your installation. Many installations have family support meetings, and individual units often have small groups that meet in addition to the family meetings. Don't miss your opportunity to receive all of the information and encouragement that these groups offer.

II/10: THE ROLE OF FAITH DURING SEPARATION

There are a wide variety of faith groups represented in the military. Whatever one's faith preference, many people are naturally inclined to turn to God and to talk about their faith during deployments. The beauty of the pluralistic expression of faith in the military system is that it provides an opportunity to talk about our beliefs.

When we're away from those we love, "thoughts of family hover close, despite the thousands of miles that separate. And for Christians and non-Christians alike, faith in God can grow or be born as mankind is reminded of his mortality and the longing for peace."[1] Both spouses can get through deployments more efficiently if they have a spiritual perspective. We often hear people talk about how God was with them during times of trial. Especially during deployment, it can be comforting to be aware of God's presence and to be willing to talk about what helps us spiritually.

When my husband suddenly deployed, our Command Chaplain sent me a note of encouragement, enclosing an excerpt of something that a theologian named Dietrich Bonhoeffer wrote while imprisoned during World War II. Bonhoeffer talked about how much he missed his family.

> In the first place nothing can fill the gap when we are away from those we love, and it would be wrong to try and find anything. We must simply hold out and win through.... It is nonsense to say that God fills the gap: He does not fill it, but keeps it empty so that our communion with another may be kept alive, even at the cost of pain.... Times of separation are not a total loss, nor are they completely unprofitable for our companionship.... In spite of all the difficulties they bring, they can be a wonderful means of strengthening and deepening fellowship.... We must commend our loved ones wholly and unreservedly to God and leave them in his hands, transforming our anxiety for them into prayers on their behalf." Dietrich Bonhoeffer, Tegel Prison, Berlin, Christmas Eve, 1944[2]

I was comforted by the chaplain's note and by Bonhoeffer's quote. I felt like I was given permission to recognize the empty spot in my heart and not expect it to go away. It's normal to feel the ache of missing someone we love. Many people feel emptiness or gaps in their lives when their families are separated or are in uncertain circumstances. That empty feeling can be turned into something positive.

The emptiness you feel when you're apart can become a reminder to pray for your spouse and to trust God to take care of him or her. The emptiness can remind us that there's a place for our loved one in our hearts, awaiting their return. A military spouse observed that when her husband left, a piece of herself went too. But, she hastened to add, that's what you want! A part of you goes along with him, and you also keep a part of him with you.

Both husband and wife feel the pain of separation. If both have the same spiritual perspective, they'll be united even when they're apart by both looking to God for the extra strength to get through it. Viktor Frankl, Holocaust survivor and Swiss psychiatrist, maintains that one can face any crisis if the person grasps some meaning or purpose in it.[3] Many couples find meaning or purpose during times of separation by thinking more deeply about their spiritual lives, individually and on the family level.

Some find that they turn to God for the first time when faced with potential danger and uncertainty during separation from their loved ones. Of course we can't call God on the phone, but I like to think of Psalm 91:1 as the 9-1-1 for deployments. Psalm 91:1 says, "He that dwelleth in the secret place of the most High shall abide under the shadow of the Almighty."[4] Let's add Psalm 91:2: "I will say of the Lord, He is my refuge and my fortress: my God; in Him will I trust."[5] I hope you'll make this Scripture your 9-1-1 too, if you haven't already.

Separation from loved ones may make people think about what life would be like if the spouse didn't return, especially if the spouse is in harm's way. The complete lack of control over the situation produces feelings of anxiety. Author David Paap is convinced that faith is the most important factor that determines how a family facing the crisis of deployment or war will deal with their member's fears. In his book *Caring For Military Families*, Paap writes that "the only practical escape from this vicious cycle of anxiety is a spiritual one: trust in God.... faith and trust differ from human optimism or self-confidence in that they are not the result of human effort or reliance upon anything within ourselves."[6]

Chaplain Cory Cathcart said, "I really believe everyone has a God-shaped vacuum inside. Many try to fill it with other things, but in the end, only God fits your heart."[7] When traumatic events occur, the media often broadcasts public references to prayer and looking to God for help. Faith gives people the hope and courage that they need to get through trials. When people feel like they have nowhere to turn, God is there. Chaplain Carver said, "There's an old saying: 'You never know Jesus is all you need until He's all you've got.'"[8] During deployments, life is very different than life at home. You don't have much privacy, no family members, and you probably don't have a very comfortable bed. But those differences from normal life may actually make it easier for you to grow spiritually during deployment.

The realization that you have no control over circumstances may draw you to God for the first time or possibly back to God. "The power is in the Person to whom faith clings.... The great things that come about through crisis are not the result of 'great faith' but of faith, even a small and flickering faith, in the greatness of God's love and mercy in Jesus Christ."[9] It is the God your faith is in, not the greatness of your faith that will get you through.

Each morning, whether you're separated from a family member or not, you may find it helpful to begin the day by looking to God for guidance and strength for the day. The military lifestyle gives you unique opportunities to experience the peace and grace of God during hard times. Chaplain Stan Beach said, "When my situation can't be changed, I can work at learning and implementing productive responses that will honor the Lord."[10] Christian military spouses have found that to be true. Denise McColl said, "A good friend once told me, 'Pray as if everything depended on God; work as if everything depended on you!' Applying this concept works wonders during deployments!"[11] Sue Roberts advises separated families "not to pray for an easy life; pray to be a strong person."[12]

Admiral Grady Jackson said, "In many ways, I've never been closer spiritually to my family than when I've been away from them for extended periods, because those are the times I fully put them into the Lord's hands. When we move out in the job that the Lord has called us to do, He will take care of our families, especially if His call requires separation."[13]

Worry about the family back home is one of the greatest concerns that military service members face, but many families find that sharing in letters how faith is active in their lives helps ease that concern. Finding things to thank God for helps keep attitudes positive. If you consider yourself a believer but do nothing special to nurture your faith, you may find that a daily personal devotional time will help keep you positive and spiritually strong.

A Christian Air Force air crew member asked her Commander for permission to have a crew prayer before each mission. The Commander agreed and even led the prayers. Before long, the maintenance troops, other air crew, and the unit chaplain heard about the pre-flight prayers. By the time the crew member returned home from her deployment, she learned that crew members' spouses knew of their prayer routine and its uplifting effects on other troops. "Although prayer blessed us as it prepared our mental and spiritual focus each flight, we were amazed that God was using this experience to reach out to others in the military and back home," she said.[14] They felt God's presence with them and were encouraged.

My husband, Ren, had a similar experience when he was deployed. His Commander asked the chaplain to give a prayer as the last item in each of their pre-takeoff briefings. When the air crews returned from their missions, a chaplain always met the planes and was the first person to greet the crew as they deplaned. Ren said that the air crews felt encouraged and strengthened to have that spiritual contact before and after each mission.

Remember that God is with you anywhere you go, even in the most isolated place that the military may send you. When Chaplain Doug Carver was deployed, his area was attacked and he had to hurry into his chemical protection suit. As he put it on, he remembered telling his wife during his training that he felt almost claustrophobic in the suit and did not look forward to having to wear it. She said: "I'm going to pray that when you put that stuff on, God sings to you. Just imagine you're in God's garden, and He is walking with you."[15] Carver hadn't thought much about what she said, but when he sat in his bunker in his chem gear, he found that "the words of the old hymn drifted through his mind—*And He walks with me, and He talks with me, and He tells me I am His own.*"[16] He was comforted by God's presence and felt peace. I think he must have also felt thankful for a praying wife back home.

However, thoughts of families back home are not always on the minds of deployed military members. When you're away from your family it's easy to feel like you aren't accountable to them; separation may offer temptations that can threaten your relationship with your spouse. Temptations can be hard to resist. Statistics tell us that many marriages break down during times of separation because of the temptation to be unfaithful. One Marine who recognized that danger and wanted to protect himself from temptation developed his own set of guidelines to follow whenever he is away from his wife. They include the following:

- Temptation is easier to resist when we are closer to God, so devote the time you would otherwise have with your family to deepening your relationship to God.
- Find others who share your faith for friendship and prayer.
- Guard your eyes. When pornography tempts you, consciously remind yourself to fill your mind with movies, books, and magazines that encourage godly living.
- Consistently communicate with your wife.
- Always be accountable for your time during times of liberty. Don't go ashore alone, but go with someone who you know will help you avoid temptations. Avoid the appearance of evil. If people know you are a Christian, they will be silently watching to see whether you practice what you preach.
- Be alert. Realize that temptation can sneak up on you.[17]

These guidelines may be points that you want to consider for yourself, or you may already have your own drawn up. The important issue is to face the fact that temptation and unfaithfulness will likely be present whether you are the deployed husband or the wife at home, and you can help yourself resist if you have a plan to stay committed to your spouse. Christians are not exempt from challenges to marriage and should assume that they too will be tempted.

God will not be overcome by the challenges or temptations that we face, so if we turn to him, we can feel safer too. His representatives, the chaplains or ministers we look to for guidance, remind us that we don't have to be afraid, and they help us direct our attention to God. Oliver North and Sara Horn put together a wonderful book entitled *A Greater Freedom: Stories of Faith from Operation Iraqi Freedom*. Their book is full of examples of how faith carried military members through the trials of deployment. It provides encouraging pictures of faith in action and encourages readers to see God's hand in their lives.

When you feel overwhelmed, turn to the Lord himself. As you cultivate your relationship with God and feel the encouragement of your chapel or place of worship, you will be more equipped to deal with separation. "I encourage you to lean on someone during this deployment. I have been going to the Darmstadt International Baptist Church, and during this time in my life when I could be feeling absolutely alone in the world, I have been overwhelmed with a sense of support and love from my church family," an Army wife said.[18] Elizabeth Hoekstra's book *Keeping Your Family Close When Frequent Travel Pulls You Apart* provides a great example of what a difference it makes to have a faith-based approach to times of family separation.

With the support of others and your sense of God's strength within, you will be able to identify with the apostle Paul when he said, "We are hard pressed on every side, yet not crushed; we are perplexed, but not in despair; persecuted, but not forsaken; struck down, but not destroyed."[19] In addition to the strength and help that you draw from your personal faith, your chapel or place of worship may offer a support group for encouragement.

Since military chaplains experience deployment and family separation too, they can identify with your feelings. When he was on duty aboard the *Truman*, Chaplain Dunn decided to take prayer walks around the ship whenever his schedule would allow him time. He got the idea to walk throughout the ship and pray for safety and for the sailors when he took part in a Foreign Object Debris (FOD) walk on the flight deck. "He believes the power of prayer changes the lives of the men and women aboard."[20] Whether you are deployed in a desert, flying a plane, aboard a ship, or anywhere else, chaplains are there to help you through the tough times. They're also available back home to help family members. Who could be better equipped to help you through tough times? God and his representatives stand ready to meet your needs.

II/11: RESOURCES TO HELP YOU DURING DEPLOYMENT

RESOURCES FOR DEPLOYING PERSONNEL

Please see chapter V/5, "Resources for All Military Personnel and Their Families," for a more complete description and contact information for the following resources:

❖ **Web Sites operated by the National Institute for Building Long Distance Relationships. Each Web site has great links, ideas, and information.**
Dads at a Distance: www.daads.com
Moms Over Miles:
www.momsovermiles.com
Long Distance Couples:
www.longdistancecouples.com
Grandparenting from a Distance:
www.longdistancegrandparenting.com

❖ *101 Ways to Be a Long-Distance Super Dad … or Mom, Too!*
by George Newman
Available from
Blossom Valley Press
5141 E. Woodgate
PO Box 13378
Tucson, AZ 85732-3378
Phone: (520) 325-1224

❖ *A Greater Freedom: Stories of Faith from Operation Iraqi Freedom*
by Oliver North and Sara Horn

❖ *Deployment Devotions*
Available from
Resource Division of the USAF
Chaplain Service Institute
525 Chennault Circle
Maxwell AFB, AL 36112

❖ *A Special Prayer Service in Support of Deploying Forces and Families*
Available from
Creative Communications for the Parish:
1564 Fencorp Drive
Fenton, MO 63026
Phone: (800) 325-9414
www.creativecommunications.com
This resource includes prayers, hymns, and Scripture selections specifically for deployed forces, their families, and our nation.

RESOURCES FOR FAMILIES

Please see chapter V/5, "Resources for All Military Personnel and Their Families," for a more complete description and contact information for the following resources:

❖ **Military HOMEFRONT:**
www.militaryhomefront.dod.mil

❖ **Military Wives Web Sites (also includes a site for military husbands)**
www.militarywives.com is the home of many great Web sites.

❖ **Keeping You in Touch:**
www.keepingyouintouch.com
5030 Bobcat Lane SE
Port Orchard, WA 98367
Phone: (253) 851-9154

The Keeping You in Touch Web site provides support to military families, especially during deployments. The Web site includes chat forums for Active Duty members, military spouses, parents of military members, kids, teens, and more. In addition to providing links to other sites of interest, it offers care package ideas and has a photo album of deployed troops.

❖ **Military Student:**
www.militarystudent.org

❖ *The Business Traveling Parent: How to Stay Close to Your Kids When You're Far Away*
by Dan Verdick

Mr. Verdick includes activities to do with your children before you leave, while you're gone, and when you get back home. He also gives resources to expand on some of his ideas.

❖ *Command* **magazine**
Fall 1989 issue, Volume 38, No. 3
Available from Officers' Christian Fellowship
3784 South Inca
Englewood, CO 80110
www.gospelcom.net/ocf

❖ *Heroes at Home: Help & Hope for America's Military Families*
by Ellie Kay

❖ *Keeping Your Family Close When Frequent Travel Pulls You Apart*
by Elizabeth Hoekstra

❖ *Holding Down the Fort*
by Peggy Sue Wells and Mary Ann Froelich

❖ *When Dad's at Sea*
by Mindy L. Pelton

The author offers free personalized and autographed messages to children on adhesive bookplates. Contact her at peltonm@earthlink.net.

❖ *Uncle Sam's Kids: When Duty Calls*
by Angela Sportelli-Rehak

❖ *Footsteps of the Faithful*
by Denise McColl

❖ *Service Separations: A Wife's Perspective*
by Beverly Moritz
Available from Focus on the Family or Officers' Christian Fellowship

❖ **Children's Booklets from Army Community Service (ACS):**
www.armycommunityservice.org
(Virtual ACS)

When you go to this Web site, click on "Deployment Readiness" on the left side then "Deployment Tools" then "Download Center." When the page comes up, click on "Children's Workbooks." You'll see the titles of booklets that talk about military separations.

Print any that you are interested in, and remember that these are for *everyone*, not just Army families!

❖ **Scriptographic Resources Published by Channing L. Bete Company**
Write From the Heart stationery kits
My Book About When My Parent Has to Go Away, for preschoolers
Know What? My Parent Is Being Deployed! for ages 6–8

Who Knew? The Deployment Issue, for ages
9–11

Until Your Parent Comes Home Again, a coloring and activities book about
deployment for ages 6–9

Let's Talk About Deployment, an information and activities book for ages 9–12

Deployment Days, a coloring calendar for
military families

*Family Readiness Groups: Caring for
Military Families*

Make the Most of Family Support Groups

*Mission: Readiness: A Personal and Family
Guide,* Active Duty Edition

❖ **Publications by The Bureau For At-Risk
Youth**

Military Family Forum Booklets:
  Deployment and Reunion
  Effective Child Discipline
  The Military Lifestyle and Children
  Loss and Change
  Family Readiness
  Stress and the Military Family
  Family Communication

Other Products:
  Military Family Writing Kit
  Our Military Family Scrapbook
  Coloring Book: *I'll Miss You* (military
  deployment)

❖ **Publications by Abbey Press**

Care Notes:
  *When You Miss Someone Deeply, During
  a Time Apart*
  *Taking Time for Yourself When You're
  Feeling Stressed?*
  Letting Faith Help You Handle Stress
  Doing Your Best as a Single Parent

Available from your chaplain or:
  Abbey Press
  One Hill Drive
  Customer Service Plant 1

Meinrad, IN 47577
Phone: (888) 374-4226 or (800) 962-4760
www.abbeypress.com

❖ ***Today's Military Wife: Meeting the
Challenges of Service Life***
by Lydia Sloan Cline

❖ **Web Sites operated by the National
Institute for Building Long Distance
Relationships. Each Web site has great
links, ideas, and information.**
Dads at a Distance: www.daads.com
Moms Over Miles:
  www.momsovermiles.com
Long Distance Couples:
  www.longdistancecouples.com
Grandparenting from a Distance:
  www.longdistancegrandparenting.com

❖ **National Military Family Association:
www.nmfa.org**
This is a national organization whose sole
focus is the military family.

❖ **Handbook for Military Families**
The April supplement to *Army Times,
Navy Times,* and *Air Force Times* (updated
yearly). Available by subscription, at military exchanges, and in many libraries.

Navy Resources

❖ ***When Dad's at Sea***
by Mindy L. Pelton
  The author offers free personalized
and autographed messages to children
on adhesive bookplates. Contact her at
peltonm@earthlink.net.

❖ ***Daddy's Days Away* (a deployment
activity book for parents and children)**

NAVY PROGRAMS AND WORKSHOPS

❖ **Keeping in Touch**

The Commanding Officer (usually of a ship) writes a familygram newsletter to keep family and friends informed about the Command. The Ombudsman is available to mediate between the military and families. An informal telephone tree consisting of Command family members passes on information of interest to everyone in the Command, such as changes to a ship's schedule.

❖ **"Gator-Aid" for Mid-Deployment**

Family members are enabled to cope with mid-deployment blues and focus on plans for the homecoming through discussion and activities.

RESOURCES FOR MILITARY CHAPEL OR CIVILIAN CHURCH CONGREGATIONS

❖ *The Other War*

Available from
    Concordia Publishing House
    Phone: (800) 325-3040
    www.cph.org
A twenty-minute video and discussion guide with an extensive resource list for use in ministering to those afflicted by war.

❖ **A Special Prayer Service in Support of Deploying Forces and Families**

Available from:
    Creative Communications for the Parish:
    1564 Fencorp Drive
    St. Louis, MO 63026
    Phone: (800) 325-9414
    www.creativecommunications.com
This resource includes prayers, hymns, and Scripture selections specifically for deployed forces, their families, and our nation.

III

REUNION

III/1: FINALLY, IT'S OUR TURN!

◩

We were still having spouse support meetings every week, but fewer and fewer wives came. Many of my friends stopped coming for the second time. They were wives of men on tanker crews, and their husbands deployed on forty-five- or ninety-day rotations, since the planes had to come back home to be serviced that often. I was one consistent attendee who had been there through the whole thing.

When Ren left, his orders, like those of many others, indicated that he would be deployed for ninety days. When Commanders began to deploy people in August, they could only guess at how long it would be. When I said good-bye to Ren, something inside told me that he wouldn't be home for Christmas. I was right.

At the support meetings, they announced when planes were coming in with people returning from the Gulf so that everyone who could and wanted to would be there to welcome them home. There was a chart in the front of the room that held yellow ribbons, each bearing the name of someone who had been deployed and returned. Yellow ribbons were everywhere, but, so far, none had Ren's name written on it. It became almost a ritual for someone to come up to me and say, "It should have been your turn before mine. Your husband has been gone longer than anyone on our base." That didn't make the waiting any easier.

On the 215th day after Ren left, it was finally my turn. He flew into the commercial airport. I wanted to have a quiet, private reunion with Ren and Dan, but a lot of people from the base wanted to welcome him home too, so our private family time would have to wait.

I was overwhelmed by the number of people at the airport to welcome him home! There were video cameras and people everywhere. I felt conspicuous, on exhibition. When he came through the security checkpoint at the airport, he was surprised to see the people there to greet him. We embraced awkwardly, conscious of the throng surrounding us waiting to shake his hand, the video camera watching every move we made.

I tried to hurry him through the handshakes. He said hello to each person, not wanting to leave anyone unacknowledged for coming to greet him.

"Get him out of here," the Commander told me.

I tried, but he didn't want to hurt anyone's feelings by hurrying away too quickly. I had to remind myself not to feel hurt that he felt that way. After 215 days apart, I could wait a few more minutes.

We finally got in the car, but we hardly knew where to start, except to agree that it sure was good to be back together. That was a good place to start. Yes, start. It may have been the end of the deployment, but we had to begin life together again after a 215-day separation.

I wasn't the only one looking forward to reunion. Here's the story from Ren's perspective:

Coming Home at Last!

It was the end of February 1991, and after almost six weeks, the war ended. What a relief! Now, the buzz throughout the camp was speculation about when we might be released to go back home. Everyone was excited and living with anticipation to get the word quickly, and "get out of Dodge!" We had been there for a long time and were weary. I remember sitting in the Commander's staff meetings, discussing the plan for releasing troops. The big question was "Who goes first?"

We talked about sending the youngest and lowest-ranking airmen back home first. Then, the idea was brought up that those who were on the island the longest should be the first to return. This got a lot of discussion. The Commander, Col. Terry Burke, was in favor of "first arrived, first to leave," and that became his policy. That was good news to many, including me. However, I felt awkward, because that meant that I would be among the first to leave, and I didn't want my staff to feel bad that I was leaving before them or the troops to feel bad that the senior chaplain was leaving them behind.

I didn't want anyone to think or feel that I was giving up my leadership and not caring for them. I shared this concern with Colonel Burke, and he said, "I don't care how noble you feel, or want to be, but you're on the first plane load out of here. You got here before most of us, so you're leaving before us. You got that?"

"Yes sir," I replied. I must admit to mixed feelings. It's tough

leaving behind people who I "went through hell with," but at the
same time, my heart was pounding with excitement to see Carol,
Mike, and Dan again. Carol and Dan were at home in Wichita,
Kansas, and Mike was in college in Grand Rapids, Michigan.

As I left Colonel Burke's office and headed back to my tent, my
heart was racing as I anticipated finally pulling out my duffle bag,
suitcase, "A" bag, and "C" bag to get ready to pack. The "A" bag
was the "All Purpose Bag," which contained my sleeping bag, mess
kit, a few items of clothing, helmet, etc. The "C" bag was my
"Chemical Bag." It contained my chemical gear, which included my
gas mask, mask filters, chemical or "chem" suit, rubber boots and
gloves, etc.

When I returned to our tent, I called my staff together to tell
them that I would be on the first plane out. They all responded with
a hand clap, smiled, and said they had hoped I would be among the
first to leave. I told them my misgivings about being the boss and
leaving them and the troops behind, but they totally supported my
departure. I knew they could do a great job taking care of the troops
until the camp was empty. I was proud of them.

Then, I found a phone to call Carol with the good news. That
was a special day for me! *Now, at last*, I thought, *we can all anticipate
the reunion phase of this deployment—something good—together*. I
thought things would be different at home. Knowing that people
change over time, I was really curious to see Dan, because he was in
high school and still growing. I wanted to see how much he had
changed.

The word soon got out that the first plane load would leave the
camp in about two weeks, and the first to leave would be those who
had arrived first. People started to come to me to say good-bye. That
made the last two weeks kind of bittersweet. There were lots of "last
things" in those two weeks. During those two weeks, we got some
good news: We did not need to carry our "A" and "C" bags back
with us. We could dump them on a pile at a drop-off point in tent
city, and Uncle Sam would take care of them. That made two less
bags for me to carry, so I wasn't going to argue.

Finally the day came for my departure. I went to the flight line,
checked my bags, and went through the out-processing line. The
other chaplains walked with me toward the plane. We prayed
together and then posed for a picture in front of the plane. After saying good-bye to everyone, I walked up the long ramp into the KC-10
Stratotanker, an air-to-air refueller. I found a sling seat along the

wall. The plane was full of cargo, cinched down with chains in the middle of the floor. Along the wall, every seat was filled with a happy GI. Beneath the floor was a fuselage half full of JP-4 jet fuel. We were tasked to do a refueling mission on our flight from Diego Garcia to Guam. So, even on our way home, we were still involved in a mission.

We took off at around four in the afternoon. As the plane lifted off the runway, I was happy to be going back home again. Yet, as I looked down at the island of Diego Garcia for the last time, I also felt fond memories for all of the experiences I had had there over the last months. I knew that many of my good friends were on the ground, looking up at our plane, waving good-bye.

We arrived in Guam around two the following morning. We were tired, sleepy, sweaty, and dirty, because it was hot inside the plane. Once we landed, we were herded onto a bus and taken to billeting. I got the key to my room and went to find it in the dark. Once in the room, I dumped my bags, took a shower, which felt wonderful, and hit the bed. This was the first "real" bed I slept in for over seven months, and man, did it ever feel good!

While on Guam, we were confined to the barracks area. Staying in the area was important because we were on notice for when our next plane would leave. We didn't know when that would be, but we had to be ready to go at any time. Believe me, no one left the area, since we knew that if we did, we might miss our flight home. We finally left later that day and flew to Castle AFB, California. It felt weird, yet good, to walk into the very same hangar that I departed from almost eight months earlier. There we went through the in-processing line and customs and then were given rooms.

There I waited, once more, for further instructions for the next leg of my trip. At Castle AFB, I could change into civilian clothes for the first time, which was nice. I found out that the connection for the next leg of my trip was a flight from Castle AFB to Barksdale AFB, Louisiana. Uncle Sam wanted to pay for a commercial ticket for the shortest distance possible, and Shreveport, Louisiana, where Barksdale AFB is located, is the closest base to Wichita, Kansas. They didn't have any military flights going to McConnell AFB, so I would have to fly into the commercial airport at Wichita.

Once I knew what the next leg of my trip would be, I called Carol, Dan, and Mike. It felt good to talk with them while standing on American soil again. I also called my brother, Al, in Southern California. He and Cindy came up to Castle AFB as quickly as they could and spent the rest of the day and evening with me. I felt a little strange to see them before I saw my own family. I spent two days at Castle AFB. The next day, I boarded the plane for Barksdale.

As we touched down in Barksdale, I heard sirens everywhere. I thought there might be a problem on the runway with another plane, or, heaven forbid, with our plane. I didn't want to come this far to have plane problems. We parked and sat in the aircraft for what seemed like a long time, and the sirens continued. I thought there must be a big problem on the ground with so many sirens and since we were stuck in position. I wondered whether mechanics might be working on our plane. There were no windows to give us a clue what was happening.

Finally, the doors opened and we heard a crowd yelling. A Chief Master Sergeant on the plane unfurled a large American flag and started waving it out the door. Then, I noticed that all of the sirens were a welcome for us. There was a large crowd assembled, along with a makeshift band. As we deplaned, we walked through a gauntlet of people standing on both sides, cheering and shaking our hands. That was an unexpected welcome I'll never forget.

Once inside the air passenger terminal, I went directly to the desk, where I showed my orders and received commercial tickets for my last leg of the trip, to Wichita, Kansas. I called Carol to give her my flight information. We connected for the last time before we would see each other. With tickets in hand, I claimed my bags, went into a holding area, and finally boarded an Air Force bus, which took many of us to the local airport. After about an hour, I was in the air again, flying home.

I arrived at the Wichita airport at approximately 10 p.m. I couldn't wait to get off the plane, run through the jetway, and see Carol and Dan. As I walked quickly down the hall and around a corner, I saw a group of people and heard someone say, "There he is."

As I walked down the ramp, Carol and Dan came up to meet me. We hugged and kissed, which was wonderful, but I was self-conscious in front of the crowd. Right behind Dan and Carol was Colonel Mangles, our Wing Commander at McConnell AFB. He patiently waited until the three of us untangled and then welcomed me back. Someone had a video camera going the whole time, but I don't think I ever did see the video.

After the Commander welcomed me back, he introduced me to others in the crowd. That got me started shaking hands with everyone who came out to greet me. It took quite a while, and once I was done with all of the hand shaking and hugging, I could finally get back to my precious, waiting Carol and Dan. I felt rotten inside that they had to wait for me to finish greeting everyone, and I just wanted to be alone with them. That was another awkward moment in the reunion phase. Over the years, as I thought of Carol and Dan waiting for me to finish shaking hands with everyone, I have always felt remorse and wish I hadn't done that. I got caught up in the moment, but nevertheless, it was not thoughtful to keep them waiting. I wish I had simply thanked everyone for coming out to greet me and then left with my family. I can't undo the past, but I certainly can learn from my mistakes.

Once we left the airport and were alone in the car, I finally felt a "finality" to my coming home and being reunited with my family. That was a defining moment for me. It ended my deployment and began the reunion.[1]

III/2: BACK HOME, SWEET HOME

◣

You've just heard when your family's separation will end and are happy to think about being a complete family again. Those at home are busy making preparations for the homecoming, while the deployed spouse envisions home as he left it. Family members at both locations have to prepare to reunite. They must realize that things will be different than they were before. If they aren't prepared for this fact, the relief of being together will soon fade into discontent.

CHANGE IS INEVITABLE

Every member of the family has probably changed during the separation. The changes can be as obvious as the physical growth of the children or the birth of a new baby, a spouse's new job, weight loss or gain, or a new hairstyle. Changes may be less definable, such as greater independence, feelings of anger about the separation, uncertainty about whether the deployed spouse will still feel the same way about the family, and fear about the changes that have occurred within each family member and how those changes will affect the family. The amount of change that takes place in the family depends on the individual family and the length of the separation.

Longer separations typically cause more emotional pain and adjustment and also produce the need for more understanding and patience when the family is reunited. The family at home may have developed a new routine or taken on extra activities to help them deal with the missing spouse's absence. Everyone in the family has to be sensitive as they decide together whether they'll continue the new pattern when he gets back, try to go back to the way they did things before the deployment, or form a different, revised version of family life.

For example, children grow and respond to different kinds of discipline as they gain understanding. Maybe when Dad left the child responded to a slap on the hand, but while Dad was gone the child progressed to the point where he responds better to being sent to his room to think about what he did, followed with a parent-child discussion about the proper behavior. Little children may not recognize Dad when he gets home or may feel afraid of him at first.

These and other differences can add stress to the joy of being reunited as a family. The "Eastern Virginia Medical Association states that reunion and homecomings are more stressful than the initial predeployment and deployment phase."[1] Author Richard D. Thompson acknowledges that most people know that reuniting the family is another beginning rather than an end and that letters cannot substitute for family experiences in life. He says that families should renew their relationships by discovering "what changes have occurred in each person"[2] rather than concentrating on the tension of the change.

Change can be negative or positive. Change often makes us feel afraid or as if we've lost something comfortable. We can choose not to dwell on the fear or loss that is involved in change, and even though the process of change often hurts, we can learn to see the growth and benefits that result from change. Of course, this process takes time.

If a wife has been attending individual or family support groups during her husband's absence, it will probably be helpful to continue attending those meetings for at least a few weeks after he returns. Attending the meetings will give the family a sense of continuity as they work through the process of reuniting the family, as well as show the husband how the family received support and encouragement when he was gone. Many returning husbands are encouraged to see for themselves the support that their families had while they were gone, and they're proud that their families participated in a support group. Attending the group meetings as a complete family can help the family find a starting point to talk about what happened during the separation and to understand each others' needs and feelings related to the deployment.

In his book *The Art of Coming Home*, Craig Storti suggests that those returning from overseas experiences have a mentor to help them adjust to returning home.[3] The military usually has sponsors to help families adjust to overseas permanent change of station assignments, so Storti's idea is one that many of us may be familiar with. You may want to consider asking a family or person you respect who has been through what you've experienced to be your mentor as you reintegrate into life as a family and at work and adjust to the cultural changes of coming home.

III/3: PREPARING YOUR FAMILY FOR REUNION

◧

Each member of the family has needs resulting from the separation, whether he or she is conscious of them or not. Many families grieve because they miss the way that the family was before the separation. They don't think about the fact that families are always in a state of change, even without military separations. Natural changes within a family occur so gradually that few members are aware of them.

Because family changes that occur as a result of military separation are often more sudden and unwelcome than life's normal progressive changes, they are harder to accept. Families may feel like separations are interruptions to life rather than changes in life. After the interruption, family life is expected to go back to what it was before. In reality, that seldom, if ever, happens.

A wife may have had to learn to change the oil in the car for the first time when her husband was gone, and after doing so, she doesn't know why she was afraid of doing it or uncomfortable doing it before. She may continue to change the oil in her car after her husband is back home again, not realizing that he expects her to want him to do it for her. The wife's growth (in car care and in other areas) could make her husband wonder if he is still needed.

Human sensitivities can make us misinterpret actions of family members and bring us to the wrong conclusions. That's why, especially after a long period of separation, family members need time to adjust to being together again and time to devote attention to understanding each other's feelings. Families should expect a time of adjustment without fearing that it will be traumatic. Don't expect family life to be perfect after a military separation. It wasn't perfect before the separation. Everyone has to adjust his or her thinking and behavior. It may help to talk about the deployment. You may want to reread letters together or talk about specific differences in the way the home operated.

Without realizing it, family members may have put Dad on a pedestal. The tendency to glamorize Dad's military service is natural, because it comes from love for him and from missing the good things about him. As the family misses Dad they tend to minimize or forget his weaknesses or bad habits. But when he returns, he will probably still have them, and the other family members will have their weaknesses too. At first the family will be so excited to be together that they will be able to ignore each other's irritations and want to party.

Families should celebrate being together again. Party and enjoy each other after the time apart. We have family parties when our family reunites. The rule with our family parties is that we only eat junk food (hot dogs, pizza, snack food, etc.) and each family member gets to choose a game that we all play together. It may take an afternoon or evening to play all of the chosen games, and the extended time together adds to the feeling of cele-bration as well as provides time for us to reconnect. Lots of casual conversation occurs during the games that helps Ren in his reentry into the family. Without formally talking about it, we end up briefing him about how things were done while he was gone and helping him understand what the boys are interested in now.

In *The Business Traveling Parent,* Dan Verdick suggests ideas for family celebrations. Make your family homecoming celebration fun! After a rea-sonable time, you will realize that you have celebrated long enough. That length of time depends on the individual family and the length of their sep-aration.

As the transition to a more normal lifestyle occurs, you'll begin to think about what you expect for the family as a whole and for each individual and examine whether the expectations are realistic. Of course, it's hard to be objective when the family has been separated for a long time, and the excite-ment of the reunion can cloud the objectivity that is there. There are some expectations that most families will have in common.

WHAT FAMILIES SHOULD EXPECT AS THEY REUNITE

To understand the changes that take place while the family is separated, each person in the family may want to answer these questions and share the answers with the rest of the family:

What do I hope has not changed?

What do I know has changed and will be different?

What am I worried about most as we get together again?

What specific problems do I think this separation might have caused in our family?

How do I think our family will respond to being together again?

How will our lives be different because of this deployment?

As you think about those questions and others that apply to your family, there are some things that you can expect as you prepare for your family's reunion:

- Expect the love of your family to be as strong as it was before the separation.

- Expect excitement and celebration, even overwhelming joy, when the missing family member arrives.

- Expect married couples to want romantic time alone. Try to take leave time both with the children and just as a couple, if possible.

- Everyone in the family should be free to tell those they've been apart from how much they missed them. People like to hear that someone missed them. Tell them often.

- Expect to see changes in the emotional and physical stamina of each family member.

- Family problems will not disappear during family separations. If children have trouble in school or you are short of money before the deployment, you can expect the problems to still be there.

- Expect some sadness or depression after the initial excitement of the homecoming wears off. If any member of the family individually or the family as a whole has trouble sharing feelings and adjusting to the changes that have taken place, don't be afraid to ask for help. Sometimes a few observations by a competent counselor are all it takes to enable families to work through the adjustment.

- Expect the adjustment to take time. If the separation has been long, the family will need more than a week or two to adjust.

- Expect each family member to need private time and space to think and adjust to the reunion.

- Expect friends and relatives to be anxious to see your spouse. If friends and relatives want to visit, make sure that you have enough time to reunite as a family *before* you have company. You might need to ask people to wait a few weeks to visit. Family comes first.

- Expect the reunion to be most satisfying if everyone is flexible.

- Expect change and be ready to do things differently rather than resist changes that will occur.

- Your family may not have the same attitude toward your military career as they did before you left. You may want to talk about how they feel about it now.

EXPECTATIONS FOR SPOUSES AT HOME

- Expect to have mixed feelings before your husband gets home. You may be excited about seeing each other but unsure about how it will feel to be together again. You may wonder what has changed. In the excitement of being together again, you may want to make everything perfect, as if you were going to entertain a celebrity, but maybe your budget won't allow for extra expenses.

- You may wonder whether your husband will look the same and fit into the family in the same way as he did before the separation. Will he approve of the way that the household has been run in his absence?

- Expect your husband to have changed. Realize that you have changed too. If you know specific ways that you have changed, discuss them with your husband.

- If your husband has been far away from home, expect him to have jet lag and to need time to physically adjust to your time zone.

- Your husband may feel culture shock when he returns. He may have become used to fewer choices at the grocery store, for example, or simple meals with no option to eat in restaurants of his own choosing. Expect him to need time to adjust to huge grocery stores with many products and other parts of our American lifestyle that he has not experienced while he was away from home.

- Your husband may feel emotionally let down or think that you don't understand what he has been through.

- Expect your husband to want you to recognize the stress that he felt while he was gone. Both of you had stress. Don't give in to the temptation to think you had it harder than he did. Support each other. Allow each other to talk. Listening is an act of love.

- Don't schedule too many activities. Expect your family to need time alone to relax. You know what the budget can handle, so don't plan to spend extra money on homecoming celebrations unless you can afford to do so.

■ If your husband has been in a dangerous area, he may be exceptionally quiet or sensitive. Expect that he will need time to open up. Be patient. He may not be ready for a structured routine right away.

■ Expect to feel concern about when he may be deployed again.

■ It's possible that sexual closeness may be awkward at first. Think of your sexual reunion as a honeymoon and be sensitive to your husband.

■ Expect to want to make up for lost time.

■ Reassure your husband of your love; tell him you love him.

■ You may wonder whether he was faithful to you while he was gone or whether he missed you. Maintaining good communication throughout the separation can make these concerns avoidable.

■ Expect your husband to need to know that your family still needs him. You've managed without him for a long time, and he may wonder whether you can get along as well without him. Make sure he knows that even though you've been *able* to get through the deployment without him at home, you don't *want* to be separated and are happy that you're together again.

■ Expect your husband to wonder how or whether he still fits into the family. Be aware of the fact that your children may come to you for everything and ignore Dad.

■ Expect your husband to feel rejected or hurt if your children hold back from him. Expect to have to help him understand the best way to approach your young children. There weren't any children deployed with him, and he may not remember everything he knows about relating to children without your gentle reminder.

■ Expect that your spouse may want to step right in to handle all of the family's responsibilities again. Talk about how to handle family responsibilities and give it time to develop.

■ Expect that it will be hard for you to give up your sole control of the family to share it with your husband.

■ Expect your husband not to notice some of the adjustments that you need to make because he is home again. He wasn't there, so he doesn't know how things went in his absence.

■ You may feel like you no longer have much time for yourself. That's because you've become used to being alone more often during the separation; you need time to adjust to being together and still having some personal time.

■ Remember that during the deployment your husband only had to think about his preferences during non-duty hours. If he forgets to include you or your children in his plans at first, don't take it personally. Try to think of it as a normal part of adjusting to being together again. Talk openly and lovingly with him about this part of the reentry process.

■ Expect to need lots of readjustment. You each adjusted to being single during the deployment, and you'll each have to adjust to being married again.

■ You may get tired of hearing your husband tell people about his deployment experiences. Listen patiently and with interest.

EXPECTATIONS FOR THE DEPLOYED SPOUSE

■ Don't develop fantasies or unrealistic expectations about what your homecoming will be like.

■ Expect to miss the excitement or glamour of the deployment. Don't expect your family to think of you as a hero because of what you did on the deployment. To them, your absence meant hardship and inconvenience, and although they appreciate your job and are proud of you, they aren't likely to see your deployment as out of the ordinary.

■ Some of your friends or family may not want to hear about your deployment experiences. That may just be a reflection of their confusion about how they should relate to you after the separation. In time, they may be ready to listen. Try to find other ways to re-connect if they don't seem interested in your deployment experiences.

■ Expect to feel concern about being deployed again.

■ Realize that you may have changed while you were gone. If you know specific ways that you have changed, you may want to discuss them with your wife.

■ You may experience culture shock when you return home. After adjusting to life in a different environment while you are deployed, you may be surprised at how you react to life back home. Simple things, like having too many products to choose from at the grocery store, may irritate or overwhelm you at first.

■ Soon after you get home, go to the commissary, exchange, and gas station to get an idea of what the prices of routine items are. This will help you understand any changes that may have been necessary in the household budget. Expect to have some concerns about the family budget.

- You may feel like no one understands what you've been through.
- You may feel emotional letdown after you get home.
- You may think that other people's concerns seem petty because of what you've been through.
- Expect to be treated like a guest when you come home. Enjoy your family's attention and celebrate being together.
- Expect that you will need to talk about your experiences.
- Expect your wife to be a little jealous that you have been able to travel places she has never been. Be sensitive about describing where you were.
- It's possible that sexual closeness may be awkward at first. Think of your sexual reunion as a honeymoon and be sensitive to your wife. Court her.
- Remember that you and your wife adjusted to living like you were single during the deployment and that it will take time and adjustment to live as a married couple again.
- Tell your wife that you love her often to reaffirm your relationship.
- You may wonder whether your wife was faithful to you while you were gone or whether she missed you. Good communication throughout the separation can make these concerns avoidable.
- Expect your wife to be more independent.
- Your wife may have new friends.
- If your wife was involved in a support group when you were gone, she may ask you to go to meetings with her. Don't hesitate to go.
- Expect your wife to want you to recognize the stress that she felt while you were gone. Both of you had stress. Don't give in to the temptation to think that you had it harder than she did. Support each other and listen to each other.
- Expect to want to make up for lost time. You can't replace the time that you were apart, so go slowly and start over instead of trying to make up for your time apart.
- Expect your wife to have new skills or possibly a new job since you left. Find ways to encourage her and let her know you're proud of her. Think about her needs and show her that her activities and interests are important to you.
- You may feel like a stranger in your own home at first, but you will soon fit in again and it will feel like home. Allow time for the feelings and adjustments.

- You may not notice that your return is causing adjustment for your family, *but it is*. Try to pay attention to what adjustments are being made.

- During your deployment you had only your own preferences to think about during non-duty hours. It may take conscious reminders to adjust your thinking to take your family's schedule and preferences into consideration again. Talk with the family about this, and see it as a normal part of your reentry into the family.

- Expect changes to occur at home. Your household probably ran differently in your absence, and you may not know how things are done now. Observe for yourself and ask your wife what family routines are like now. Knowing what to expect will help you fit into the routine as everyone adjusts to your homecoming.

- Try not to come home and take control of everything right away. Take time to see how the family managed without you and ease back into your roles. The family had to do everything while you were away and probably managed quite well in your absence. If decisions were made that you would have handled differently, remember that those decisions were probably made under stress and your family might not have been used to making decisions, so try to be positive. Show appreciation for their management, and talk about how the roles will change now that you are home again. Be patient.

- Expect to wonder whether you handled everything right from a distance while you were gone, as well as upon your arrival back home. You'll probably wonder when things will return to normal. What was normal before your time away will be different from the normal pattern that you will establish after your return.

- Enjoy partying and celebrating. Just don't lose your common sense.

- Expect it to be difficult to know what to say to each family member at first. If you have been gone for a long time, you will probably have to ease back into communicating with the family before you feel as intimate with each member as you did before you left. As you have time, talk to and listen to each child and your wife.

- Expect your children to need your reassurance.

- Expect your children to continue the habits that they developed while you were gone. They may not remember to ask you if they want to do something but go only to your wife. It will take time for them to remember that now they can ask you as well as your wife for permission to do things. If your children come to you first, try to find out how things were done while you were gone before you respond to their requests so that you don't give them different rules than your wife does or contradict her answers.

- Expect to see growth and change in your children. They won't be just like they were when you left. They may have new interests or skills.

- Familiar sights or neighborhoods may seem different than you remember them. There may be new buildings or streets, or old buildings may be gone.

- Don't avoid people or withdraw if you don't feel like you fit in immediately.

- Your friends may seem different than they were before you left.

- You may miss those who deployed with you at first.

- You may want to talk to someone who has gone through what you have about how it feels to adjust to being home again.

- You receive ribbons, awards, or medals for doing a good job in the military. Remember that your spouse's only appreciation for supporting you and enduring deployments may be your words of thanks!

COMING HOME TO A BABY

If your wife gave birth to a child while you were gone, your relationship will be very different when you return, especially if the baby is your first child. You may need to talk about how to share the joy of your child and the responsibilities of parenthood. To ease your transition into your new family, you may want to consider the following:

- Ease in slowly. Ask your wife for hints about how to relate to and care for the baby.

- Remember how your wife last described the baby's stage of growth and abilities so that you have an idea of what the baby is like.

- Try to be realistic about what you expect of the baby and your wife. Your wife may be exhausted, fatigued, and in need of relief. The baby may cry a lot.

- They will be happy to see you, and that may make your reunion seem perfect. Try to be helpful and concentrate on the joy, rather than the extra work or loss of freedom that may result from having a new baby.

- Small babies will need lots of cuddling, skin contact, and time to study your face and eyes.

- If your child is seven months of age or older, he or she may need more time to accept you because you seem like a stranger to him or her.

- Expect that you and your wife will handle and care for the baby differently. As long as you don't handle the baby too roughly, that's OK. The baby will enjoy getting to know you and the way you relate to him or her.

- You may be frustrated about what you've missed in your baby's life while you were gone. If you can be patient and persistent, you will establish your relationship to the child and will feel caught up in time.

One father returned home from a deployment, and the daughter that was a baby when he left acted like he was a stranger. It broke his heart at first, but after a couple of days she came to him. He said, "Now I make sure to do the little things, like bathing her, changing her, teaching her lessons. My wife says I'm a much better man, that I'm more patient." After you adjust to changes in your family life, you may become more patient, and you will surely be a better person too!

CHILDREN'S FEELINGS AND REUNION

Children may not be aware of their emotional needs or understand the changes that take place when Daddy is home again. You may want to read them books that relate family changes and transitions in a manner that they can identify with. You may want to consider these ideas:

- Don't expect children to be miniature adults. They may respond to your return in childish ways.

- Babies born during the deployment or less than a year old will probably not know who Daddy is and may cry when he holds them or pull away from him. Hug and hold them as much as you can, and become involved in bathing and feeding them.

- Children between one and three years of age may be unsure about Daddy and avoid him, hide from him, or be slow to approach him. Don't force holding them or showing them affection. If you give them space and time to warm up to you they will. Sit at their level and relate to them in a gentle and fun way.

- Children three to five years old may be afraid of Daddy or have feelings of guilt about making him go away. They may talk a lot to bring you up to date or misbehave to get your attention. Listen to them and accept their feelings. If you play with them and ask them to show you what new programs they like on TV or what their favorite books are, they will sense your reinforcement of your love for them.

- Children six to twelve years old may want a lot of Dad's time and attention.

They may dread your return out of fear that they will be disciplined. At the same time, they may boast about how proud they are of you. Draw closer to them by looking at their school work with them, looking at family pictures, and praising them whenever you can. Try not to criticize them.

- Teenagers may be excited or moody or act like they don't care about the reunion. They may feel guilty because they're afraid that they didn't live up to your expectations while you were gone. They will wonder how your return will affect their responsibilities and the household rules, and they may not want to change anything to accommodate you. Listen to them without judging them. Don't tease them about fashion, style, or music. Respect their privacy. Try to get to know their friends. Share what happened to you while you were gone, and ask your teenagers to share what they did while you were gone.

- Children of any age might feel guilty about not living up to Dad's expectations. This can especially be true if they were warned as they were disciplined that there would be consequences when Dad got home.

- Resist the urge to take over disciplining the children right away. They're used to their mother's style of discipline and need time to adjust to your presence before you begin to do a lot of the discipline. Go easy on them for a while.

- Children may feel caught between loyalties for Mom and Dad. Some children may resent Dad because he replaced them in Mom's affections.

- Expect to take time to talk to and listen to your children. It will take time to regain their trust and closeness. Do something with each child individually that he or she will enjoy. Maybe she'd like to repeat the special activity that you did with her before you deployed. Your child may need extra time alone with Mom and with Dad.

- Remember that the children are adapting to the change in routine since Dad got home, and change is stressful for them. You may want to ease up on some of the rules and try not to be too rigid about things that aren't very important.

III/4: DISSOLVING REUNION TENSION

⬙

Thinking about expectations before your husband gets home will help prepare your family for a smoother transition from coping with the separation to living as a complete family again. Often, wives whose husbands have been deployed become more independent and self-confident than they were before the separation. They've had to do many things that they weren't used to doing for the family and feel good about their ability to cope with the added responsibilities.

When their husbands return home, wives may find it hard to give the leadership of the family back to their husbands. One military wife, Denise McColl, said, "It's difficult, but necessary! Children are involved in this entire transition and are observing just how the … marriage operates, not to mention the other onlookers who are observing our adjustments (whether we want them to or not). Others will either be encouraged and inspired by us, or discouraged and disillusioned."[1] If you are in a position of leadership and are also experiencing homecoming from a deployment, you may need to help others with their transitions as you try to reunite your own family.

Successfully reuniting families requires sensitivity to each family member's feelings and needs. If religious faith guided the family as they went through the separation, their shared faith may enable them to adjust during the homecoming transition as they look to God for what they need rather than relying on their expectations of what they want each other to do or to be. If you think about how your actions or what you say will sound to your family, you may be more careful about how you act or what you say.

"This is where a sensitive wife must help her husband to understand that being *able* to get along without him is very different from *wanting* to get along without him!"[2] Both spouses have changed over the time of the separation, and the "months of changes may be tough to take all at once. But you can't go back. Accept the new person your spouse is"[3] as you get to know him.

Think back to when you were first married and you wanted to learn as much as you could about each other and make each other happy. See the reunion as a new beginning to your relationship. Think about what made you fall in love with your husband or wife. What attracted you to him or her? You now have the advantage of shared experience, so as you rebuild your relationship you can incorporate good times from your past.

As you discover changes that have taken place in each other and the marriage, decide to find a way to see them as positive improvements rather than disruptions. Wives who feel more independent than they did before a military separation may feel torn between enjoying their new sense of accomplishment and the need to restore their husbands in their roles at home. If both spouses realize that because the wife had to do everything by herself she gained a stronger sense of leadership, neither has to be threat-ened by it. The deployment has helped the wife develop, and both spouses can appreciate the growth while they sort out how they will share the household responsibilities now that the husband has returned.

Before my husband deployed, I'd ask him to fill my car up, and he'd do it for me. I learned to do it myself after he left, and I also learned to get the oil changed. Then I wondered why I hadn't been comfortable doing those things earlier. When Ren came home, I was so used to getting gas that I just did it, and I even got the oil changed one day after he returned. He won-dered whether I still needed him and felt left out.

After Dan and I both got used to driving Ren's car, Dan asked me whether he could drive Dad's car to school. I thought that was reasonable, so I gave him permission. Ren came home during the school year, in March. The first day after Ren's return, Dan went off to school, like he always did. Ren decided to go somewhere later in the morning, and he said, "Where's my car?"

"Dan's got it at school," I replied.

"When did that start?" We thought we'd told Ren everything while he was gone, but apparently we forgot to tell him that Dan was driving the car to school. Now that Ren was home, who would drive the car? We had to sort that out.

If you had a family change-of-command ceremony before Dad left, you may want to have another one now that he's back. This can help sort out the family responsibilities and begin the shift to make Dad part of daily activities again. If you choose to do that, it may be helpful to have a family meeting to draw up lists of responsibilities and distribute them among family members. You can call it your planning meeting for the change of command, held to be sure that the ceremony will be a success. Children might enjoy taking part in listing responsibilities, planning the ceremony, and planning a reception for after the family ceremony. Make it a fun event.

III/5: WELCOMING SINGLE SERVICE MEMBERS HOME

Military members who are married are usually welcomed home by their families, but who welcomes single service members when they come back from deployment? Many single members have friends who welcome them, but they may miss their families as they see family members embracing their married friends to welcome them home. If you have a single friend who is returning after a deployment, you may want to think of ways to make her or him feel the warmth of a family greeting. Here are a few ideas that you may want to consider:

- Make a sign or banner to welcome your friend home.
- Decorate your friend's room, car, apartment, or house with balloons, ribbons, or flowers.
- Surprise your friend with his or her favorite snacks.
- Throw a welcome home party.
- Ask your friend to tell you about the experiences of the deployment.
- Tell your friend that you missed him or her and that you are happy he or she is back.
- Your friend may need time to adjust to jet lag.
- If your friend was out of the country for a length of time, he or she may have culture shock when he or she returns. Be understanding if he or she becomes easily irritated or overwhelmed at first. New products or too many choices in the grocery store may seem like larger issues than you'd expect.
- Your friend will probably be surprised at how much things have changed. You can help by taking him or her on a drive to show him or her new buildings, new roads, or places that you know have changed during the time he or she was away.
- Remind your friend that if utilities where he lives haven't been used during his absence, the water may need to be tested to be sure that it hasn't been contaminated from lack of use.

III/6: REUNION RESOURCES

RESOURCES FOR FAMILIES

Please see chapter V/5, "Resources for All Military Personnel and Their Families," for a more complete description and contact information for the following resources:

❖ **Military Wives Web Sites (also includes a site for military husbands)**

www.militarywives.com is the home of many great Web sites. Please see chapter V/5 for a complete listing.

❖ **Military Student:**
www.militarystudent.org

❖ *The Business Traveling Parent: How to Stay Close to Your Kids When You're Far Away*
by Dan Verdick

❖ *Today's Military Wife: Meeting the Challenges of Service Life*
by Lydia Sloan Cline

❖ *Heroes at Home: Help & Hope for America's Military Families*
by Ellie Kay

❖ *Footsteps of the Faithful*
by Denise McColl
Available from
    Campus Crusade for Christ
    c/o Integrated Resources
    100 Lake Hart Drive

Orlando, FL 32832
Phone: (800) 729-4351

❖ *The Art of Coming Home*
by Craig Storti

❖ **Publications by The Bureau For At-Risk Youth**
Military Family Forum Booklets:
    Deployment and Reunion
    Stress and the Military Family
    Loss and Change
    Family Communication
Coloring Book:
    Welcome Home! (military reunion)

❖ **Scriptographic Resources Published by Channing L. Bete Company**
    Let's Talk About Reunion, an information and activities book for ages 9–12
    Your Parent Is Coming Home, a coloring and activities book for ages 6–9
    Who Knew? The Reunion Issue, for ages 9–11
    Know What? I'm Ready For Reunion! for ages 6–8
    About Reunion
    Preparing For Reunion
    Mission: Readiness: A Personal and Family Guide, Active Duty Edition

Navy Workshops and Programs

❖ **Return and Reunion**

Return and Reunion includes a workshop and support group meetings for families of deployed personnel. Some of the meetings target children. Families learn to understand the expectations that each family member has for reuniting the family. Counseling and Ombudsman support is also available. A parallel program is conducted aboard returning ships to discuss topics that include reestablishing family intimacy, financial planning, and setting goals.

❖ **Shipboard Return and Reunion**

A team from the Navy Family Support Center comes aboard the ship during the transit home from an extended deployment to present a workshop on family, children, and financial issues. The emphasis is placed on making a good thing better as the family is reunited. The workshop is presented during the last month at sea.

❖ **Homecoming Program**

In a discussion format, preparations for reunion are presented by addressing emotional aspects of reunion and changes that may occur upon return. In some areas a play, *Coming Home Again*, is featured as part of the program, which is presented just before the return date.

Resources for People Who Support Military Families

❖ *Reunion! Training Resources for the Unit Ministry Team*

Department of the Army, Office of the
Chief of Chaplains

❖ **Rebonding and Rebuilding**

A reunion seminar that is part of the USAREUR and Seventh Army Personal Redeployment Readiness Plan

❖ *Caring for Military Families: Facing Separation, War, and Homecoming*

by David A. Paap
Available from
Stephen Ministries
2045 Innerbelt Business Center Drive
St. Louis, MO 63117-1449
Phone: (314) 428-2600
www.stephenministries.com

❖ *The Art of Coming Home*

by Craig Storti

IV

SOME DON'T RETURN

IV/1: WE REGRET TO INFORM YOU ...

◥

Some families who send loved ones off on deployments don't have the happiness of reunion at the completion of the duty. According to Department of Defense statistics, an average of 2,000 service members have died each year for the last 15 years. That means about five military deaths occur every day.[1] Those statistics were compiled before the September 11, 2001, terror attacks. With our military involvement in more countries as part of the War on Terror, the numbers are undoubtedly higher today. Deployed servicemen and women face the possibility that they may not return, and so must their families.

One wife said, "God forbid, if anything should happen to where he will not be returning, my comment will be that Daddy died doing what is right and protecting his family ... make the best out of every day that God gives us."[2] She faced the possibility of death with a good attitude. Not all military families have her perspective. Many military members and their families live in denial that anything could ever happen to them. If they don't admit that they could die, they don't have to think about it.

Some may think it's a sign of weakness to admit their own mortality. But the fact remains that some military members die in accidents or by hostile action while on duty. Some are taken prisoner or are unaccounted for. In his book, *Return With Honor*, Captain Scott O'Grady wrote, "I'd known four pilots lost to bad luck or bad weather or some malfunction that defied the best maintenance in the world. None of them died in combat; it didn't take a war to make our business risky. But until you faced it foursquare, death remained a tragedy that happened to someone else."[3] He suggests that servicemen may not face the possibility of death until they find themselves in a situation in which they have no other choice.

Don't let the denial that anything could happen to you prevent your family from talking about and preparing for the possibility that you may not return from duty. If you are taken prisoner or listed as missing, your family may not know where you are or whether you're healthy. The uncertainty can continue for months or years. How do you prepare for that possibility? Among military couples, those who discuss the possibilities that military members could be killed, taken prisoner, or declared missing in action, "the possibility of something happening, which would prevent the return of the military man, those wives were better able to handle the ambiguous separation.... There were predictably fewer problems in coping with the separation."[4] Wives who learn to discount and ignore rumors also have fewer problems. Know who to ask for the truth, and ignore other sources of information as much as possible.

IV/2: POW/MIA

◨

To prepare for the possibility of your spouse being taken prisoner or listed as missing, you may need to think about many of the same issues that you would have to address if he were to die. To help understand them, think a moment about past experiences of military spouses.

For example, during the Vietnam War some of the Prisoner of War/Missing in Action (POW/MIA) families had to move out of government housing on their installations. Even though some families had that unfortunate experience, the wives of POWs and MIAs should have been entitled to their husbands' pay and benefits as long as they were not declared dead. To add to the traumatic uncertainty of their husbands' conditions, these wives had to move knowing that their husbands didn't even know where they were going. They also had to deal with the emotional shock of being cut off from their military lifestyle, surroundings, and support.

After the Vietnam conflict, some spouses felt like their husbands had vanished from the military. Those feelings, combined with the order not to talk about their situations publicly, led some of the wives of Vietnam-era POW and MIA service members to form two organizations to bring their concerns to public attention.

The National League of Families of American Prisoners and Missing in Southeast Asia began in the late 1960s when the wife of one prisoner thought that the government was wrong to tell the families not to tell their stories publicly. The first POW/MIA story was published in 1968. That publication resulted in wives networking and forming a group that led to the National League of Families. The League is still active today.

The National Military Family Association (NMFA) began in 1969. Military wives and widows lobbied for financial security and benefits for survivors of service members. The NMFA is now a strong voice for military families in Washington, DC. Its work has resulted in government policies that affect Active Duty families as well as surviving families and retirees.

Today it may not seem likely that service members will be taken as prisoners or listed as missing in action. However, the peace-keeping missions in various parts of the world, regional conflicts we become engaged in, and the threat of terrorism make both the POW and the MIA status for servicemen and women possible. Military families should discuss the possibilities of POW, MIA, and of death. Preparing your family for the possibility of your death will also equip them for the possibility that you could be missing in action or taken prisoner.

It's hard for a wife to prepare for how she will go on if she doesn't know when or if her husband will return. Eva Moore, wife of a former prisoner of war, said, "From personal experience I will go on record as saying that the thing that kept me going when he was a POW ... was FAITH. Faith in him, faith in myself, and, above all, faith in a higher being."[1] Faith carries many wives through uncertain times. If they have children, they must also find ways to carry the children through. The uncertainty of the husband's welfare can make it more difficult to help children understand what is happening to Daddy. But uncertainty also gives the family room to hope that Daddy will return.

Barbara Eberly, whose husband was a prisoner of war in 1991, encourages wives in that situation to "keep their faith in our system, our government, their husbands and themselves."[2] Col. (ret.) David Eberly adds that he would tell captives to concentrate on resisting and staying alive and not to worry about their families.[3] The Eberlys' religious faith, support at their base, and hope to see the family reunited brought them through their experience. Each family facing POW/MIA status has to consciously decide to have hope that the family will be reunited.

Yet, how long can a family hold out hope when there appears to be no end to the uncertainty of the husband's status or return? Holding out hope is different than going on with life. Some wives whose husbands were taken prisoner or declared missing during the Vietnam War have still not received information about their husbands. Some of them may still hope to see their husbands return.

They have all found ways to go on with their lives during the uncertainty, though. Author Edna Hunter says that "wives who had closed out the husband's role (that is, made decisions and took actions as if the husband were no longer in the family) actually coped better than those who did not."[4] They found the strength to make the decisions that they had to make as they hoped for their husbands' return. You will also be able to find that strength if it's necessary.

The strength to hope for his return may come in unexpected ways. If your husband is held prisoner, he may not be able to correspond with you, but he may get a message through.

> One captured pilot ... followed the Iraqi script and unemotion-
> ally mumbled a few words of propaganda into the television camera.
> But then, he seized the chance to add those otherwise mundane
> words: "Honey, I love you. Tell the kids to study hard." In four short
> words a husband assured a waiting wife that no matter how many
> miles separated them, and no matter what danger threatened him,
> his love for her was the first priority in his mind. In six more words
> the children were reminded that they still had a dad, that he wanted
> them to work hard, to achieve the most they could.[5]

Essentially, he asked his family to remember him while they carried on their daily lives. If you should face those circumstances, it will be best if you maintain your daily routines too. You may not want to plan for more than a few days, weeks, or months at a time, but you'll have to go on with life while you wait for news about your husband.

Your relatives will also be waiting for word about him, so you'll probably want to stay in close communication with them. They may encourage you. Whether you find support from them or elsewhere, you'll need someone to talk to who will understand how you feel. You may find that understanding in a relative, a friend, your husband's unit, the chapel or church you attend, or a service organization. Think about where you receive encouragement and support.

When many people are in stressful situations, they are helped most by others who have experienced the same thing they're going through. You may want to contact the National League of Families of American Prisoners and Missing in Southeast Asia for advice and support (see the "Support Group Information" section of the resources in chapter IV/9 for information about how to contact them).

Studies of families separated in uncertain circumstances during the Vietnam War gave researchers the information that they needed to give suggestions to help families who would face the same uncertainty in the future.

They emphasize the importance of an "outreach program from the very beginning because that is when the need for support from others is the greatest."[6] The stress that wives face can be eased a lot if they meet other women who are in the same situation as they are in. They also need a place where they can talk about their frustrations. There they can benefit from the advice and experiences of women who have been in the same situation before or for a longer time.

Research confirms the idea that the military should not lose contact with families but continue to support them and give them information until the status of their husbands has been resolved or they have returned.[7] If your husband is a POW or MIA and you want to talk with someone who has been a POW or the spouse of a former POW, contact your Casualty Assistance Office or the National League of Families.

If your husband is listed as a POW or MIA, you'll receive an official message from the Casualty Assistance Officer. They, or your installation Public Affairs Office, will give you advice about how to respond to media inquiries and tell you what information you are free to share with the public. You should call relatives who may be contacted by media to let them know what should or should not be said. What families say *can* have a direct affect on how a POW is treated. Keep the Public Affairs Office or Casualty Assistance Office informed about any contact you have with the media.

Some specific things to remember if your loved one is a POW or MIA are the following:

- You may feel upset or tired, lose your appetite, have trouble sleeping, or be preoccupied. Those are normal responses to your situation. It's OK to be sad.
- Expect to wonder whether you should have said or done something more for and with your husband before he left.
- Expect to experience different stages of grief after learning of his status.
- Expect news of his welfare to be irregular and non-specific for an indefinite period of time.
- If pictures of your husband are shown on TV by his captors, try to take comfort in knowing that he is alive and knows that you will likely be seeing the broadcast, even though he may not be allowed to speak. See any communication as a connection that draws you together and points to your reunion.

- Determine to be a survivor, as well as to expect that he will survive. When her husband was MIA in Vietnam, and a year later when she knew that he was a POW, Myrna Borling said that it helped her to think about their past together and the future together, even though she couldn't think about the present. As her daughter grew from the baby her husband had left into the seven-year-old that she was when he returned, Myrna talked about Daddy to keep him in the family and to be sure that the girl knew who her father was.[8] You, like Myrna, can get through, one day at a time if necessary.

- Try to keep up your normal routine as much as you can.

- Eat balanced meals.

- Don't turn to alcohol or drugs.

- Get enough sleep. Exercise regularly.

- It may help you to talk to other people who have been in your situation.

- Continue with family vacations and activities that you would normally be involved in.

- You may gain strength through your religious faith and church group. Allow them to support you.

- Don't wait next to the phone for news every day. If there is new information, you will know it as soon as it is available.

- You may want to keep a journal during this time.

CHILDREN OF POW/MIA

If your husband is a captive or missing, your children may worry about him and may be confused or afraid. They will hear parts of conversations and may jump to wrong conclusions. To help them, you may want to consider the following:

- Small children may not understand what happened apart from the fact that Daddy is gone and they miss him. They will sense the emotional strain around them, especially in Mommy.

- Children may think that Daddy left home because they were naughty and that now they are being punished. They may feel guilty and responsible. You may want to talk to them and tell them that sometimes children feel like it's their fault, but that is not true. Then tell them what happened in terms that they can understand.

- Explain to your children what it means to be a prisoner of war or missing in action. They need to understand that Dad didn't do anything wrong and is not like a criminal in jail.

- Be prepared to talk about rumors that your children may hear from their friends.

- If watching news on TV bothers your children, limit their exposure to it.

- Children may fear that since Dad is already missing, something bad will also happen to Mom.

- Children may over-identify with Dad, pretending to be him in the kind of captivity that they imagine he is in.

- Children may react with anger, fear, resentment, guilt, or anxiety. They need to know that those are normal ways to respond under the circumstances.

- Children will feel more secure and stable if you maintain their regular routines.

- Children may cry a lot, have nightmares, rebel, become shy, bite their nails, or become afraid of the dark. They may lose interest in schoolwork or misbehave in school. All of these behaviors can be reactions to Dad's status. Don't neglect necessary discipline, but try to show them that you love them more often, be more understanding, and give them the attention that they need.

- Don't give the oldest child responsibility that he or she is not ready for. He or she should not be asked to fill the role of the man or woman of the house.

- Children look to you for guidance. They watch how you react and imitate your behavior in their own ways.

- Don't make promises you can't keep. You shouldn't tell them that you are sure that Dad will come home.

- Children need someone to talk to and a safe place to vent frustrations. Be open and honest with them, and communicate freely within your family.

- Don't hide your feelings or tears from your children. Teach them by example that strong people talk to their families about what's bothering them so that they don't feel alone. When we all know how the others feel we can help each other through the hard times.

- If you need help supporting your children, ask your Family Support Center, your chaplain, or your church. They will be happy to help you or refer you to the help that you need.

IV/3: WHAT IF YOUR SPOUSE COMES BACK BUT A FRIEND DOESN'T

◩

Your spouse may come back safely while one of your military friends does not return. If a friend dies, you may experience grief as intense as if you've lost a relative. "In the civilian community when you lose a friend, you mourn. In the military community when you lose a friend, you wonder if your husband will be next."[1] If you're the military member, the death of a friend can be a sudden reminder that you could have been the one to die or lose your spouse.

If a friend dies you will probably want to show your care and sympathy to his widow and family. You may wonder what you can say to convey your feelings. You may not know how to help. The best thing you can do is to continue to be a friend. If you don't know what to say, it's OK to tell her that, hug her, and just be there without talking. She will probably be in a state of shock and may not know what she wants or needs, but your presence will be a comfort to her.

People react to death in a variety of ways. Some become angry and don't know how to express their feelings. Others become moody, talkative, or lash out at those who are trying to support them. Love and stand with your friend regardless of how he or she reacts to the trauma of death. Immediately after a person has been notified of the death of her spouse, she needs the freedom to react in whatever way is natural for her and to know that her friends are there and accept her response to the death without judgment.

You may be able to reassure her by reminding her that mixed-up emotions and difficulty trying to focus her attention are normal responses to death. As the grieving spouse faces the reality of the death, she may be able to tell you how you can help her. Before she is able to express specific requests for help, you can still help her if you are sensitive to her needs and willing to offer assistance.

HELPING A FRIEND DURING GRIEF

When you hear that a friend has died, be sure that the information you have is correct before you tell anyone. You may want to call the surviving spouse to ask her if what you heard is true and to offer your help. Your friend will appreciate specific offers of help; she is probably not able to think about details since her mind is numb with grief. If you want to help a grieving friend, you may want to consider the following ideas:

- Offer to make phone calls for her, and if she accepts your offer, ask her what she wants you to say. When you make the calls, don't use too much detail but calmly tell the individuals what they need to know. Allow them time to absorb the news and ask them if they know others who should be notified. Keep the calls focused and short.
- Offer to clean house for her, or just pitch in and clean if she is close enough to you that she would be comfortable with it.
- Answer the phone for her. Be sure to note who called, the phone number, the date, and the message.
- Keep a list of food that people may bring over and list what dishes have to be returned to what individuals.
- Babysit the children, take them to the park, feed them, or put them to bed. Be sensitive to their needs too.
- Pick up dry cleaning, groceries, mail, etc.
- Pick up people from the airport and find them a place to stay.
- Help select clothes for the funeral and do shopping that may be necessary.
- Help make travel arrangements for relatives or for your friend if the funeral will be held in another area.
- Offer to go along to the funeral home to make the arrangements.
- Offer to call the chaplain or minister.
- Ask if there will be a reception at the church or their home after the funeral. Offer to help organize and plan it.
- Make yourself available to talk.
- Ask questions that require more than a yes or no answer. Avoid doing a lot of talking or telling your friend what to do.
- Be a good listener. Let your friend talk about her husband if she wants to.
- Don't try to reassure your friend by saying things like "You're still young, and I'm sure you'll find another husband." She wants her husband, not a replacement. Understand and respect her feelings.

- Share your memories of the deceased with your friend.

- Let your friend cry and grieve. Don't be afraid to cry with your friend or let your friend see your emotions.

- Encourage your friend to rest.

- Don't keep your friend so busy that she avoids her grief. She needs comfort and time to absorb and work through her loss, not extra activity.

- Expect your friend to be in shock for as long as a month. She may not remember what has been done or said, even if she seems to be normal.

- Don't make decisions for your friend.

- Don't encourage your friend to become too dependent on you.

- Don't dominate your friend's time.

- Patiently repeat information that may not sink in the first time your friend hears it.

- Help your friend pace herself.

- Visit her regularly after the funeral when the activity is slowing down.

- Ask your friend if she wants you to help her write thank-you notes or address envelopes for them.

- Suggest that your friend become involved in a support group. Tell her if you hear of seminars or workshops that may help or interest her.

IV/4: DEATH NOTIFICATION

◩

The way that you hear about the death of your spouse will be an important part of your response to the news. With today's on-location television coverage of events, you could be informed of your spouse's death by a news report before the military has a chance to notify you. That kind of notification is obviously traumatic. If your spouse dies in an event that is reported on the news, you may be besieged by reporters who want to interview the family, and your privacy may be compromised.

Notoriety makes grief more difficult for the family because their personal grief processes are complicated by and interrupted by the attention focused on them. They may be confused emotionally, waiting for official confirmation or notification of the death, and holding out some hope that their loved one is still alive. "Once the deceased becomes a public persona entering the public domain, families have lost yet another part of that person during a time that they have not learned how to cope with their initial loss. Since the nature of news is what is 'new,' the pace in which the press intrudes in the victims' families is uncaring and often quite relentless."[1] It's better for families to have time to absorb the shock of the death before they're faced with public attention.

If your spouse dies while on Active Duty you can expect to be notified in the following manner:

■ The duty officer receives news of the death and assembles a Casualty Notification Team (CNT) made up of the Casualty Assistance Officer (CAO) [or Casualty Assistance Calls Officer (CACO)], a chaplain, and a medical representative.

■ The CNT comes to your home and the CAO introduces himself and the other members of the team.

■ The CAO tells you what happened and gives you the official notification letter.

- The CNT answers any questions that you have and helps you as you react to the news.

- The CAO tells you to expect to be contacted by a military Casualty Assistance Representative (if you are eligible to receive this service), who will visit you within twenty-four hours.

- When the Casualty Assistance Representative meets with you, he or she will explain what benefits are available to you and tell you how to use them.

Some of the military benefits that you may be eligible for if your spouse dies are a monthly amount of pay, a lump-sum death benefit, ninety days to stay in government housing, an advisor to help you with arrangements and benefits, cremation or embalming, a casket or urn, transportation of remains to the final resting place, an American flag, military honors, burial in a national cemetery, provision of burial arrangements, and a grave headstone or marker.

The notification process is much the same for Active Duty members and Reserve or Guard members who are on Active Duty or deployed. Benefits will vary according to the sponsor's duty status and rank.

IV/5: THE FUNERAL OR MEMORIAL SERVICE

◩

Many people wonder why it's important to have a funeral or memorial service. The service helps survivors through their grief. The service gives comfort to the grieving, helps them face the reality of the death, and gives a sense of closure to the shock of the death. This enables the mourners to say good-bye to the deceased and begin to move on with life again.

Funerals are services at which the remains of the deceased are present. After the service, those who attend may join the procession to the cemetery and the grave site where the interment will take place. Memorial services are much the same as funeral services, but the body is not present. Usually a picture of the deceased is displayed at a memorial service.

To make a funeral or memorial service most meaningful to those who will grieve your death, you may want to plan for it now. Planning eases the burden for your family if you die suddenly, because they will have fewer decisions to make during the first days after the death. You may want to consider the following items as you plan for your funeral or memorial service:

- Is it important that you are buried close to your hometown or relatives?
- Decide what city and cemetery you want to be buried in, and buy a plot.
- Make tentative arrangements if you want to be buried in a national cemetery. Where is the national cemetery that is closest to your hometown?
- Can you pick out and pay for a burial marker now? Are you eligible to have a marker placed at your grave at government expense?
- To which funeral home will your remains be sent?
- What kind of casket do you want?
- What kind of service do you want at the funeral home or church?
- Do you want military honors?

- What customs do you or your family or church observe?

- Are there specific songs that you would like to have sung at the service?

- Does your spouse or family want pictures or videos taken of the casket, service, or cemetery?

- Do you want to be cremated? If so, do you want the bone fragments pulverized? What do you want done with your ashes? They can be interred at a cemetery in a columbarium (a wall with recesses for ashes and a place for a plaque marker), taken home in an urn, or scattered in a special place. If you choose to have your ashes scattered or kept in an urn, will your family want a cenotaph (a monument to honor a dead person whose remains are not available for burial)? Where?

- If your remains were not found and not available for burial, would you like the family to have a memorial service? Where would you want a cenotaph placed?

IV/6: If Your Spouse Dies

If your spouse dies suddenly, you won't be able to prepare for the death or say good-bye like you would if there were a prolonged illness. The shock of an unexpected death makes it more difficult to accept. When you receive the news you may be numb, cry, or be thinking of what will happen next. The initial reaction is not necessarily an indication of how you will go through the grieving process.

The amount of support that you have will impact how you grieve. It will probably be good for you to talk about your feelings with someone who will listen without trying to influence how you feel. Having people around you whom you feel close to will help you remember that you have meaningful relationships that continue, even though you've lost the person you're closest to on earth.

When you're told about the death, ask for the details about how it happened. Those details can help you accept the reality that the death happened. View your spouse's body if it's possible. Facing the reality of the death and the body helps people accept the changes that will occur in their lives. Your spouse's death will result in a lot of changes in your life. You will suddenly be responsible for the provision and nurture of the family. While you assume that new role, you'll still be grieving.

You may wonder how long the grieving process will take. Since everyone handles grief in his or her own unique way and on his or her own timetable, there is no predictable amount of time that it should take. One thing that everyone has in common is the need to bring closure to a tragic death and to feel like they've said good-bye to the deceased. For some, that closure may come when they see the body. Others may feel closure after the funeral or burial.

You can't prepare yourself to know when closure will occur for you, but you can prepare yourself for the possibility of losing your spouse. Military families may be more prepared for the possibility of losing a spouse than they realize they are. "One woman told me that her husband, a military man, often would be gone for six months at a time. She said she hated those long absences, but found that they helped her to deal with her husband's death."[1] She had learned to make decisions on her own.

You'll have a lot of decisions to make quickly if your husband dies. If you can put any of them off until later, do so. If you live in military housing or overseas when he dies, you can't delay some decisions, like where you'll live. You'll have a limited amount of time to move out of government housing or move back to the States. Try to avoid rushing into decisions about moving too quickly, and avoid moving to escape memories.

PREPARATION FOR A SPOUSE'S DEATH

Here are some of the things to think about as you prepare yourself for the possibility of your spouse's death:

- Where would you want to live if your spouse died? Would you want to buy a house? How will you make that decision?
- Expect grief to take time.
- Expect it to be difficult to realize that you are a widow or widower.
- Expect to wonder whether life will ever be normal again.
- Expect to have trouble concentrating and remembering things. You may be less organized than you'd normally be. Allow yourself a slower pace for a while.
- Expect to be preoccupied with what faces you and with the shock of your loss.
- Expect to have to remind yourself to get enough rest, eat right, and get some exercise.
- Expect that life will be different and won't return to the way it was before.
- If you have children, you'll have to help them grieve while you are working through your own grief. It's difficult to help someone when you're in need yourself. Planning in advance how to help your children if their other parent dies will equip you to go through the difficult process if it should become necessary. Ideas about helping children follow this discussion.

WHEN DEATH OCCURS

As a military wife, you may not have the established support systems around you that your civilian counterparts have, such as extended family, a church you've belonged to for most of your life, long-term friendships, or long-term relationships at work. Military people do support one another, but depending on the length of your assignments, you may not have the depth in your military relationships that you need when your spouse dies. In addition to the uncertain availability of support, a military wife is dependent on the military for information about the death. Sometimes official reports about military deaths are classified and families don't have access to the information.

After the casualty assistance has been provided, you may be on your own, seemingly abandoned by the military. "The military widow is coping not only with grief but her 'new' life outside the confines and security of the military safety net, which once provided structure and emotional safety to her world. The civilian world, along with grief, is foreign. These are factors documented to predispose the survivor to a more complicated grief."[2] Women who had experienced these things came to realize that military widows often need more support than the military system offers. In response, they formed the Tragedy Assistance Program for Survivors, Inc. (TAPS). TAPS is a group of survivors who are committed to reaching out to help others heal. If your husband dies, you may want to contact TAPS (for information, refer to "Support Group Information" in chapter IV/9).

Even if you've done all that you can to prepare for the possibility of your spouse's death, it will be a shock if it occurs. No amount of planning can take away the emotional impact of such a tragic loss. You will probably have a flood of emotions as well as things to do, and as a result you may have trouble accomplishing anything. In addition to the preceding preparation, you may want to remember the following concerns as you face the death of your spouse:

- You'll have to decide whether you want to be a survivor or a victim. Choosing to survive will enable you to face what lies ahead.
- Expect your feelings to fluctuate. Grief is not a predictable or orderly process. Expect to use a lot of your energy as you grieve, and do not put your own needs aside.
- Expect to feel overwhelmed with wonder about how you can go on without your husband. Instead of thinking about the long-term, it may help to concentrate on getting through hours, days, and weeks at first.
- Don't try to hide your grief from your children. Try to express it to them in

words that show that you love them and that, although you are sad that Dad died, you'll feel better soon.

- Get help with running the household while you're adjusting to the death if you need it. Maybe you need to take relatives and friends up on their offers to babysit, cook, clean the house, do the laundry, go to the grocery store, or run errands for you. Don't wait for people to offer to help you; ask for help. Your friends and relatives may be hesitant to volunteer because they don't want to intrude, but they may be ready to help.

- Expect to spend some time reflecting on your marriage and life together.

- You may feel like all the security in life is gone or that nothing is safe. Don't demand too much of yourself while you're feeling like that. For example, if you aren't comfortable driving, ask someone to help until you feel ready to drive again.

- Shield your children from feelings of despair or wondering how you'll cope with the loss. They need to feel secure in your care. If you need to talk about those feelings, talk to an adult out of the child's earshot. You may want to talk to a counselor or chaplain.

- Don't be in too much of a hurry to dispose of your spouse's clothes and personal belongings. Everything does not have to be done at once.

- Go through your spouse's personal things yourself rather than allowing someone else to dispose of them for you. You may find yourself remembering special moments that you'll cherish as you decide what to do with his things.

- Expect your mind to wander easily, so be careful driving.

- You may not remember all of the details of the funeral and burial afterward.

- Try to develop a new routine or schedule for yourself.

- Set reachable goals.

- Don't turn to drugs or alcohol for comfort.

- Expect holidays and special anniversaries to be filled with memories and emotion. The anticipation could be worse than the pain that you think you'll feel, though, so don't completely avoid celebrations. You may want to celebrate in a different way than you did in the past. Don't force yourself to keep old traditions alive if you don't want to.

- Expect to need some time to know who you are apart from your spouse.

- You'll have to decide whether you want to wear your wedding ring. Maybe you'll be comfortable replacing it with another ring. Do what is best for you.

- Although it may seem distant, you'll come to a point of release from the emotion of grieving, a little at a time.

- Find a support group (such as TAPS) to participate in, where you'll be with others who have shared your experience.

- How often will you want to visit the grave? You'll probably be shocked when you see the grave marker for the first time with your spouse's name engraved on it. Visiting the grave may help you work through your grief.

IV/7: CHILDREN AND DEATH

◪

It's natural to want to shelter children from pain and try to minimize the effect of death in their lives. Although the intention is understandable, you won't be able to shield them. When you're notified that your husband died, you must decide whether you'll tell the children yourself, have someone else do it, or a combination of both. Your explanation to your children will depend on their ages and levels of understanding. When you tell them, be honest and straightforward, using simple language that they will have no trouble understanding.

Children respond to the news of death in a wide variety of ways, just like adults do. However, they may not fully understand what is happening, so their reactions may reveal that confusion. They may imitate the responses of the adults around them, become withdrawn, exhibit attention-getting behavior, become angry, deny death's reality, refuse to talk about it, or even want to die to join Daddy. They'll probably be affected most by watching their mother's response to get an idea of how they should act. They probably have no experience with the death of someone they know and don't know what to expect. Adults can help them by remembering that children need to be told what is happening.

Children sense the emotional pain around them and recognize that something bad has happened. They need to know why everyone feels so sad. Rather than let them rely on information that they overhear, tell them what's causing the emotion that they sense. Someone special is dead. Give them direct answers to their questions. In their book *How Do We Tell the Children?*, Dan Schaefer and Christine Lyons list questions that children often ask, giving appropriate answers. They explain that "dead" means that a person's body won't work or do what it used to do any more.[1] Their answers to questions that children often ask may be a great help to a parent or friend who has trouble knowing how to say things in ways that children can relate to. Schaefer and Lyons also provide excellent explanations of events connected with death and funerals for children.

Children need to grieve just like adults do. Seeing the body will help them accept the reality of the death, but they should be told first what they'll see. If they don't know what really happened, they will imagine what they think happened, and a child's imagination is usually worse than anything that could have happened. If childhood misunderstandings aren't corrected, they can be carried into adulthood.

A child should be allowed to go to the visitation at the funeral home, the wake, the funeral, and the cemetery if he wants to, but he should not be required to go. He should know that people there will be crying and what will happen. He will also be helped by a description of the room and the flowers in the funeral home, the casket, the clothes that Daddy is wearing if the body is available for viewing, who will be there, and the service.

Knowing exactly what to expect may help a child decide whether he really wants to go along to the funeral home, wake, or funeral service. Attending the funeral and seeing how adults express their grief will help children learn how to express their own emotions and learn that grieving is a part of life. The funeral also gives children the opportunity to say good-bye to Daddy. They can't go to the funeral later if they change their minds, so it is important to be sure that they have the opportunity to attend.

You may want to tell children how different people in the family will act at the funeral. If your children know that Aunt Jane will cry and Uncle Jim will say that real men don't cry, it will help them when they observe those behaviors. Then you will also have a chance to tell them that many adults do not know how to express grief very well, so they say things that aren't exactly true to help themselves feel better, like Uncle Jim will probably do. Tell them that other adults may tell them things to make them feel better. They should remember that what Mom tells them is true, even if some of the adults make it sound mixed-up. Children don't understand everything you do, and they may need more explanations than you think they do.

In addition to their lack of understanding, the whole world of military children is shaken up when their sponsoring parent dies, because they have to leave the military community and lifestyle that they identify with. As a result, they lose the security of a parent and the predictability of their lifestyle at the same time. However, the military lifestyle does help children learn flexibility, which helps them deal with the changes that they must face.

Helping Children Through Grief

It's difficult to prepare children for news as tragic as the death of a parent. It may be more realistic to think about how to help children if a death occurs so that the surviving adults in the children's lives will be prepared to care for children in crisis. If you have the occasion to help your children or the children of a friend when a parent dies, you may want to consider the following:

- Don't assume that children know that Daddy will be lying down in the casket.

- It's good for children to see Daddy in the casket, but whatever age your children are, never leave them standing alone at the casket. They need the warmth and support of your presence as they view their dead father.

- Always refer to the deceased by name; don't refer to him as "the body."

- The children need reassurance that they won't be abandoned.

- Children may not understand what is happening, and that may upset them. Try to help them understand.

- Be consistent about keeping your promises to your children. For example, be sure to get home at the time that you tell them you'll be back, not later.

- Expect children to ask questions over and over again as the death sinks in. Patiently give them direct answers each time. If it becomes emotionally difficult to answer at the time they ask you a question, ask them if it is OK if you talk about it later, and then don't forget to follow through.

- Try to avoid situations in which the children will feel uncertain. Explain what will happen so that they know what to expect if they will be exposed to new experiences.

- If you are the surviving parent, never leave the child without telling him or her. If you'll be getting a sitter, tell the child when you'll be leaving and when you'll return, even if the child will be in bed sleeping at the time.

- Be sure that children know who would take care of them or who to call if something happened to you.

- Children may wake up during the night and come to sleep in their parents' bed. Allow the child to feel the comfort of falling asleep next to you, but take the child back to her own bed after she is asleep so that she will wake up in her own bed. This will help her maintain normal life without showing any rejection.

- Be available when the children need your attention or want to talk, even if you have to drop something to give them your full attention. Let them know that they're important to you. Listen to what they say and be sensitive to their feelings.

- If you think the child needs professional help, get it. You can ask your pediatrician, chaplain, or Family Services (or Support) Center for referrals.

- Try to help children understand that sometimes things happen that are nobody's fault. "Ruth achieved this by drawing a special book for her young son, Michael. It showed a family of birds, in which the father bird was killed accidentally and the mother bird and baby bird lived in the nest alone. This became Michael's favorite book, and he would read it to his toys, explaining death to them. It was very hard, and sad, for adult relatives to hear him do this … but it removed all elements of guilt, allowing Michael a very early acceptance of what had happened."[2] You can find books like the one described here in your library or bookstore.

- Don't be afraid to share memories of the dead parent with the children. Remembering the parent reminds the children of the important relationship that they shared and reassures them that their parent isn't forgotten, even if there are tears.

- Don't try to hide your grief from your children. They'll see that you're sad, and verbalizing why will help them learn to talk about and express their own feelings.

- Children may become preoccupied with thinking about Daddy. During the times when the children miss Daddy most, they may say they want to go to him or die too. That's their way of saying that they want to see him again.

- Don't feel like you need to have all of the answers for your child. He or she may just need to talk without hearing much response from you. A hug or your shoulder to cry on may be more important than what you say.

- Some adults may want to conduct a special memorial service just for the children, which the children can help plan and participate in. The children could invite their friends.

- Give children the opportunity to participate in activities that they enjoy. Returning them to school and their regular routines will help children feel more stable and secure.

- Be sure that the children's teachers know that a parent died.

- Try to give the children some degree of control in their lives. Perhaps they could choose what clothes to wear or what food to eat.

- Encourage children to foster relationships with extended family members or friends who love them and express that they care.

- Don't forget that children need to get enough rest, to exercise, and to eat right, just like adults do.

DEVELOPMENTAL STAGES OF GRIEF

It's important to relate to children in ways that are appropriate to their levels of development. No matter what ages the children are, it's good to keep the family together as much as possible. Closeness to the surviving parent will promote feelings of security and care. Following are some characteristics of grieving associated with each stage of growth.

BIRTH THROUGH THREE YEARS OF AGE

A child's first understanding of death is his awareness of separation. Babies know that things are different but don't know why. They sense emotional changes in the adults who care for them and notice when there are more people around than normal. A baby's response to death may include becoming irritable, changing eating or sleeping routines, or showing fear of strangers.

These little ones need to know that adults are always going to be there to take care of them. Adults can communicate that care by rocking them, cuddling, singing songs, or whatever the child feels soothed by. They may ask questions, which should be answered simply in terms that they can relate to. Some may be ready to look at books that explain death on their level.

AGES THREE THROUGH SIX

Young children tend to think that the world revolves around their experience. They can't conceive of life without their parents because they are dependent on them for daily care. Their inability to separate their existence from their parents makes the death of a parent hard to understand. Children between the ages of three and six think death is temporary, like a nap or a trip to the grocery store. They may seem to understand that their Daddy is dead but actually think that he'll be back later. Thinking like that is reinforced in cartoons, where children see a character die and then reappear alive in another scene.

Because they think of death as temporary, they may not seem to be affected by it. These children will eventually realize that Daddy won't come back, and then they may need reassurance that they won't be abandoned by Mommy too. They may be clingy and afraid to let their mother out of sight.

Once children in this age group understand that death is final, they'll think about how events relate to each other and will probably connect thoughts that don't belong together. They may think that if Daddy died in an airplane, when they get in an airplane they'll die too. (Or that if Grandma is coming to visit on an airplane, she may be in danger.) They may ask indirect questions to find out if someone else is going to die. For example, if they wonder whether they are going to die they may ask you if they are going to go in an airplane.

Fairy-tale thinking is common in young children, and they may think that Daddy's death is like a magical story. To be sure that your children are sorting out their thoughts and emotions realistically, if you have children between the ages of three and six you may want to consider the following concepts:

- Help them understand that they did not cause the death.
- Daddy's death is not connected to any event that they experienced or thought about.
- Everyone cries when people die, and crying is OK.
- Everyone feels sad when people die, and they miss the dead person. These young children know how they feel but can't understand grief.
- Expect them to ask the same questions over and over again.
- Their understanding of death may be reflected in their play. It's common for young children to recreate the death in some way as they play. The playtime helps the death become more real for them.
- Tell them, "We'll miss Daddy a lot, but we'll be able to live without him now that we have to. We can remember him every time we look at his picture."
- Tell them, "We may not want to eat or sleep when we're supposed to. This happens because death upsets us, and after awhile we'll be OK again."
- They may regress in behaviors like thumb sucking, bed wetting, or not sleeping through the night. These are responses to the death and will likely be temporary.
- They may become fearful. If you sense fear, ask them if they feel afraid. Try to limit the amount of adult conversation about the death and its circumstances that these children hear to help minimize their fear.

AGES SIX THROUGH NINE

Before children are ten years old they may think of death as a person, maybe a bogeyman or a ghost. To them, death comes to get you. They may think that death is contagious, like the flu or a cold. They usually understand that death is final and are ready for a short description of how their daddy died. As you explain things to children this age, remember that they don't know that many words sound alike but have more than one meaning (for example: soul and sole).[3] Be sure that they know what the words that you use mean.

Children may feel embarrassed and not know how to act, so they may react in what seems to be an inappropriate manner. For example, they might act silly or become totally withdrawn. They may have trouble concentrating in school, and their schoolwork may suffer. Some children in this age group may have sleeping problems, headaches, or stomachaches or develop stuttering or nail biting. Since they usually don't know how to act when someone dies, they need adults to help them know what to say and do. You may want to talk to children ages six through nine about the following concepts:

- Be sure that they understand that they did nothing to cause the death. Their understanding and emotions will probably not match.
- Tell them, "Daddy's death is not going to make any of us die if we are near him."
- Tell them, "Everyone cries when someone dies, and that is OK."
- Tell them, "Everyone feels bad when someone dies."
- Encourage them to talk about their memories of life with Daddy.
- Children may be afraid or angry when someone they love dies.
- When someone dies we feel like something important is missing.
- Adults feel mixed-up too when someone they love dies. You may want to talk about your feelings to help the children talk about theirs.
- They may react by fantasizing about the way the death occurred and how it might have been different. In their imagination they may even think of ways that they could have affected the death or changed what happened. Tell them what happened in terms that they will understand so that they don't have to guess or imagine. Let them ask questions, and give them answers.
- Encourage the children to use communication that is different than talking

to express how they feel. Maybe drawing a picture or play-acting with toys will help. Some children might want to "play violent games in which cars crash and burn to get their feelings out."[4]

AGES NINE THROUGH TWELVE

As children grow, they develop a strong sense of what is right and wrong. They'll apply this to areas of their lives that they think it applies to, and as a result they may think that Daddy's death could be a punishment for something they did. They may think that every time there is a death a baby is born and that is related to their dad's death. Although those ideas are not realistic, children between the ages of nine and twelve do understand what death is and that death is final. They are often conscious of the affect that the death has on their lives and may even think about how it relates to the family structure. Children in this age group may wonder how the family will be able to pay the bills and buy groceries now that Dad died. You may want to tell them, at least in a general way, how the family will be supported financially.

Children in this age group are likely to show what they feel as a response to the death, but they may not show their feelings in ways that are obvious to you. They may have trouble concentrating in school, and their schoolwork may suffer. Some children in this age group may have sleeping problems, headaches and stomachaches or start stuttering or biting their nails. If you see any of these behaviors in your children, help them understand that they are probably responses to their father's death. Ask your children to repeat what you've said to be sure that they understand. You may also want to talk to them about the following concepts:

- Tell them how the death occurred and encourage them to ask questions. As you support them, let them talk whenever they're ready.
- If they aren't comfortable talking to you, offer others they can talk to. Some children are afraid to talk to the surviving parent because they don't want to upset him or her.
- They weren't responsible for the death.
- We can't kill someone by wishing he or she would die.
- They may feel anger about the death. Anger may be a result of their strong desire to fit in with other children, but the death sets them apart as different.
- Everyone feels sad and cries when someone dies; that's OK and expected.

■ They may not be sure how they should act or become very judgmental. Reactions vary from criticism to kind sensitivity.

■ Assure them that the family will have enough money to live even though Dad died, although there may be changes.

TEENAGERS

Teenagers understand death, although their responses are different from what adults may expect. They may have adult-like responses but at the same time may become critical, philosophic, or spend time day-dreaming. Don't assume that they can handle their grief and emotion alone. They may be trying to hold it all inside to be strong for those around them. They may wonder whether Dad's death changes their roles in the family. They may feel like it's their duty to help run the family and get them through the grieving.

You may want to talk with teenagers about the following ideas:

■ People often feel like they have to be strong when someone dies, so they may not want to let others know how they feel. It isn't necessary to be strong to show friends a good image. Everyone feels bad when someone dies, and many people show that by crying. Crying is OK.

■ Ask your teenagers what Dad's death means for them.

■ They may be nervous or complain of physical ailments. Without discounting their pain, help them understand that often people feel as they do when they face deaths in their families. Reassure them.

■ They may have trouble sleeping. Encourage them to end the day with relaxing and pleasant experiences. Teenagers may like to play video games or listen to music that includes violence or that excites them. Try to help them realize that playing electronic games or listening to high-energy music before bedtime doesn't help them relax as they get ready to sleep for the night. Help them find other activities to relax at night. Maybe they'd like to read before going to bed or listen to soothing music. Perhaps your teenager would enjoy the old comedy routines of Abbott and Costello, the Marx brothers, or Sid Caesar and find that relaxing. Try to help them find relaxing activities that will leave them feeling happy or encouraged about life.

■ Help them understand the importance of getting enough rest, exercising, and eating right.

■ We don't use drugs, alcohol, or anger to help kill our pain. If they engage in unacceptable behavior, talk to them frankly about it, asking why they did what they did, and ask them how they think you should handle it. They'll know that you respect them even if you don't approve of their behavior. They may not show it, but they want you to tell them that you are in control and hold them accountable to live within their boundaries. Help them find acceptable ways to respond to Dad's death.

- Expect emotions to fluctuate. Teenagers are often confused about their emotions and express them in a variety of ways. "A wildly hysterical outburst may be followed by embarrassed laughter as the child tries to get a grip on himself, to act like an adult. One moment he may idealize the dead person, making him superhuman, the next moment condemn him."[5]

- They may lose interest in school or have trouble concentrating.

- They may not want to continue with activities, like sports, that they shared with Dad. The avoidance may be their way of denying the expression of the emotions that they feel.

- Expect teenagers to look for support outside of the family rather than within it. They're likely to talk to friends, including other adults in their lives, and you shouldn't feel threatened by that.

- Their tendency to talk with others isn't an excuse to ignore their needs. Talk to them and comfort them.

- Encourage teenagers to become involved in community activities after the pain of Dad's death begins to subside. Helping others may help them regain a positive outlook and give their lives renewed purpose.

- Involvement in extracurricular activities at school (music, art, sports, etc.) may help relieve their stress.

- They don't have responsibility for the family now. Don't let older children try to fill the gap left by the parent who died. A teenager cannot be the "man of the house" or "take over for Mom." Give them responsibilities that they can handle. You may want to give them the responsibility for yard work, keeping gas in the family car, helping with cooking meals, or doing laundry. They aren't ready to assume control of the family budget or constant care of younger children.

- Try to help them focus on the future to enable them to plan for how life will continue without Dad.

IV/8: PARENTS OF MILITARY MEMBERS WHO DIE

If your son or daughter is in the military, you may wonder how you'd ever be able to bear the news if he or she was killed. I pray that you never receive that kind of message, but I want to talk about it in case you ever need the information. Please read all of the chapters in section 4 of this book. They give you information that applies to you as much as to the spouse or friend of your military loved one, so this chapter does not address concerns already discussed in the earlier contexts.

If you receive notification that your military offspring dies, you will react in your own unique way. You can expect to feel numb and to spend time wondering whether your son or daughter is really gone. A flood of memories may engulf you as you deal with the emotions. After one mother received news that her son had been killed in Iraq, she reflected that he had always loved Army life. When he was five years old, he told his mom that he was going to be a soldier. When he was eight years old, he dug trenches for his toy soldiers. "He put those little plastic men through basic," she said.[1]

Grief is individually felt and experienced, so don't expect that your response to the death of an adult child will be the same as anyone else's. As parents, we invest a lot of time and emotion nurturing our children and bringing them to adulthood. After they're grown and on their own, we may find that we don't spend as much time with them as we once did, but our love for them doesn't diminish. Combined with pride in seeing our children function as adults, our love is deepened. That's one reason it's so devastating to face the death of an adult child.

There's a wonderful booklet available on the Internet that has a chapter titled "Adults, Trauma, and Death." You can find it at www.aboutourkids.org; click on "Article Archive." Then, toward the bottom of the page you'll find a search by keyword. Enter "War," and a list of articles will be available. Open the booklet entitled "Caring For Kids After Trauma and Death" and look at the chapter that begins on page 37. Page 47 of the same booklet discusses the involvement of grandparents when a parent dies. It emphasizes the importance of the continuity that grandparents provide as children adjust to the death of a parent.

If you have to face the trauma of losing an adult son or daughter, be sure to give yourself time to grieve and heal. Males tend to internalize their emotions, and females are more free to express their emotions outwardly. Grieve in the way that's natural for you. As you go through this process, try to be sensitive to the grieving spouse of your child, if there is one. Your own pain may be so intense that you forget that the spouse's bond with your son or daughter was as important as your relationship with him or her.

I know a widow whose husband was an Air Force pilot. When his plane crashed and he was killed, his parents came to their home immediately. The woman dearly loved her in-laws, but they were so grief-stricken that she had to try to care for them at the same time that she was grieving and needed support herself. That complicated her grief. She had not realized that her in-laws' grief would be so overwhelming. Her in-laws didn't think about the tremendous loss that the daughter-in-law felt because of their own pain, so they didn't help or support her. Everyone feels intense pain when a loved one dies. Try to be aware of the feelings of others, and try to support each other.

If your son or daughter was married, you should expect that your relationship with his or her family will change after the death. You'll all adjust to the new family identity as it develops. The change in the relationships is not a sign of separation or lack of love for one another but, rather, a reflection of the fact that the person who brought you together to form the closeness that was there during his or her life is now missing.

You may maintain closeness, or more likely your relationship with your son or daughter's family may not be as close as it once was. Don't mistake the drifting to be a lack of love, though. It may be painful for you, and for your in-laws, the deceased's family, to spend a lot of time together, because being together emphasizes the absence of the loved one. Be patient and understanding as you all discover the ways in which you're comfortable relating to each other as your relationships change after your son or daughter's death. You'll find that if you express the care you have for one another, whether you remain close or see less of one another, you'll still feel encouraged and comforted in the relationship that you share.

You'll *never* forget the son or daughter who died, but you *will* have to go on with your life. The life of your deceased loved one can inspire you to find positive ways to work through your grief. One mother decided to honor her son's memory by supporting families affected by the war in Iraq.[2] Her pain was eased as she reached out to others and moved on in life.

IV/9: RESOURCES TO PREPARE AND HELP THOSE WHO GRIEVE

❖ *The Art of Condolence*
by Leonard Zunin

❖ *The Art of Helping*
by Lauren Littauer Briggs

❖ *An Early Journey Home*
by Mary Ann Froehlich

❖ *Talking About Death: A Dialogue Between Parent and Child*
by Earl Grollman

❖ *Today's Military Wife: Meeting the Challenges of Service Life*
by Lydia Sloan Cline

❖ **Handbook for Military Families**
The April supplement to *Army Times, Navy Times,* and *Air Force Times* (updated yearly). Available by subscription, at military exchanges, and in many libraries.

❖ **Publications by Abbey Press**
Care Notes:
Cherishing Your Memories of a Loved One
Finding Your Way After the Death of a Spouse
Finding Strength to Survive a Crisis or Tragedy
Taking the Time You Need to Grieve Your Loss
Getting Through the Annual Reminders of Your Loss
Learning to Live Alone
Helping a Child Grieve and Grow
Planning the Funeral of Someone You Love
Searching for God When You Lose Someone Close
Sharing Your Grief, Easing Your Loss
Taking Care of Yourself While Grieving
Walking With God Through Grief and Loss
When Grief Won't Go Away
When Death Comes Unexpectedly to Someone You Love
Coping in a Time of Trauma
Letting Tears Bring Healing and Renewal
Comforting a Friend or Loved One at the Funeral Home
Finding Ways to Help Someone Who Is Grieving
Losing Someone Close
Being a Friend to Someone Who Hurts
Care Notes for Teens:
Bad Things: Wanting to Know Why They Happen
Sadness: When Life Hurts Too Much
Prayer Notes:
Letting God Be With You at a Time of Loss
Hope Notes:
Feeling God's Love ... in the Midst of Suffering
Finding Comfort ... When You've Lost Someone Close
Books:
Grief: How to Live with Sorrow

Children Facing Grief: Letters from Bereaved Brothers and Sisters

Walk on in Peace: A Thoughtful Companion for Those Who Suffer the Pain of Loss

Self-Help Books:

Grief Therapy

Consolation Books Series:

Finding Your Way Through Grief

Grief Quest: Reflections for Men Coping with Loss

A Pilgrimage Through Grief: Healing the Soul's Hurt After Loss

What Helps the Most … When Hope Is Hard to Find: 101 Insights from People Who Have Been There

What Helps the Most … When You Lose Someone Close: 101 Insights from People Who Have Been There

Available from your chaplain or:

Abbey Press
One Hill Drive
Customer Service Plant 1
St. Meinrad, IN 47577
Phone: (888) 374-4226 or (800) 962-4760
www.abbeypress.com

❖ **Publications by The Bureau For At-Risk Youth**

Military Family Forum Booklets:

Loss and Change

Stress and the Military Family

Family Communication

Available from

The Bureau For At-Risk Youth
www.at-risk.com or
www.militaryfamily.com
Phone: (800) 99-YOUTH

Some of these products must be ordered in packages, so ask your Family Support Center or your chaplain if they can provide them for you.

❖ **The Air Force Enlisted Men's Widows and Dependents Home Foundation, Inc.**

92 Sunset Lane
Shalimar, FL 32579
Phone: (800) 258-1413
www.afenlistedwidows.org

This foundation provides homes for widows of Air Force, Air National Guard, or Air Force Reserve enlisted personnel. Although they normally accept widows only age fifty-five or older, younger widows may be admitted.

❖ **Army Emergency Relief (AER): www.aerhq.org**

200 Stovall Street, Room 5-N-13
Alexandria, VA 22332-0600
Phone: (703) 428-0000

❖ **The Air Force Aid Society: www.afas.org**

1745 Jefferson Davis Highway, Suite 202
Arlington, VA 22202
Phone: (703) 607-3064

The Air Force Aid Society has a small headquarters in the Washington, DC, area, but most of its assistance is managed on a decentralized basis on Air Force bases worldwide. They will consider any valid request for emergency financial help.

❖ **Coast Guard Mutual Assistance: www.cgmahq.org**

Commandant (G-ZMA)
2100 2nd Street SW, Room 5502
Washington, DC 20593-0001
Phone: (800) 881-2462; Office hours: M–F, 7 a.m.–4 p.m. EST

❖ **Navy-Marine Corps Relief Society: www.nmcrs.org**

847 North Randolph Street, Second Floor
Arlington, VA 22203

Phone: (703) 696-4904; DSN: 226-4904; Office hours: M–F, 8:15 a.m.–4:15 p.m. EST

The Navy-Marine Corps Relief Society helps meet basic living needs such as rent, utilities, and food in times of emergency. They can loan money for emergency leave travel for either spouse's immediate family or grandparents if you have a Red Cross message or verification from a doctor that requests your presence.

❖ **Civilian Health and Medical Program of the Department of Veterans Affairs (CHAMPVA)**
CHAMPVA Registration Center
PO Box 65023
Denver, CO 80206-5023
Phone: (800) 733-8387
www.va.gov

This medical benefits program helps pay for health care for surviving family members. Families must be registered with DEERS to receive CHAMPVA. For information or if you have questions about whether you are eligible, contact them at the address above.

❖ **Air Force Village Foundation, Inc.: www.airforcevillages.com**
5100 John D. Ryan Boulevard
San Antonio, TX 78245-3502
Phone: (800) 762-1122

Air Force Village is a retirement complex for Air Force officers and widows of officers. Younger widows of Air Force officers may also live there for a year while they decide where they may want to live. (See also www.afvw.com for Air Force Village West in Riverside, CA.)

❖ **Other Web Sites:**
Department of Veterans Affairs: www.va.gov
Provides information about burial benefits.
The Pentagon's Funeral Information: www.militaryfuneralhonors.osd.mil
Provides information about military funeral honors.
The National Cemetery System: www.cem.va.gov
Phone: (800) 827-1000
ACCESS: Air Crash Casualty Emotional Support Services: www.accesshelp.org
1594 York Avenue, Suite 22
New York, NY 10028
Phone: (877) 227-6435
This organization aids and facilitates the grieving process of people affected by or involved in an air crash.
Grief Recovery Online Widows and Orphans: www.groww.org
Sena Foundation: www.sena.org
Phone: (804) 633-7575
Works with those who are going through catastrophic loss.
Widow Net: www.widownet.org
Self-help resource by and for widows and widowers.
Wings of Light: www.wingsoflight.org
Phone: (623) 516-1115
Nonprofit organization to support families, friends, and rescue and support personnel.
Society of Military Widows: www.militarywidows.org
Phone: (800) 842-3451
This Web site has many great features, including a new widow's checklist.

SUPPORT GROUP INFORMATION

❖ **Tragedy Assistance Program for Survivors, Inc. (TAPS): www.taps.org**
2001 S. Street NW, Suite 300
Washington, DC 20009
Phone: (800) 959-8277

TAPS supports surviving families and helps them after a serviceman's death. They provide comfort, peer support, information and referral, and assistance to military casualty officers and Commanders and hold camps for children who have lost a parent.

❖ **National League of Families of American Prisoners and Missing in Southeast Asia: www.pow-miafamilies.org**
1001 Connecticut Avenue NW, Suite 918
Washington, DC 20036
Phone: (202) 223-6846

❖ **Gold Star Wives of America: www.goldstarwives.org**
PO Box 361986
Birmingham, AL 35236
Phone: (888) 751-6350

Gold Star Wives is an organization of women whose husbands have died in military service. They are the widows of servicemen of all ranks, races, and creeds. The organization offers information about entitlements and understanding of the problems that are unique to the service widow.

❖ **The American Gold Star Mothers, Inc.: www.goldstarmoms.com**
2128 Leroy Place NW
Washington, DC 20008
Phone: (202) 265-0991

Gold Star Mothers is the mothers'

parallel organization to Gold Star Wives of America.

❖ **Parents Without Partners: www.parentswithoutpartners.org**
1650 South Dixie Highway, Suite 510
Boca Raton, FL 33432
Phone: (561) 391-8833

This organization is international. They teach practical parenting and help single parents learn how to be alone without being lonely, how to communicate more effectively, and how to enjoy life as a single parent.

RESOURCES FOR HELPING CHILDREN

❖ *Saying Goodbye When You Don't Want To*
by Martha Bolton
This book addresses teens dealing with loss.

❖ *Straight Talk About Death for Teenagers: How to Cope with Losing Someone You Love*
by Earl Grollman. For ages thirteen and up.

❖ *Helping Teens Work Through Grief*
by Mary Kelly Perschy

❖ *Helping Children Cope with Separation and Loss*
by Claudia L. Jewett

❖ *A Child's View of Grief* and *Sarah's Journey: One Child's Experience with the Death of Her Father*
by Alan D. Wolfelt

❖ *How It Feels When a Parent Dies*
by Jill Krementz. For ages eleven and up.

❖ *Lifetimes: A Beautiful Way to Explain Death to Children*

by B. Mellonie and R. Ingpen. For ages three to eight.

❖ *What on Earth Do You Do When Someone Dies?*

by T. Romain. For ages nine and up.

❖ *50 Facts About Grieving Children*

by Erin Linn

❖ *When My Daddy Died* and *When My Mommy Died*

by Janice M. Hammond. For ages five to eight.

❖ *Learning to Say Goodbye: When a Parent Dies*

by Eda LeShan. For age eleven and up.

❖ *The Kid's Book About Death and Dying*

by Eric Rofes. Age eleven and up.

❖ *Death as a Fact of Life*

by David Hendin (refer to chapter 6, "Children and Death").

❖ *How Do We Tell the Children?*

by Dan Schaefer and Christine Lyons

❖ **Web Sites**

All Kids Grieve: www.allkidsgrieve.org

All Kids Grieve offers books, classroom strategies, and information on how to start support groups for kids. The site also includes grief and loss book lists and other links.

American Academy of Child & Adolescent Psychiatry: www.aacap.org

Children grieve differently from adults, and parents may be so shaken by grief that they are not able to cope with the normal responsibilities of child care. Here they offer resources to help. On the left side of the home page, click on "publications." Then, click on "Facts for Families and Other Resources," then "Facts for Families." Scroll down the list to find "Grief."

New York University Child Study Center: www.aboutourkids.org

This Web site has articles to help talk with children about death. On the home page, click on "article archive." Then enter a keyword search for "death." When the page comes up you'll find a list of resources including a booklet titled "Caring for Kids after Trauma and Death." See pages 18–26 of the booklet.

V

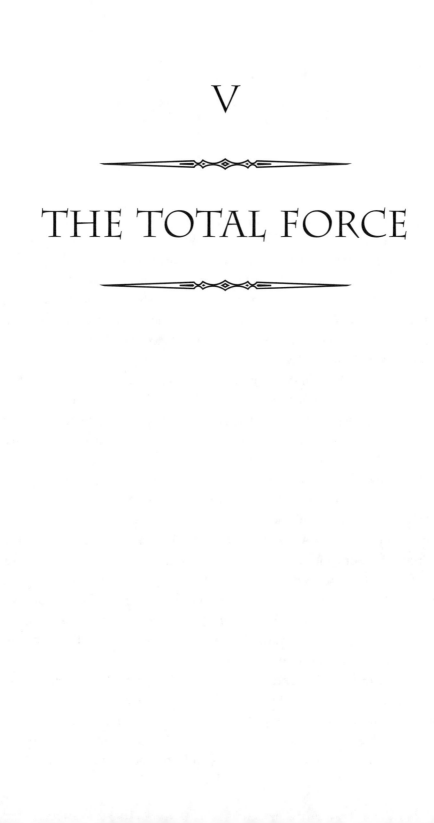

THE TOTAL FORCE

V/1: TOTAL FORCE DEPLOYMENT

◧

When thinking of the military services, many people automatically think of Active Duty forces. However, the military components are made up of more than just Active Duty forces. Today's military in the United States consists of Active Duty Army, Air Force, Navy, Marines, and Coast Guard, with Reserve components of each, as well as the Air National Guard and Army National Guard. Each component has its own mission and works to coordinate with the other components to meet the missions of the Department of Defense (DOD).

In 1969 the DOD first announced the Total Force Policy. This policy views all components of the military as a single military force in which each component has equal standing. The DOD draws the components together in joint training and missions to enable them to function as one total force rather than as individual components.

The equal standing of the components makes all components equally susceptible to deployment. Some people believe that those in the Reserve and Guard and their families are more affected by deployment than Active Duty personnel, since Active Duty personnel already live in the military environment. Some of the needs of personnel in the Reserves and Guards are different than the needs of Active Duty personnel, but neither should be minimized. Deployment disrupts life and causes pain for *all* families involved in military service. Instead of talking about who is impacted more by deployments, families need to find ways to help each other through family separations and to support each other.

Families of Reservists and Guard members may find more support from the Active Duty community than they dreamed was available to them. Before you're deployed, whether you're Active Duty, Reserve, or Guard, be sure that your family has someone to call when they need help. It will be most helpful if the person they call knows and understands the military system. Anything

your family can do to connect with the Active Duty,
Reserve, and Guard com-
munities will make them
feel less isolated or alien-
ated when the family is
separated for military reasons. Preparation for
inevitable family separa-
tions helps your family
appreciate the military
lifestyle even during the
unpleasant times.

To best understand

"A major finding in this survey of Reservist and National Guard spouses is that they live in a civilian, rather than a military, world.

Only about one-fifth reside within twenty-five miles of a military installation while 37 percent live more than one hundred miles from one. It is per- haps not surprising that most of these spouses have had no experience with a variety of Army Services.... The services with which they are famil- iar tend to be non-installation based: 45 percent have experience with CHAMPUS, 28 percent with the Family Assistance Center (these were estab- lished at Reserve centers) and 25 percent with the Red Cross." Rosenberg, 37.

the Total Force Policy, your family should know some general information
about all of the military components, programs, and services.

V/2: THE ACTIVE DUTY COMPONENTS

The Active Duty components of the military are the Army, Air Force, Navy, Marines, and Coast Guard. Here's a review of the role and responsibility each has in the military mission.

ARMY

The Army is responsible to organize, train, and equip ground forces for operations on land. Their mission includes orders to defeat enemy land forces and to seize, occupy, and defend land. The Army may have a part in some air and missile defense and space control operations.

Army forces in today's military take part in joint operations, special operations, and occupation of countries outside the continental United States. They are also involved in civil works programs and natural resource development.

AIR FORCE

The Air Force is responsible to organize, train, and equip forces to defend the United States against air attack, to gain and maintain air supremacy, to defeat enemy air forces, and to conduct space operations. The Air Force is also responsible for missile defense and strategic warfare. In the joint environment of the Total Force, the Air Force provides close air support and air logistical support to the other forces, including airlift, air-to-air refueling, resupply, and reconnaissance. They too are involved in special operations.

NAVY

The Navy is responsible to organize, train, and equip Navy and Marine Corp forces for combat in operations at sea. The Navy has sea-based aircraft and land-based naval air components, as well as ships at sea. The

Navy mission includes seeking and destroying enemy naval forces, suppressing enemy sea commerce, maintaining superiority in an area of naval operations, and seizing and defending naval bases. They accomplish their mission through land, air, and space, with joint amphibious operations. The Navy may use strategic nuclear warfare, reconnaissance, anti-submarine warfare, protection of shipping, aerial refueling, and mine laying, as well as afloat forces. They operate sea lines of communications and special operations and coordinate with the Coast Guard.

MARINE CORPS

The Marine Corps organizes, trains, and equips forces to work together with supporting air components in the seizure or defense of naval bases and in land operations necessary to enable the naval campaigns. Marines may be stationed on naval vessels, provide security at naval stations and bases, or work at other duties in a joint environment.

COAST GUARD

The Coast Guard is responsible to enforce or assist in enforcement of the law and has power to arrest, search, and seize people or property suspected in federal law violation. Obviously, that includes drug enforcement. They regulate and promote safety on the seas and waters subject to United States jurisdiction and enforce port safety and security. They are involved in search and rescue and maintain readiness to function as a specialized arm of the Navy.

The Coast Guard was switched to the Department of Homeland Security after September 11, 2001.The new strategy that the change includes is identifying and intercepting threats before they reach the United States' shores—in effect, pushing the borders outward. The Coast Guard also plays a role in deployment, as their Reservists are called to Active Duty, often overseas. In addition, the Coast Guard continues with its mission of search and rescue, drug enforcement, and environmental protection.[1]

SEPARATE BRANCHES, BUT PARALLEL IN ORGANIZATION

All branches of the military work hard to provide a good quality of life for service personnel and their families. Military members should be sure that their families know what benefits they have and how to use them. You are welcome to use services that you are entitled to *on any installation* of any branch of the military. Each branch of the Active Duty force has the following services available to members and their families:

MILITARY OFFICES AND SERVICES

1. Billeting Office

Billeting is short-term housing that is used for families in transition, visitors to an installation, or military members on temporary duty assignments. The accommodations can be as small as a hotel room or as large as a guest house. Accommodations are usually assigned based on rank and availability.

2. Casualty Assistance

The Casualty Assistance Office notifies and assists family members if their active-duty sponsor dies or becomes unaccounted for. They provide guidance and counseling relating to survivor benefits, arrange for the funeral and burial, and provide immediate assistance to next of kin.

3. Chaplain Services

Chaplains are responsible for the spiritual, religious, moral, and personal well-being of military personnel and their families. They offer pastoral care, religious services, Sunday school, other religious education, Bible study groups, and family fellowship events. Chaplains are available for counseling and are sworn to confidentiality. If you have a specific problem that they are not able to deal with or if you want to counsel with a chaplain of your specific faith, they will refer you to the appropriate places. Chaplains are available for emergencies after duty hours through the Command duty officer.

4. Child Development Center

Child Development Centers are daycare facilities that provide structured activities based on age group. They are responsive to the needs of military families, so they may have flexible hours.

5. Civilian Personnel Office

The Civilian Personnel Office is responsible to oversee and manage civilian employees on an installation. They advertise available positions, hire workers, and take care of issues related to employee benefits and evaluations.

6. Clubs

Installations traditionally provide a separate club for officers, NCOs, and enlisted personnel. Each club offers food and beverages at affordable prices, entertainment, and social activities. There are normally check-cashing privileges for members, as well as facilities for banquets or parties. In recent years many club memberships have decreased, so each of these clubs may not be available on every installation. Some installations have combined clubs or all-rank clubs.

7. Commissary

Commissaries are installation grocery stores. They sell products close to cost, so there can be significant savings compared to shopping in civilian stores.

8. Exchange

Installation exchanges are parallel in each component of the military. The Army refers to them as Post Exchanges (PX), the Air Force refers to them as Base Exchanges (BX), the Navy refers to them as Navy Exchanges (NEX), the Marine Corps refers to them as Marine Corps Exchanges (MWX), and the Coast Guard refers to them as Coast Guard Exchanges

Large installations may have a Main Exchange, a convenience store called a shoppette, and possibly a liquor store referred to as Class VI. Exchanges are department stores, but they also may offer a variety of services, which may include an automotive shop, gas station, barber shop, beauty salon, optical shop, garden shop, florist, toy store, dry cleaner, food court, photo-developing service, and theater.

9. Family Services

Each branch of the military has a family services organization to help meet the needs of personnel and their families. The Army has Army Community Service (ACS) Centers. The Air Force has Family Support Centers (FSC). The Navy and Marine Corps have Family Service Centers (FSC) and Family Readiness Groups (FRG). The Coast Guard has Work-Life Centers. The Family Service Centers in all branches of the military offer parallel services that may include the following: youth programs; job search assistance; information and referral; informational meetings and counseling for budgeting, investments, credit management, and personal financial planning; opportunities to do volunteer work; relocation assistance; a twenty-four-hour hotline; transition assistance for those leaving Active Duty; career workshops; résumé workshops; and individual counseling. Ralph F. Nelson gives a good picture of how their services work in his book *The Sailor's Savvy Spouse*. (See chapter V/5, "Resources for All Military Personnel and Their Families," for more information.)

Family services programs help people in transition, have information about other military installations, and operate loan closets where you can borrow household items while you're between moves. The centers are also able to refer you to other organizations.

The Military Assistance Program Site, MAPsite, is a twenty-four-hour cybercenter run by the Family Policy Office at the Defense Department to support military families around the world. The MAPsite enhances the military family centers and can be accessed at the following address: http://www.dod.mil/mapsite.

10. Federal Credit Union

Most installations have a federal credit union that provides loans and financial services including checking and savings accounts. Some installations also have a civilian bank.

11. Finance and Accounting

The finance office can help you set up automatic allotments from your regular pay and answer all pay-related questions. If there is a special pay to which you are entitled because of deployment (such as hazardous duty pay or family separation pay) talk to them about it.

12. Golf Course

Many installations have golf courses that offer a driving range, a club house, rental equipment, and lessons. They are not usually open to the public.

13. Gymnasium

Most installations have a fully equipped gym with athletic programs, weight rooms, and various sport courts.

14. Health Care

The government has a medical program to supply health care for military members and their families. Complete medical and dental care is provided for the Active Duty member. Medical and dental care are provided to family members by the military medical treatment facilities and supplemented by civilian care when necessary. Not all installations have full hospitals, but most have at least a clinic for routine care. Health care offered may range from only a routine care clinic to the full range of specialties.

* DEERS

The Defense Enrollment Eligibility Reporting System (DEERS) verifies that individuals are eligible to receive military health benefits. Active Duty members are automatically enrolled in DEERS, but they must register family members at the installation personnel office. Family members cannot receive medical care at government expense or use CHAMPUS or TRICARE unless they are enrolled in DEERS. If you have questions about DEERS, ask at your military personnel center.

* Civilian Health and Medical Program of the Uniformed Services (CHAMPUS)

CHAMPUS is a benefit for dependents of service members to help with medical care if it isn't available at the local military facility or in an emergency when the closest hospital is not military. You pay a deductible and a small percentage of the bill and CHAMPUS pays the rest. See the TRICARE information below for more details. (You can also ask the Health Benefits Advisor at the military clinic or hospital nearest you for information.)

* TRICARE

TRICARE is a health-care program that expands CHAMPUS coverage. TRICARE addresses the increasing need for military families to receive care from civilian providers when military medical treatment facilities can't meet their needs. TRICARE offers a choice of health-care plans. TRICARE is now the comprehensive health-care plan for the military; what was known as CHAMPUS is now called TRICARE Standard, which is one of the options within TRICARE. Ask the Health Benefits Advisor in the TRICARE or CHAMPUS office of the military medical treatment facility nearest you for more information. If you don't live near an installation, you can find information about TRICARE at your unit.

* PRIMUS and NAVCARE

In some areas there are satellite medical-care clinics located off of the military installation. They have been called PRIMUS (Primary Care for the Uniformed Services) and NAVCARE centers in the past. In the TRICARE plan they are called TRICARE outpatient clinics.

* TRICARE Active Duty Family Member Dental Plan

The TRICARE Active Duty Family Member Dental Plan is the DOD dental insurance plan offered to families of Active Duty personnel. You pay a small monthly fee and receive care from civilian dentists. The Health Benefits Advisor at your TRICARE or CHAMPUS office can give you details about the dental plan and answer your questions.

15. Housing

Housing helps military families find acceptable housing either in government quarters or in the civilian community. If you have housing problems they can advise you.

16. Inspector General (IG)

One of the purposes of the IG is to be available for service members and their families to help to resolve problems related to the military if the chain of command can't solve the problems. They also conduct investigations of improprieties and inspections to be sure that missions are performed according to regulation.

17. Legal Assistance

Legal assistance is available at no charge to Active Duty service members and their spouses. The legal office can draft powers of attorney for specific or general needs, draw up wills, and provide counseling relating to sworn statements, debts, insurance, personal property, automobiles, real estate, houses, sales and leases, taxes, estates, and claims. They can tell you what your legal rights are in specific situations and can contact people to whom you owe money to try to make arrangements with them before any legal action is taken against you. Many legal offices also have notary service. Legal assistance can't represent you in civil or criminal matters that fall under civilian law.

18. Liaison Offices

Each branch of the military has a liaison office to serve family members. Here are the addresses and phone numbers of those offices:

* ARMY: HQDA

Army Family Liaison Office: www.aflo.org
Room 2D653, The Pentagon
Washington, DC 20310-0300
Phone: (703) 695-7714 (in Virginia) or (800) 833-6622; hours: 7:30
    a.m.–5:00 p.m. EST
E-mail: ArmyFamily.link@hqda.army.mil

* AIR FORCE: Air Force Family Matters Office: www.afcrossroads.com

HQ USAF/DPPH
The Pentagon
Washington, DC 20330-5060
Phone: (703) 697-4720

* NAVY: Navy Family Support Office

The Naval Services FamilyLine: www.lifelines2000.org/familyline
Washington Navy Yard, Building 172
1254 9th Street SE, Suite 104
Washington, DC 20374-5067
Phone: (202) 433-2333; DSN: 288-2333; Office hours: M–F,
    10 a.m.–1 p.m. EST

* MARINE CORPS: Marine Corps Family Programs Branch

Marine Corps Family Team Building (MCFTB):
    www.usmc-mccs.org/MCFTB
MCCS HQ USMC
Manpower and Reserve Affairs
3280 Russell Road
Quantico, VA 22134-5103
E-mail: mcftb@manpower.usmc.mil

* COAST GUARD: US Coast Guard Family Programs

Commandant (G-WKW)
Office of Work Life

2100 2nd Street SW, USCG HQ Room 6320
Washington, DC 20593-0001
Phone: (202) 267-6160 or (202) 267-6263

19. Library

Most installations have a library where military members and their families can check out books and other resources. Usually there are computers and study areas available for use.

20. Military Clothing Sales Store

This store sells military clothing and equipment to personnel. Military Clothing Sales is run by the Exchange Service, so the store may be located with the Exchange but more often is located in a separate building.

21. Military Personnel

The military personnel office includes a variety of services. They issue and renew ID cards for military members and eligible family members and maintain records such as DEERS, military service documents, etc.

22. Military Police/Shore Police/Security Force

The Military Police, Shore Police, and Security Force are the military installation police departments.

23. Public Affairs

The Public Affairs Office manages contact between the military and the civilian media. They contribute to or produce an installation newspaper. In some locations, they produce radio or television programs. Public Affairs is the installation liaison with the civilian community.

24. Recreation Services

Recreation services offer activities and entertainment for both single military members and families. Some of the services that they may have available are the following: Information, Tickets, and Travel (ITT) Office, with information and tickets for tourist attractions, cultural events, and sports events, often at a discount; theaters; picnic parks; softball fields, volleyball, and horseshoe areas; hobby, sewing, and craft classes; ceramic and pottery studios; wood shops; picture framing; photo labs; auto hobby shops; retail stores to support hobbies; bowling; golf; camping and rental of outdoor equipment.

25. Scheduled Airline Ticket Office (SATO)

SATO works in cooperation with the Transportation office to arrange moves that require airline tickets and other official travel. Installations may have a branch of SATO that can be used by family members to arrange personal travel.

26. Transportation

The Transportation Management Office (TMO) coordinates your moves as well as other official travel-related issues, including movement of household goods and automobiles. They also maintain vehicles and provide them to military organizations for official use.

27. Veterinary Service

The veterinary service inspects food items brought to the installation, provides veterinary care for government-owned animals, and, subject to time and duty requirements, may offer vaccinations or care for animals owned by military personnel at the installation.

PRIVATE ORGANIZATIONS

1. Armed Services YMCA

Armed Services YMCAs try to provide recreational services needed at military installations to supplement what the installation offers. In addition to the usual services available at YMCA branches, the Armed Services YMCA branches offer special programs geared to the needs of military families. They do not charge fees, but a valid ID card is required to use their facilities. To learn more about them, access their Web site at www.asymca.org.

2. Red Cross

The Red Cross is available twenty-four hours a day. Most people know that they are there to help during disasters or death notification, but they offer much more than that. The services that they have available may include communication to help with requests for emergency leave; financial assistance for food, clothing, shelter, and transportation to help you through unexpected financial emergencies; swimming lessons; lifeguard instruction; CPR classes and certification; babysitting classes; opportunities to volunteer your time to help others; and their worldwide communication network will send a message to request information on the health and welfare of a family member if it's been more than three weeks since you've heard from him and you would like to find out if everything is all right (this is a drastic and last-resort step to take, since the Commander and chaplain will then become involved).

3. Relief Societies

The Army Emergency Relief (www.aerhq.org), Air Force Aid Society (www.afas.org), Navy-Marine Corps Relief Society (www.nmcrs.org), and Coast Guard Mutual Assistance (www.cgmahq.org) are parallel charity organizations to help service members and their families with financial emergencies. Policies vary between them, but they all work in much the same way. The relief societies are usually located in Family Service Centers on military installations. They don't charge for their services and rely on donations for funding. They usually offer help in the form of interest-free loans or grants for basic needs such as rent, utility bills, food, travel for a funeral, moving, or car repair. They consider any valid request for emergency transportation and emergency financial help. The aid societies also offer Guaranteed Parent Loans and other forms of tuition assistance, budgeting advice, and assistance to families when a military member dies. Information about the relief societies can be found online at each of their Web sites, and contact information for each is listed in chapter V/5.

4. United Service Organization (USO)

The USO runs airport centers, Navy fleet centers, and community centers to help military members and their families adjust to unfamiliar surroundings. They provide tours, activities, and discount tickets for local events. They also encourage Americans stationed overseas to participate in the events of their host nations.

5. Wives' Clubs/Spouse Clubs

Wives' or spouse clubs exist on most military installations. There are usually separate clubs for wives/spouses of officers and wives/spouses of enlisted members. They provide a social environment to help wives/spouses make friends and are involved in charitable projects. Most of the members are wives, although husbands may and do join these clubs.

V/3: THE GUARD AND RESERVE COMPONENTS

☒

The Reserves and Guard members have long been referred to as citizen soldiers. Historically, they serve a weekend a month on drill duty, other specific days of duty, or maybe for two weeks of duty sometime during each year. There are a variety of options for fulfilling part-time military duty. In recent years, these part-time military members have been mobilized as never before, and they are a vital part of the Total Force. To help appreciate what they do, I'd like to give a sketch of who they are.

RESERVE COMPONENTS

Reserves are part-time military personnel who are trained and ready to serve full-time if they are needed to augment the Active Duty arm of the component to which they belong. Their missions and responsibilities parallel the corresponding Active Duty missions and responsibilities. There are three general categories of personnel in the Reserves. The Ready Reserve consists of military members in the Reserve and National Guard who are available to be called to Active Duty to augment the Active Duty components during a war or national emergency. The Standby Reserve includes personnel who don't perform drills in units but who could be involuntarily called to Active Duty during a war or national emergency. Standby Reserves aren't mobilized unless there aren't enough members available in the Ready Reserve. The Retired Reserve is made up of personnel who receive retirement pay because of their military service. The personnel in the Retired Reserve aren't normally eligible to be ordered to Active Duty.

The Ready Reserve can be activated in three ways: volunteerism, presidential call-up, and mobilization. Volunteerism allows a member to be placed on Active Duty with his consent. The president may order selected Guard or Reserve members to Active Duty to augment the Active Duty forces for specific missions or for national emergencies. Mobilization brings

Ready Reserve units and individual members to Active Duty in times of war or national emergency. Each Reserve and Guard unit has its own mission.

The Reserve component of the Army is the largest Reserve component. In addition to the Reserve components of the Army, Air Force, Navy, Marine Corps, and Coast Guard there are the Fleet Reserves. When enlisted Navy or Marine Corps members retire from Active Duty after twenty or more years, they are automatically transferred to the Fleet Reserve. Members of either Fleet Reserve component are eligible to be involuntarily recalled to Active Duty or called to active training until they finish thirty years of service, when they are transferred out of the Fleet Reserves.

Reservists, like Active Duty personnel, are entitled to military benefits because of their military service. While serving on Active Duty or drill, they are normally entitled to the following benefits: Serviceman's Group Life Insurance, the use of military exchanges, limited use of military commissaries, medical care for injuries connected with their duty, access to military clothing stores, access to military dining facilities, access to military theaters, space-available access to military billeting, space-available access to air transportation within the United States, and certain survivor benefits.[1]

NATIONAL GUARD

The National Guard includes the Army National Guard (ARNG) and the Air National Guard (ANG). They augment the Active Duty military and meet state and local needs relating to natural disasters and civil uprisings. The National Guard has an important role in America's Homeland Security. This role added another focus to the Guard mission that has become foremost. As the oldest component of the Armed Forces, the National Guard has been part of every major military campaign in our nation's history.[2] It has an established position as a vital element of the Total Force. The National Guard Bureau works to develop and maintain Army and Air Guard units. The bureau also acts as a liaison between individual states and the Departments of the Army and the Air Force. The role and focus of the Guard in Homeland Security has resulted in many changes to its organization and status.

In July 2003, The National Guard Bureau was reorganized into one joint organization. The new structure makes it easier for the National Guard to communicate with and support the Active Duty components and therefore to perform its mission more efficiently. So now each state's Army Guard

and Air Guard are in a joint headquarters that may also include other components, such as the Army Reserve, the Air Force Reserve, and the Navy,
Marines, and Coast Guard. This change is an example of the Total Force
concept in action.

There is an increased emphasis on readiness levels as the Guard takes
part in more Active Duty missions. The National Guard's top priorities are
the security and defense of the homeland, both at home and abroad; the
support of the combatant commands with trained, equipped, and ready
troops as they fight the war on terrorism; and to remain a relevant, reliable,
and ready force.

V/4: WILL YOU BE READY?

◩

I hope that military families of all components prepare themselves for deployments and military separations so that when they face separations they'll be equipped to cope with them. Now more military personnel than ever are called on to take a turn, or a second or third turn, on deployments that separate them from their families. Tech. Sgt. Michael Gilbertson spoke for many military members and their families when he said that every successive deployment becomes more difficult.[1]

My husband was deployed on only two hours' notice. We had no idea that he would be sent because another chaplain was designated as the mobility chaplain. When crises occur, however, all rules and predictability are subject to change. I was blessed because we were stationed at a base where there was a wonderful support program set up for families within the first weeks of the deployment. Weekly meetings continued until everyone returned home and the regular three-month replacement rotations were begun.

The meetings provided me with a sense of connection with my husband because they brought the most recent information to us and a sense of connection to other deployed spouses whom I met at the meetings and formed friendships with. My husband said that he felt good knowing that the base was taking good care of us.

My friend, who was stationed at another base, went through the deployment of her husband with no base support. Not all families have supportive environments during separations. However, most installations are prepared to help the families who are left behind. I hope that this book helps you prepare for deployment or military separation so that you know where to look for help when it's your turn. If you're at an installation that doesn't provide a supportive environment, you may be able to bring ideas to key people who can begin a family support program. You'll be happy that you did!

Let me close with this quote from Dianne Collier's book *My Love, My Life:*

> "While other couples argue often about small things, military marriages are an ongoing battle to let go of someone you love, explain to the children why daddy has to leave, cope while he is away, and finally, get reacquainted with a new man each time he comes home. I believe that there is a special place in heaven for the military."[2]

God bless your family as you serve!

V/5: RESOURCES FOR ALL COMPONENTS OF THE MILITARY

Remember: You can use resources from any service component, so don't limit yourself to the areas that relate to your branch of the military. Check them all out!

RESOURCES FOR SINGLE MILITARY MEMBERS

❖ *The Savvy Sailor, The Savvy Naval Officer,* and *The Savvy Marine Officer*
by Ralph F. Nelson
$19.95 per book, plus $2 shipping (MD, add 5% tax)
Available from
Master Plan, Inc.:
www.savvy.onweb.com
500 N. Washington Street
PO Box 10071
Rockville, MD 20849
Fax: (301) 340-1581 (credit-card purchases only)

❖ **Publications by The Bureau For At-Risk Youth: www.at-risk.com or www.militaryfamily.com**
Military Family Forum Booklets:
Single in the Military
The Single Military Parent
Available from
The Bureau For At-Risk Youth
Phone: (800) 99-YOUTH
These booklets must be ordered in packages, so ask your Family Support Center

or your chaplain if they can provide them for you.

❖ *Starting Your Military Career: A Guide for Single Service Members*
A Scriptographic resource published by Channing L. Bete Company

RESOURCES FOR ALL MILITARY PERSONNEL AND THEIR FAMILIES

❖ **Military HOMEFRONT: www.militaryhomefront.dod.mil**
Military HOMEFRONT is a central Web site to help service members and their families to locate information relevant to their quality of life. This site features sections for families, troops, and Commanders, forums for discussion, and much more. You'll want to take some time to explore this site, whether you are Active Duty, Reserve, or Guard. Whatever your military affiliation or involvement, you'll find information you can use at Military HOMEFRONT. You may want to add it to your favorites list for easy access.

❖ **Military Wives Web Sites (also includes a site for military husbands)**
www.militarywives.com is the home of many great Web sites. In addition to the sister sites listed below, the home page has access to their newsletter; an online

e-zine; news links; military hymn information; information about military ribbons,
medals, and ranks and their history; medical links; support forums; information
about shopping, government departments,
travel, moving, and military weddings;
Space-A information; and the complete
Uniform Code of Military Justice (UCMJ).
Go to www.militarywives.com, to find
links to the following:

Military Wives Web site
Army Wives Web site
Air Force Wives Web site
Coast Guard Wives Web site
Marine Corps Wives Web site
Navy Wives Web site
Reserve Wives Web site
Military Kidz Web site
Military Husbands Web site
Military Chapel
Military Wives Store

These Web sites can also be found individually by going to
www.armywives.com,
www.airforcewives.com, etc.

❖ **More Internet Resources**

There are many Web sites offering support for military families.

**World Wide Web Military Pages-
Group Family:
www.militarydataresource.com/
group_family.htm**

A good place to start looking for
military family information.

There you will be offered a
variety of Web pages such as
Military Wives and Moms:
www.militarywivesandmoms.org

**Patriot Greeting Cards:
www.patriotgreetings.com**

Patriot Greetings is an online
store that was founded by two

veterans. They have cards for each
military branch, as well as cards that
are appropriate for all branches.
You'll find cards for almost any
occasion you can think of.

**Military Student:
www.militarystudent.org**

Military Student is a Web site of
the Department of Defense
Educational Opportunities
Directorate. It has sections that
address kids from six to twelve
years old, teens thirteen years and
older, parents, special needs families, military leaders, school
educators, and more. There are
links to "Family Life Deployed" in
each of the military components.
This is a great Web site for information regarding deployments.

**Deployment LINK:
www.deploymentlink.osd.mil**

This Web site is offered by the
Health Support Office. It covers current deployments, medical
readiness, and more.

**Deployment Connections:
www.deploymentconnections.org**

This Web site is all about readiness for the Joint military
community with component-
specific links and resources for
everyone in uniform and those who
love military members.

Military.com: www.military.com

This Web site has areas for Active
Duty, Reserve, National Guard, and
more. You can browse your specific
area or look at them all, and each
presents deployment information.

**4 Military Families:
www.4militaryfamilies.com**

This site offers service-specific

areas, support, and an impressive list of links to other Web sites.

Military Spouse Support Network: members.aol.com/widowclub/index. html

This site offers support for spouses during deployments or family separations. It connects spouses who are going through family separation and offers a chat room and personal Web pages.

These sites provide peer support for spouses of all branches:

www.spousenet.com

www.militaryfamily.com

www.CincHouse.com

(short for Commander-in-Chief of the House; includes an online chat room and resources for military women and spouses)

Sgt. Mom's: www.sgtmoms.com

This site provides links to all branches and covers a variety of military issues.

Military City: www.militarycity.com

This site gives military news and related information from the Military Times Publishing Group.

Parent Center:

www.parentcenter.com or www.babycenter.com

Parent Center features two great Web sites that are linked. They have excellent resources, arranged by topic, that include articles, advice, and specific chat rooms. Take your time as you explore this extremely helpful Web site.

Fatherhood Online:

www.fatherhood.org

National Fatherhood Initiative
101 Lake Forest Boulevard.,
Suite 360

Gaithersburg, MD 20877
Phone: (301) 948-0599

The National Fatherhood Initiative (NFI) is an organization dedicated to helping fathers be better dads and making families stronger. They offer a weekly e-mail service, lots of great advice, and excellent resources. They specifically address deployed fathers and families and provide e-mail links between them. Look at their great list of affordable resources. Brochures include topics such as becoming a new father, ways to stay in touch during deployment, being a single father, and much more. Don't miss their Deployed Fathers & Families, an excellent planning guide for deployments for both enlisted and officer families.

❖ *Today's Military Wife: Meeting the Challenges of Service Life*
By Lydia Sloan Cline

❖ *Keeping Your Family Close When Frequent Travel Pulls You Apart*
by Elizabeth Hoekstra

❖ *Heroes at Home: Help & Hope for America's Military Families*
by Ellie Kay (www.elliekay.com)

❖ *Uncle Sam's Brides: The World of Military Wives*
by Bonnie Domrose Stone and Betty Sowers Alt

❖ *The Savvy Sailor, The Savvy Naval Officer,* **and** *The Savvy Marine Officer*
$19.95 per book, plus $2 shipping (MD, add 5% tax)

The Sailor's Savvy Spouse
   $26.95 per book, plus $2 shipping
   (MD, add 5% tax)
   by Ralph F. Nelson
Available from
   Master Plan, Inc.:
   www.savvy.onweb.com
   500 N. Washington Street
   PO Box 10071
   Rockville, MD 20849
   Fax: (301) 340-1581 (credit-card
   purchases only)

❖ *When Dad's at Sea*
   by Mindy L. Pelton
   The author offers free personalized
and autographed messages to children on
adhesive bookplates. Contact her at
   peltonm@earthlink.net.

❖ *While You Are Away*
   by Norma Kimrey Colwell
   Illustrated by Gloria Sallings
Available from
   MAR*CO Products, Inc.
   Department S97
   1443 Old York Road
   Warminster, PA 18974
   Phone: (800) 448-2197 (Mon.-Fri.)
   Fax: (215) 956-9041
   While You Are Away (order # WA910)
can be used to help pre-kindergarten
through sixth-grade students with temporary family separation. The program
contains plans and activities to be used
with individuals or small groups. (It is
used by the Parents Away Group.)

❖ *Uncle Sam's Kids: When Duty Calls*
   by Angela Sportelli-Rehak

❖ *Footsteps of the Faithful*
   by Denise McColl

Available from
   Campus Crusade for Christ
   c/o Integrated Resources
   100 Lake Hart Drive
   Orlando, FL 32832
   Phone: (800) 729-4351

❖ *Married to the Military: A Survival Guide for Military Wives, Girlfriends, and Women in Uniform*
   by Meredith Leyva

❖ *A Greater Freedom: Stories of Faith from Operation Iraqi Freedom*
   by Oliver North and Sara Horn

❖ **My Love, My Life**
   by Dianne Collier
      US$19.95; CAN$23.95
   Available from
      Creative Bound, Inc.
      www.mylovemylife.ca
      Phone: (800) 287-8610

❖ **Web Sites operated by the National Institute for Building Long Distance Relationships. Each Web site has great links, ideas, and information.**
   Dads at a Distance: www.daads.com
      This site helps fathers who are away
      from their children maintain and
      strengthen their relationships during
      their absence. They also offer an activi-
      ties book titled *Dads at a Distance*.
   Moms Over Miles:
      www.momsovermiles.com
      This site helps mothers who have to be
      away to maintain and strengthen the
      relationships that they have with their
      children while they're gone. They also
      offer an activities book titled *Moms Over Miles*.

Long Distance Couples:
www.longdistancecouples.com
This site helps couples maintain relationships with each other when they're separated.
Grandparenting from a Distance:
www.longdistancegrandparenting.com

❖ *Uniformed Services Almanac* [**Annual Editions**]
Ronald S. Hunter, MSG Gary L. Smith, USA (ret.), and Debra M. Gordon, Editors
Available from
Uniformed Services Almanac, Inc.
www.militaryalmanac.com
PO Box 4144
Falls Church, VA 22044
Phone: (703) 532-1631 or (888) 872-9698

❖ **Children's Booklets from Army Community Service (ACS): www.armycomminutyservice.org (Virtual ACS)**
When you go to this Web site, on the left side of the home page click on "Deployment Readiness" then "Deployment Tools" then "Download Center." When the page comes up, click on "Children's Workbooks." You'll see the following booklet titles:
My Goodbye Book, for ages 3–5
Goodbyes Are Hard, for ages 6–8
"I Can Do That!" for ages 9–12
Separations Happen, for ages 13–15
Print any you are interested in; remember that they're for everyone, not just Army families!

❖ **Booklets to Help Children of Deploying Parents: www.dma.state.mn.us**
The Minnesota National Guard has some great resources for families of any military component, whether they are

Active Duty, Reserve, Guard, full-time, or part-time. The following Discovery Guides deal with deployment:
Discovery Guide for Ages 2–4:
Let's Take a Trip! About Deployment
Discovery Guide for Ages 5–7:
My Travel Trunk
Discovery Guide for Ages 8–10:
Travel Journal: A Discovery about Deployment
Discovery Guide for Pre-Teens Ages 11–12:
Trip Ticket: About Deployment
A Deployment Information Guide for Teens Ages 13–18:
Travel Pack
The following Emotional Intelligence Activities help deal with and understand emotions:
Emotional Intelligence Activities Booklet for Ages 2–4
Emotional Intelligence Activities Booklet for Ages 5–7
Emotional Intelligence Activities Booklet for Ages 8–10
Emotional Intelligence Activities Booklet for Pre-Teens Ages 11–12
Emotional Intelligence Activities Booklet for Teens Ages 13–18
To find these great resources, click on "Family Programs." Then click on "Soldiers & Families." Then click on "Youth & Development" and then on "Youth & Deployment." As you scroll down, you'll see the booklet titles. They will take time to download, as the note on the Web site says, but they are worth the effort. Print them out for your family's use.

❖ **Mothers of Preschoolers (MOPS): www.gospelcom.net/mops**
MOPS International
2370 South Trenton Way

Denver, CO 80231

Phone: (303) 733-5353

Fax: (303) 733-5770

MOPS is an organization that offers support to mothers with small children. They usually meet twice a month, offering a morning of relaxing support, discussion about marriage and parenting, crafts, and friendship to young mothers while their children are cared for in age-appropriate classes where they play games, sing, listen to stories, and have a craft time. To find out if there is a MOPS group in your area, consult the phone book, ask at your chapel or church, or contact the international headquarters.

❖ **Military Child Education Coalition: www.militarychild.org**

108 East FM 2410, Suite D

PO Box 2519

Harker Heights, TX 76548-2519

Phone: (254) 953-1923

They have some great booklets, including "How to Prepare Our Children and Stay Involved in Their Education During Deployment" and "How Communities Can Support the Children and Families of Those Serving in the National Guard or Reserves."

❖ *Daddy, You're My Hero* **and** *Mommy, You're My Hero*

by Michelle Ferguson-Cohen

This sensitive author is a "military brat," and she uses these books to help children understand and appreciate the military lifestyle. You can read them online at www.booksforbrats.net or order a copy. She also offers online kid-safe communities.

❖ **TCK World: www.tckworld.com**

This is a wonderful Web site dedicated to supporting Third Culture Kids (TCKs), including military brats and others who grow up in a variety of cultures. It has lots of resources for adults and children. Check out the story of Mr. Roundhead and the rest of this site. When you visit this Web site, be sure to check out the extensive list of links to other related sites.

❖ **Families in Global Transition: www.figt.org**

This site addresses the challenges of global moving and living outside the continental United States. It has some good resources for moving with children.

❖ **Scriptographic Resources Published by Channing L. Bete Company**

Write from the Heart stationery kits

Deployment Planner, a guide for military families

Family Preparation = Family Readiness, a deployment planning kit

Protect Your Family with a Family Care Plan

Terrorism: Living with Uncertainty

Bioterrorism: Understanding the Threat

Make the Most of Family Readiness Groups

Family Readiness Groups: Caring For Military Families

Mission Readiness: A Personal and Family Guide, Active Duty Edition

Available from

Channing L. Bete Co., Inc.

200 State Road

South Deerfield, MA 01373-0200

Phone: (800) 477-4776

www.channing-bete.com

These resources may be available from your Family Support Center or your chaplain. Some of them can only be ordered in packages.

❖ **Publications by The Bureau For At-Risk Youth**

Military Family Forum Booklets:
Family Communication
The Military Lifestyle and Children
Effective Child Discipline
Successfully Parenting Your Teen
Parenting Your Young Child
The Single Military Parent
Deployment and Reunion
Family Readiness

Coloring Books:
I'm Proud to be a Military Kid
I'll Miss You (military deployment)
Welcome Home! (military reunion)

Other Products:
Military Family Writing Kit
Our Military Family Scrapbook
Inspirational Magnets for Military
   Families

Available from
The Bureau For At-Risk Youth:
www.at-risk.com or
www.militaryfamily.com
Phone: (800) 99-YOUTH

Some of these products must be ordered in packages, so ask your Family Support Center or your chaplain if they can provide them for you.

❖ **Handbook for Military Families**

The April supplement to *Army Times*, *Navy Times*, and *Air Force Times* (updated yearly) available by subscription, at military exchanges, and in many libraries.

❖ **Armed Forces Hostess Association (AFHA): www.army.mil/afha**

Pentagon Room 1D110
Washington, DC 20310

Phone: (703) 697-3180; DSN: 227-6857

This organization maintains files on guest facilities at military installations of all services throughout the world.

❖ **USO World Headquarters: www.uso.org**

1008 Eberle Place SE, Suite 301
Washington Navy Yard, DC 20374-5096
Phone: (202) 610-5700

❖ **National Military Family Association: www.nmfa.org**

2500 North Van Dorn Street, Suite 102
Alexandria, VA 22302-1601
Phone: (701) 931-6632

This is a national organization whose sole focus is the military family. They have lots of resources and links on their Web site. One notable project that they offer is Operation Purple, a summer camp for children.

❖ **Military Family Resource Center: www.mfrc.calib.com**

CS4, Suite 302, Room 309
241 18th Street
Arlington, VA 22202-3424
Phone: (703) 602-4964; DSN: 332-4964

The Military Family Resource Center is an invaluable tool for helping military families. They have a wide variety of Web sites and programs to provide help, referrals, and information. The Web sites that they run include Military Children and Youth, Military Family Week, Parenting Initiatives, Child Abuse Prevention, and many more special issues. Visit their Web sites to research how they address topics of interest to you or your organization.

❖ **American Legion Family Support Network: www.legion.org**

PO Box 1055

Indianapolis, IN 46206

Phone: (317) 630-1200

The American Legion supports and responds to the needs of service members and their families who face long-term separations. Reserve and Guard families have been very appreciative of their efforts.

❖ **American Red Cross: www.redcross.org**

Military/Social Services

National Headquarters

17th and D Street NW

Washington, DC 20006

Phone: (202) 737-8300

❖ **Armed Forces Services Corporation: www.afsc-usa.com**

2800 Shirlington Road, Suite 350

Arlington, VA 22206-3601

Phone: (888) 237-2872 or (703) 379-9311

RESOURCES FOR PARENTS OF MILITARY MEMBERS

❖ **Mothers of the Military (MOM): www.mothersofthemilitary.com**

MOM is an organization that holds monthly meetings to bring mothers together for mutual support. The meetings are usually informal and open to any mother, father, grandparent, or sibling of a military member.

❖ **Keeping You in Touch: www.keepingyouintouch.webpointusa. com**

5030 Bobcat Lane SE

Port Orchard, WA 98367

Phone: (253) 851-9154; hours: M–F,

7 a.m.–3 p.m. PDT, Sat. by appointment

The Keeping You in Touch Web site provides support to military families, especially during deployments. The Web site includes chat forums for Active Duty members, military spouses, parents of military members, kids, teens, and more. In addition to providing links to other sites of interest, it offers care package ideas and has a photo album of deployed troops.

❖ **Military Wives And Moms: www.militarywivesandmoms.org**

Military Wives and Moms is a wonderfully supportive faith-based Web site. They have articles and poems to uplift and empathize with the challenges of deployments and with military life in general.

❖ **4 Military Families: www.4militaryfamilies.com**

This Web site covers many aspects of military life. Click on "Support for Parents" and check out the links to other helpful sites. Among the links are Army Moms USA, Marine Moms, Mom of Marine, and Navy Moms Online.

❖ **Operation: MOM: www.operationmom.org**

4061 East Castro Valley Boulevard

Castro Valley, CA 94552

Phone: (925) 706-1736

Operation: MOM shows support to loved ones of military members and to those in all branches of the military. They send letters, care packages, etc.

ARMY RESOURCES

❖ **Army Wives Web site**

Army Wives Web site is a sister site of www.militarywives.com. Access Army Wives by way of the link provided at www.militarywives.com or directly at www.armywives.com. The www.militarywives.com home page also offers access to their newsletter; an online e-zine; news links; military hymn information; information about military ribbons, medals, and ranks and their history; medical links; support forums; information about shopping, government departments, travel, moving, and military weddings; Space-A information; and the complete Uniform Code of Military Justice (UCMJ).

❖ *The Army Wife Handbook: A Complete Social Guide*
by Ann Crossley

❖ **Army Family Team Building**
US Army Community and Family Support Center
ATTN: CFSC-FST (AFTB)
4700 King Street
Alexandria, VA 22302-4418
Phone: (703) 681-7401
    Army Family Team Building (AFTB) is a comprehensive training resource to help families understand and become comfortable with Army life. Some of the topics included are military customs and organizational charts, acronyms, pay charts and explanations of them, schools for children, relationships, meeting people and volunteering, résumés, stress, support groups, elder care, and the Army Family Action Plan. Ask about AFTB at your Army Community Service (ACS) or Family Support Center. It is used by both Active Duty and Reserve components.

❖ **Soldier/Family Assistance**
Addresses issues that affect the duty environment of soldiers and civilians and the living conditions of soldiers and their families. Sponsors a Family Life

Communication Line (FLCL) to family members located anywhere in the United States. Ask your ACS for more information.

❖ **Army Family Liaison Office:**
www.aflo.org
DAIM-ZAF
Room 2D665
Assistant Chief of Staff for Installation Management
600 Army Pentagon
Washington, DC 20310-0600
Phone: (703) 695-7714 (in Virginia) or (800) 833-6622; DSN: 225-7714
E-mail: ArmyFamily.link@hqda.army.mil

❖ **Army Emergency Relief (AER):**
www.aerhq.org
200 Stovall Street, Room 5-N-13
Alexandria, VA 22332-0600
Phone: (703) 428-0000; DSN: 328-0000

❖ **Army Community Service (ACS):**
www.armycommunityservice.org

❖ **Army One Source:**
www.armyonesource.com (user ID: army; password: onesource)
Phone: (800) 464-8107 (United States) or (484) 530-5889 (international collect)
    The Web site is interactive and is meant to help reach families who are unable to come to Family Support Programs at installations.

❖ **Association of the United States Army:**
www.ausa.org
PO Box 1560
2425 Wilson Boulevard
Arlington, VA 22201
Phone: (703) 841-4300 or (800) 336-4570
    (for family programs, ask for extension 150 or 151)

❖ **Army Community and Family Support Center Homepage: www.armymwr.com**

❖ **Scriptographic Resources Published by Channing L. Bete Company**

Army Community Service: Your Partner in Readiness

Army Community Service: For Help When You Need It

Available from

    Channing L. Bete Co. Inc.

    200 State Road

    South Deerfield, MA 01373-0200

    Phone: (800) 477-4776

    www.channing-bete.com

These resources may be available from your Family Service Center or your chaplain. Some of them can only be ordered in packages.

AIR FORCE RESOURCES

❖ **Air Force Wives Web site**

Air Force Wives Web site is a sister site of www.militarywives.com. Access Air Force Wives by way of the link provided at www.militarywives.com or directly at www.airforcewives.com. The www.militarywives.com home page also offers access to their newsletter; an online e-zine; news links; military hymn information; information about military ribbons, medals, and ranks and their history; medical links; support forums; information about shopping, government departments, travel, moving, and military weddings; Space-A information; and the complete Uniform Code of Military Justice (UCMJ).

❖ *Balancing Work & Life in the U. S. Air Force*

(includes helpful checklists and forms)

Available from your Family Support Center.

❖ **Air Force Family Matters Office: www.afcrossroads.com**

HQ USAF/DPPH

The Pentagon

Washington, DC 20330-5060

Phone: (703) 697-4720

❖ **The Air Force Aid Society: www.afas.org**

1745 Jefferson Davis Highway, Suite 202

Arlington, VA 22202

Phone: (703) 607-3064

The Air Force Aid Society has a small headquarters in the Washington, DC, area, but most of its assistance is managed on a decentralized basis on Air Force bases worldwide. Air Force Aid offers help for families with financial emergencies, usually in the form of interest-free loans or grants for basic needs such as rent, utility bills, food, travel for a funeral, moving, or car repair. They will consider any valid request for emergency financial help. The Air Force Aid Society also offers Guaranteed Parent Loans and other forms of tuition assistance.

❖ **Family Advocacy Program**

This program was created to deal with the prevention, identification, evaluation, treatment, reporting, and follow-up of child and spouse abuse and neglect, sexual assault, and rape. They conduct parent education and provide crisis intervention, treatment, and follow-up. Family Advocacy exists worldwide on Air Force bases. Look for Family Advocacy in your base directory, and if you have trouble finding them, your chaplain or Family Support Center will be able to assist you.

❖ Key Spouses

The Air Force is also beginning a Key Spouse program. Like the Marine Key Volunteer Network, Air Force Key Spouses will be made up of volunteers who are available to help families when they need assistance. To find out whether there is a Key Spouse program available at your base, ask at your unit or your base Family Support Center.

❖ Ombudsmen

The Air Force has an Ombudsman program to help families with deployments. The Ombudsman is an Active Duty member, spouse, or family support expert chosen by the Wing Commander. Like the Navy Ombudsmen, those in the Air Force are not there to solve problems but to help families find resources and to serve as a liaison between the families and Command. Not every base has an Ombudsman. To find out if you have an Ombudsman, contact your unit. If there is no Ombudsman, call the Family Support Center and the Family Readiness NCO may be able to help you.

❖ Family Readiness NCO

The Air Force has appointed and trained Active Duty NCOs (non-commissioned officer) to help meet the needs of the families of deployed personnel. They are well-trained and happy to help deployed families. To talk you your Family Readiness NCO, call the Family Support Center on your base, and ask for the Family Readiness NCO, or stop at the FSC to meet him or her at the office. They also coordinate with other caregivers on base to hold support group meetings and to help ease the stress of separation. They are advocates for families, and some have

videophones or computers available for families to use to keep in touch with the deployed members. Often resources like these are underused, so be sure to contact your Family Support Center to see what resources are available on your base and to talk with your Family Readiness NCO.

❖ Air Force Crossroads: www.afcrossroads.com

This site will give you information about all Department of Defense installations and also has an Air Force Spouse Forum. The forum is designed specifically for spouses and provides communication on a variety of Air Force issues and assists them during times of military duty that result in family separation. Spouses can post messages and participate in the following manner:

1. Click on the category entitled "Spouse Network."
2. Register as a new user, creating your own user name and password.
3. You will receive an e-mail verifying your approval (usually within about five minutes).
4. Once approved, you can sign in and access the Spouse Forum.
5. Don't worry about having to provide your Social Security number, full name, birth date, and personal e-mail address to access sections of this Web site. The information is verified through the DEERS records to be sure that each user is authorized, and it is submitted using Secure Socket Layer (SSL) encryption in order to provide the best security available and honor the privacy act. Remember that if DEERS does not have correct information, you will be denied access to the password-protected sections of the site. You may want to check

to be sure that your DEERS records are accurate.

❖ **Air Force One Source: www.airforceonesource.com (user ID: airforce; password: ready)**

Phone: (800) 707-5784 (United States) or (484) 530-5913 (international collect)

The Web site is interactive and is meant to help reach families who are unable to come to Family Support Programs at installations.

❖ **Heart Link**

The Heart Link Program helps spouses understand the Air Force and maximize their military lifestyle. Its stated purpose is to strengthen military families and enhance mission readiness. The Heart Link name reinforces the feeling that spouses are the heart of the Air Force. As spouses become more comfortable with the Air Force, they will be more likely to encourage their loved ones to continue their military career and support the mission. Call your Family Support Center to sign up for this interactive and enjoyable program.

❖ **Air Force Sergeants Association: www.afsahq.org**

5211 Auth Road
Suitland, MD 20746
Phone: (800) 638-0594 or (301) 899-3500

❖ **Air Force Association: www.afa.org**

1501 Lee Highway
Arlington, VA 22209-1198
Phone: (800) 727-3337

NAVY RESOURCES

❖ **Naval Services FamilyLine/LIFELines Network**

The Naval Services FamilyLine
Washington Navy Yard, Building 172
1254 9th Street SE, Suite 104
Washington, DC 20374-5067
Phone: (202) 433-2333; DSN: 288-2333;
Office Hours: M–F, 10 a.m.–1 p.m. EST
www.lifelines.navy.mil/familyline or
www.lifelines.usmc.mil/familyline

Naval Services FamilyLine was formerly known as The Navy Wifeline Association. FamilyLine expanded and now includes Marine Corps and Coast Guard families. No membership fee or registration is required. They offer printed materials as well as a complete Web site, which is full of great quality-of-life information, deployment advice, and links to other sites. Be sure to check out the "Deployment Readiness" topics and articles.

❖ *Navy Family Lifeline*

Navy Family Lifeline is a quarterly newspaper for Navy and Marine Corps spouses and dependents. It is available through the Naval Services FamilyLine.

❖ *Sea Legs*

Sea Legs is a handbook for Navy spouses available from Naval Services FamilyLine.

❖ *Social Customs and Traditions of the Sea Services*

This booklet is written and published by the Naval Services FamilyLine.

❖ **COMPASS: A Spouse's Guide to Navy Life**

COMPASS is a program to educate new Navy spouses about the Navy system. It has been called the spouse version of boot camp and officer's candidate school. You can learn more about COMPASS on the LIFELines Web site.

❖ **Navy Wives Web site**

Navy Wives Web site is a sister site of www.militarywives.com. Access Navy Wives by way of the link provided at www.militarywives.com or directly at www.navywives.com. The www.militarywives.com home page also offers access to their newsletter; an online e-zine; news links; military hymn information; information about military ribbons, medals, and ranks and their history; medical links; support forums; information about shopping, government departments, travel, moving, and military weddings; Space-A information; and the complete Uniform Code of Military Justice (UCMJ).

❖ **There are more Web sites specifically for Navy wives such as, www.navymoms.org**

❖ **Navy One Source: www.navyonesource.com (user ID: Navy; password: sailor)**

Phone: (800) 540-4123 (United States) or (484) 530-5914 (international collect)

The Web site is interactive and is meant to help reach families who are unable to come to Family Support Programs at installations.

❖ **Navy Mutual Aid Association: www.navymutual.org**

Henderson Hall

29 Carpenter Road
Arlington, VA 22212
Phone: (800) 628-6011

❖ **Navy-Marine Corps Relief Society: www.nmcrs.org**

847 North Randolph Street, Second Floor
Arlington, VA 22203
Phone: (703) 696-4904; DSN: 226-4904;
Office hours: M–F, 8:15 a.m.–4:15 p.m. EST

The Navy-Marine Corps Relief Society helps meet basic living needs such as rent, utilities, and food in times of emergency. They can loan money for emergency leave travel for either spouse's immediate family or grandparents if you have a Red Cross message or verification from a doctor that requests your presence. They may be able to help you with a loan for emergency repairs if your car breaks down. The society also handles Guaranteed Student Loans and may have an emergency food pantry and thrift shop.

❖ *Navy Spouse's Guide*
by Laura Hall Stavridis

❖ *The Savvy Sailor, The Savvy Naval Officer, and The Savvy Marine Officer*
  $19.95 per book, plus $2 shipping (MD, add 5% tax)
  The Sailor's Savvy Spouse
  $26.95 per book, plus $2 shipping (MD, add 5% tax)
  by Ralph F. Nelson
  Available from
    Master Plan, Inc.
    www.savvy.onweb.com
    500 N. Washington Street
    PO Box 10071
    Rockville, MD 20849

Fax: (301) 340-1581 (credit-card
purchases only)

❖ *E-mail to the Front*
by Alesia Holliday

❖ *When Dad's at Sea*
by Mindy L. Pelton
   The author offers free personalized
and autographed messages to children on
adhesive bookplates. Contact her at
peltonm@earthlink.net.

❖ *Footsteps of the Faithful*
by Denise McColl
Available from
   Campus Crusade for Christ
   c/o Integrated Resources
   100 Lake Hart Drive
   Orlando, FL 32832
   Phone: (800) 729-4351

❖ **Ombudsmen**
The Ombudsman, a volunteer, is an official representative of Navy families and
works to establish and maintain good
communication between the Command
and the families of personnel. As a liaison
for community resources, the
Ombudsman works to find ways to help
families use the programs and services
that are available to them and guides shy
or reluctant people to the service or
agency that they need. The Ombudsman
communicates care from the Command to
the individual but is not there to address
problems between the military sponsor
and the Command or fill the role of a professional counselor. If you aren't sure
how to contact your Ombudsman, ask
your unit or your chaplain.

❖ **Navy Family Advocacy Program**
The Navy Family Advocacy Program was

created to deal with the prevention, identification, evaluation, treatment,
reporting, and follow-up of child and
spouse abuse and neglect, sexual assault,
and rape. They conduct parent education
and provide crisis intervention, treatment, and follow-up. To contact Family
Advocacy, look in your installation directory or ask your chaplain for help.

❖ **The Chaplains Religious Development
   Operation (CREDO)**
CREDO, which means "I believe" in
Latin, is a Chief of Naval Operations
(CNO) sponsored program that is conducted by chaplains. CREDO addresses
issues such as personal growth, parenting, stress management, and marriage
enrichment. The foundational program
offered is a seventy-two-hour personal
growth retreat. It is an opportunity for
individuals to pursue personal and spiritual growth in a residential setting. The
major aims of the retreat are to provide
participants with the opportunity to
develop new perspectives in their relationships with God, family, friends,
shipmates, the Navy, and the broader
world in which they live. Each person is
encouraged to explore the basis of his or
her inner spiritual resources. For more
information or to sign up for the program, call your chaplain.

MARINE CORPS RESOURCES

❖ **Marine Corps Wives Web site**
Marine Corps Wives Web site is a sister
site of www.militarywives.com. Access
Marine Wives by way of the link provided at www.militarywives.com or
directly at www.marinewives.com. The
www.militarywives.com home page also

offers access to their newsletter; an online e-zine; news links; military hymn information; information about military ribbons, medals, and ranks and their history; medical links; support forums; information about shopping, government departments, travel, moving, and military weddings; Space-A information; and the complete Uniform Code of Military Justice (UCMJ).

❖ **There are more Web sites specifically for Marine Corps wives, such as:**
www.marinemoms.online.virtualave.net

❖ **Naval Services FamilyLine/LIFELines Network**
The Naval Services FamilyLine
Washington Navy Yard, Building 172
1254 9th Street SE, Suite 104
Washington DC 20374-5067
Phone: (202) 433-2333; DSN: 288-2333;
Office Hours: M–F, 10 a.m.–1 p.m. EST
www.lifelines.navy.mil/familyline or
www.lifelines.usmc.mil/familyline
    Naval Services FamilyLine was formerly known as The Navy Wifeline Association. FamilyLine expanded and now includes Marine Corps and Coast Guard families. No membership fee or registration is required. They offer printed materials as well as a complete Web site. The Web site is full of great quality-of-life information, deployment advice, and links to other sites. Be sure to check out the "Deployment Readiness" topics and articles.

❖ **Key Volunteer Network (KVN)**
The KVN is the official Marine Corps family support and communication network within a Command. Key Wives assist incoming Marines and their families and make them aware of the services that are available to them. They also support families when sponsors are separated from their families. This program is similar to the Ombudsman program in the Navy and Coast Guard. If you don't know how to contact your Key Volunteer, consult your installation directory or ask your unit or your family support center for help.

❖ **L.I.N.K.S. (Lifestyle, Insights, Networking, Knowledge, and Skills)**
L.I.N.K.S. is a program to help Marine Corps families understand the Marine Corps and the benefits offered to them. To learn more about L.I.N.K.S., see the Marine Corps Family Team Building Web site, www.usmc-mccs.org/MCFTB.

❖ **Marine Corps Family Team Building (MCFTB)**
MCCS HQ USMC
Manpower and Reserves Affairs
3280 Russell Road
Quantico, VA 22134-5103
www.usmc-mccs.org/MCFTB
    MCFTB provides educational resources and services and enhances the readiness of Marine Corps families. It offers a variety of helpful programs, such as PREP, CREDO, and L.I.N.K.S. Check out the Web site for details.

❖ **Marine Corps Community Liaison Office**
Phone: (800) USMC-CLO (876-2256)

❖ **Marine Corps One Source:**
www.mccsonesource.com (user ID: marine; password: semper fi)
Phone: (800) 869-0278 (United States) or (484) 530-5908 (international collect)

The Web site is interactive and is meant to help reach families who are unable to come to Family Support Programs at installations.

❖ **Navy-Marine Corps Relief Society:**
www.nmcrs.org
847 North Randolph Street, Second Floor
Arlington, VA 22203
Phone: (703) 696-4904; DSN: 226-4904;
Office hours: M–F, 8:15 a.m.–4:15 p.m.
    EST

The Navy-Marine Corps Relief Society helps meet basic living needs such as rent, utilities, and food in times of emergency. They can loan money for emergency leave travel for either spouse's immediate family or grandparents if you have a Red Cross message or verification from a doctor that requests your presence. They may be able to help you with a loan for emergency repairs if your car breaks down. The society also handles Guaranteed Student Loans and may have an emergency food pantry and thrift shop.

❖ **Marine Corps Association:**
www.mca-marines.org
715 Broadway Street
MCCDC
Quantico, VA 22134
Phone: (703) 640-6161 or (800) 336-0291;
Office hours: M–F, 8 a.m.–4:30 p.m. EST

❖ **Marine Corps League:**
www.mcleague.org
Mailing:
    PO Box 3070
    Merrifield, VA 22116
Street:
    8626 Lee Highway, Suite 201
    Fairfax, VA 22031

Phone: (800) 625-1775 or (703) 207-9588

❖ *The Savvy Sailor, The Savvy Naval Officer,* **and** *The Savvy Marine Officer*
    $19.95 per book, plus $2 shipping
    (MD, add 5% tax)
The Sailor's Savvy Spouse
    $26.95 per book, plus $2 shipping
    (MD, add 5% tax)
by Ralph F. Nelson
Available from
    Master Plan, Inc.:
    500 N. Washington Street
    PO Box 10071
    Rockville, MD 20849
    Fax: (301) 340-1581 (credit-card purchases only)
    www.savvy.onweb.com

COAST GUARD RESOURCES

❖ **Coast Guard Wives Web site**
Coast Guard Wives Web site is a sister site of www.militarywives.com. Access Coast Guard Wives by way of the link provided at www.militarywives.com or directly at www.coastguardwives.com. The www.militarywives.com home page also offers access to their newsletter; an online e-zine; news links; military hymn information; information about military ribbons, medals, and ranks and their history; medical links; support forums; information about shopping, government departments, travel, moving, and military weddings; Space-A information; and the complete Uniform Code of Military Justice (UCMJ).

❖ **Naval Services FamilyLine/LIFELines Network**
The Naval Services FamilyLine
Washington Navy Yard, Building 172

1254 9th Street SE, Suite 104
Washington, DC 20374-5067
Phone: (202) 433-2333; DSN: 288-2333;
Office hours: M–F, 10 a.m.–1 p.m. EST
www.navy.mil/familyline or
www.lifelines.usmc.mil/familyline

Naval Services FamilyLine was formerly known as The Navy Wifeline Association. FamilyLine expanded and now includes Marine Corps and Coast Guard families. No membership fee or registration is required. They offer printed materials as well as a complete Web site. The Web site is full of great quality-of-life information, deployment advice, and links to other sites. Be sure to check out the "Deployment Readiness" topics and articles.

❖ **US Coast Guard Family Programs**
Commandant (G-WKW);
Office of Work Life
2100 2nd Street SW,
USCG HQ Room 6320
Washington, DC 20593-0001
Phone: (202) 267-6160 or (202) 267-6263

Obtain the services of or information about the Work Life Program by contacting the EAPC specialist at your regional Work Life Staff. Regional staffs are located at each Integrated Support Command (ISC) in the Coast Guard.

To contact the Work Life Staff nearest you, call (800) 872-4957, followed by the extension of the appropriate ISC location:

Alameda, ext. 252
Boston, ext. 301
Cleveland, ext. 309
Honolulu, ext. 314
Ketchikan, ext. 317
Kodiak, ext. 563
Miami, ext. 307
New Orleans, ext. 308

Portsmouth, ext. 305
San Pedro, ext. 311
St. Louis, ext. 302
Washington, DC, ext. 932

❖ **My Coast Guard:**
www.mycoastguard.com
This Web site offers a chat area, a message board, and Coast Guard merchandise.

❖ **Ombudsman**
The Ombudsman, a volunteer, is an official representative of Coast Guard families and works to establish and maintain good communication between the Command and the families of personnel. As a liaison for community resources, the Ombudsman works to find ways to help families use the programs and services that are available to them and guides shy or reluctant people to the service or agency they need. The Ombudsman communicates care from the Command to the individual but is not there to address problems between the military sponsor and the Command or fill the role of a professional counselor. If you don't know how to contact your Ombudsman, consult your installation directory or ask your unit or your chaplain for help.

❖ **The Coast Guard Employee Assistance Program**
Phone: (800) 222-0364 (available 24 hours)
Callers can request help through a counselor outside the military system, and most information is kept confidential.

❖ **Coast Guard Chief Petty Officers Association: www.cgea.coastguard.org**
Coast Guard Enlisted Association:
5520 G Hempstead Way

Springfield, VA 22151
Phone: (703) 941-0395

❖ **Chief Warrant Officers Association, USCG**
200 V Street SW
Washington, DC 20024
Phone: (202) 554-7753

❖ **Coast Guard Mutual Assistance:**
www.cgmahq.org
Commandant (G-ZMA)
2100 2nd Street SW, Room 5502
Washington, DC 20593-0001
Phone: (800) 881-2462; Office hours: M–F,
7 a.m.–4 p.m. EST

RESOURCES FOR RESERVE AND GUARD PERSONNEL AND THEIR FAMILIES

❖ **Reserve Affairs: www.defenselink.mil/ra**
The Department of Reserve Affairs and the Office of Family Policy worked together to develop the National Guard and Reserve Readiness Strategic Plan. From the Reserve Affairs home page, click on "Publications" to find the Family Benefits Handbook, the Family Readiness Toolkit, and many more helpful resources. The Web site addresses all of the components of the Reserve, including the Army National Guard, Army Reserve, Naval Reserve, Marine Corps Reserve, Air National Guard, Air Force Reserve, and Coast Guard Reserve. The Web site includes many useful links:
Family Readiness:
www.defenselink.mil/ra/
family readiness
Army Reserve: www.army.mil/usar
Naval Reserve: www.navres.navy.mil

Marine Corps Reserve:
www.marforres.usmc.mil
Air Force Reserve: www.afreserve.com
Coast Guard Reserve:
www.uscg.mil/hq/reserve
Army National Guard:
www.arng.army.mil
Air National Guard: www.ang.af.mil

❖ **Booklets to Help Children of Deploying Parents: www.dma.state.mn.us**
The Minnesota National Guard has some great resources for families of any military component, whether they are Active Duty, Reserve, Guard, full-time, or part-time. The following Discovery Guides deal with deployment:
Discovery Guide for Ages 2–4:
Let's Take a Trip! About Deployment
Discovery Guide for Ages 5–7:
My Travel Trunk
Discovery Guide for Ages 8–10:
Travel Journal: A Discovery about Deployment
Discovery Guide for Pre-Teens Ages 11–12:
Trip Ticket: About Deployment
A Deployment Information Guide for Teens Ages 13–18:
Travel Pack
The following Emotional Intelligence Activities help deal with and understand emotions:
Emotional Intelligence Activities Booklet for Ages 2–4
Emotional Intelligence Activities Booklet for Ages 5–7
Emotional Intelligence Activities Booklet for Ages 8–10
Emotional Intelligence Activities Booklet for Pre-Teens Ages 11–12

Emotional Intelligence Activities
Booklet for Teens Ages 13–18

To find these great resources, click on "Family Programs." Then click on "Soldiers & Families." Then click on "Youth & Development" and then on "Youth & Deployment." As you scroll down, you'll see the booklet titles. They will take time to download, as the note on the Web site says, but they are worth the effort. Print them out for your family's use.

❖ *National Guard Almanac* and *Reserve Forces Almanac*

Annual Editions

Ronald S. Hunter, MSG Gary L. Smith, USA (ret.), and Debra M. Gordon, Editors

Published by

Uniformed Services Almanac, Inc.
PO Box 4144
Falls Church, VA 22044
Phone: (703) 532-1631 or (888) 872-9698
www.militaryalmanac.com

❖ **Military Child Education Coalition: www.militarychild.org**

108 East FM 2410, Suite D
PO Box 2519
Harker Heights, TX 76548-2519
Phone: (254) 953-1923

They have some great booklets, including "How to Prepare Our Children and Stay Involved in Their Education During Deployment" and "How Communities Can Support the Children and Families of Those Serving in the National Guard or Reserves."

❖ *Keeping Your Family Close When Frequent Travel Pulls You Apart*

by Elizabeth Hoekstra

❖ **Handbook for the Guard & Reserve**

Annual insert to the *Military Times* newspaper, available every August.

Available by subscription, in military exchanges, or in libraries.

❖ **National Committee for Employer Support of the Guard and Reserve: www.esgr.org**

1555 Wilson Boulevard, Suite 200
Arlington, VA 22209-2405
Phone: (800) 336-4590

This group acts as a mediator for disputes between employers and employees.

❖ **Military Wives Web Sites (also includes a site for military husbands)**

www.militarywives.com is the home of many great Web sites. In addition to the sister sites listed below, the home page has access to their newsletter; an online e-zine; news links; military hymn information; information about military ribbons, medals, and ranks and their history; medical links; support forums; information about shopping, government departments, travel, moving, and military weddings; Space-A information; and the complete Uniform Code of Military Justice (UCMJ). It's a tremendously supportive and informative resource. Go to www.militarywives.com, and you'll find links to the following:

Military Wives Web site
Army Wives Web site
Air Force Wives Web site
Coast Guard Wives Web site
Marine Corps Wives Web site
Navy Wives Web site
Reserve Wives Web site
Military Kidz Web site
Military Husbands Web site
Military Chapel

Military Wives Store

These Web sites can also be found individually by going to www.armywives.com, www.airforcewives.com, etc.

❖ **Scriptographic Resources Published by Channing L. Bete Company**

A Family Guide to Annual Training
Annual Training
The National Guard Family Program
You're Part of the National Guard Family
Sharing the Challenge: The National Guard Family
Preparing for Mobilization
United in Readiness: The U.S. Army Reserve Family
Make the Most of Family Readiness Groups
Family Readiness Groups: Caring for Military Families
Mission: Readiness: A Personal and Family Guide for National Guard and Reserve Members, Reserve Duty Edition
  Available from
    Channing L. Bete Co. Inc.
    200 State Road
    South Deerfield, MA 01373-0200
    Phone: (800) 477-4776
    www.channing-bete.com

These resources may be available from your Family Support Center or your chaplain. Some of them can only be ordered in packages.

ARMY RESERVE RESOURCES

❖ **Family Readiness Online**

The Army Reserve offers Family Support Programs to help families prepare for deployments. Many of these programs are courses that are part of the Army Family Team Building (AFTB) program. Operation Ready specifically addresses readiness for families. To access information online, look at: www.trol.redstone.army.mil/acslink and www.military.com.

❖ **Army One Source:**
www.armyonesource.com (user ID: army; password: onesource)
Phone: (800) 464-8107 (United States) or
  (484) 530-5889 (international collect)

The Web site is interactive and is meant to help reach families who are unable to come to Family Support Programs at installations.

❖ **Army Reserve Association:**
www.armyreserve.org
PO Box 711
Winfield, KS 67156
Phone: (800) ARMY-RES

❖ **Army Family Team Building**
AFTB Office
US Army Community and Family Support Center
ATTN: CFSC-FST (AFTB)
4700 King Street
Alexandria, VA 22302-4418
Phone: (703) 681-7401

Army Family Team Building (AFTB) is a comprehensive training resource to help families understand and become comfortable with Army life. Some of the topics included are military customs and organizational charts, acronyms, pay charts and explanations of them, schools for children, relationships, meeting people and volunteering, résumés, stress, support groups, elder care, and the Army Family Action Plan. Ask about AFTB at your Army Community Service (ACS) or Family Support Center. It is used by both Active Duty and Reserve components.

❖ **Association of the United States Army:**
www.ausa.org
PO Box 1560
2425 Wilson Boulevard
Arlington, VA 22201
Phone: (703) 841-4300 or (800) 336-4570
(for family programs, ask for ext. 150 or
151)

❖ **Army Emergency Relief (AER):**
www.aerhq.org
200 Stovall Street, Room 5-N-13
Alexandria, VA 22332-0600
Phone: (703) 428-0000; DSN: 328-0000

❖ **Army Reserve Headquarters Hotline**
Phone: (800) 359-8483, ext. 464-8995

❖ **Army Reserves: www4.army.mil/USAR**

AIR FORCE RESERVE RESOURCES

❖ **Air Reserve Headquarters Hotline**
Phone: (800) 223-1784, ext 71294

❖ **The Air Force Aid Society: www.afas.org**
1745 Jefferson Davis Highway, Suite 202
Arlington, VA 22202
Phone: (703) 607-3064
    The Air Force Aid Society has a small
headquarters in the Washington, DC,
area, but most of its assistance is managed on a decentralized basis on Air
Force bases worldwide. Air Force Aid
offers help for families with financial
emergencies, usually in the form of interest-free loans or grants for basic needs
such as rent, utility bills, food, travel for a
funeral, moving, or car repair. They will
consider any valid request for emergency
financial help. The Air Force Aid Society
also offers Guaranteed Parent Loans and
other forms of tuition assistance.

❖ **Air Force Reserve: www.afreserve.com**

❖ **Air Force Sergeants Association:**
www.afsahq.org
5211 Auth Road
Suitland, MD 20746
Phone: (800) 638-0594 or (301) 899-3500

❖ **Air Force Association: www.afa.org**
1501 Lee Highway
Arlington, VA 22209-1198
Phone: (800) 727-3337

❖ **Air Force One Source:**
www.airforceonesource.com (user ID:
airforce; password: ready)
Phone: (800) 707-5784 (United States) or
    (484) 530-5913 f(international collect)
    The Web site is interactive and is
meant to help reach families who are
unable to come to Family Support
Programs at installations.

NAVAL, COAST GUARD, AND MARINE CORPS RESERVE RESOURCES

❖ **Naval Services FamilyLine/LIFELines**
Network
The Naval Services FamilyLine
Washington Navy Yard, Building 172
1254 9th Street SE, Suite 104
Washington DC 20374-5067
Phone: (202) 433-2333; DSN: 288-2333;
Office Hours: M–F, 10 a.m.–1 p.m. EST
www.lifelines.navy.mil/familyline or
www.lifelines.usmc.mil/familyline
    Naval Services FamilyLine was for-
merly known as The Navy Wifeline
Association. FamilyLine expanded and
now includes Marine Corps and Coast
Guard families. No membership fee or
registration is required. They offer

printed materials as well as a complete Web site. The Web site is full of great quality-of-life information, deployment advice, and links to other sites. Be sure to check out the "Deployment Readiness" topics and articles.

❖ **Ombudsman**

The Naval Reserve Ombudsmen are appointed by Unit Commanders to help meet family needs. Many of these volunteers are married to Reservists and have a firsthand understanding of family separation. If you don't know how to reach your Ombudsman, call the Human Resources Program Manager for Ombudsmen at (800) 621-8853.

The Marine Corps Reserves have liaisons in their training centers, as well as Key Volunteers, who are comparable to Navy Ombudsmen, available to help families.

The Coast Guard Reserve Work/Life Program supports their family members. Ombudsmen are also assigned to be liaisons with the Work/Life Program staffs. To contact the Work Life Staff nearest you, call (800) 872-4957, followed by the extension of the appropriate ISC location:

Alameda, ext. 252
Boston, ext. 301
Cleveland, ext. 309
Honolulu, ext. 314
Ketchikan, ext. 317
Kodiak, ext. 563
Miami, ext. 307
New Orleans, ext. 308
Portsmouth, ext. 305
San Pedro, ext. 311
St. Louis, ext. 302
Washington DC, ext. 932

❖ **Naval Reserve Association:**
www.navy-reserve.org
1619 King Street
Alexandria, VA 22314-2793
Phone: (703) 548-5800

❖ **Marine Corps Reserve Association:**
www.mcroa.com
337 Potomac Avenue
Quantico, VA 22134
Phone: (703) 630-3772

❖ **Naval Enlisted Reserve Association:**
www.nera.org
6703 Farragut Avenue
Falls Church, VA 22042-2189
Phone: (800) 776-9020

❖ **Coast Guard Reserve Web Site:**
www.uscg.mil

❖ *The Savvy Sailor, The Savvy Naval Officer,* **and** *The Savvy Marine Officer*
   $19.95 per book, plus $2 shipping (MD, add 5% tax)
   The Sailor's Savvy Spouse
   $26.95 per book, plus $2 shipping (MD, add 5% tax)
by Ralph F. Nelson
Available from
   Master Plan, Inc.
   500 N. Washington Street
   PO Box 10071
   Rockville, MD 20849
   Fax: (301) 340-1581 (credit-card purchases only)
   www.savvy.onweb.com

❖ **Navy-Marine Corps Relief Society:**
www.nmcrs.org
847 North Randolph Street, Second Floor
Arlington, VA 22203
Phone: (703) 696-4904; DSN: 226-4904;

Office hours: M–F, 8:15 a.m.–4:15 p.m. EST

The Navy-Marine Corps Relief Society helps meet basic living needs such as rent, utilities, and food in times of emergency. They can loan money for emergency leave travel for either spouse's immediate family or grandparents if you have a Red Cross message or verification from a doctor that requests your presence. They may be able to help you with a loan for emergency repairs if your car breaks down. The society also handles Guaranteed Student Loans and may have an emergency food pantry and thrift shop.

❖ **Coast Guard Mutual Assistance: www.cgmahq.org**
Commandant (G-ZMA)
2100 2nd Street SW, Room 5502
Washington, DC 20593-0001
Phone: (800) 881-2462
Office hours: M–F, 7 a.m.–4 p.m. EST

❖ **Fleet Reserve Association: www.fra.org**
125 N. West Street
Alexandria, VA 22314-2754
Phone: (703) 683-1400

❖ **Marine Corps Association: www.mca-marines.org**
715 Broadway Street
MCCDC
Quantico, VA 22134
Phone: (703) 640-6161 or (800) 336-0291;
Office hours: M–F, 8 a.m.–4:30 p.m. EST

❖ **Marine Corps League: www.mcleague.org**
Mailing:
PO Box 3070
Merrifield, VA 22116

Street:
8626 Lee Highway, Suite 201
Fairfax, VA 22031
Phone: (800) 625-1775 or (703) 207-9588

❖ **Coast Guard Reserves: www.uscg.mil/hq/reserve**

❖ **Marine Reserves: www.marforres.usmc.mil**

❖ **Naval Reserves: www.navalreserve.com**

❖ **Navy and Marine One Source:**

Navy Corps Source:
www.navyonesource.com (user ID: Navy; password: sailor)
Phone: (800) 540-4123 (United States) or (484) 530-5914 (international collect)
Marine Corps Source:
www.mccsonesource.com (user ID: marines; password: semper fi)
Phone: (800) 869-0278 (United States) or
(484) 530-5908 (international collect)

These Web sites are interactive and are meant to help reach families who are unable to come to Family Support Programs at installations.

NATIONAL GUARD RESOURCES

❖ **National Guard Bureau Family Program: www.guardfamily.org or www.guardfamilyyouth.org**

These Web sites focus on predeployment, deployment, and reunion information. Don't miss the Family Separation/Deployment Survival Booklets that you can download or print. They are presented for children from two to eighteen years old in age-appropriate groups. Additional topics are also found there. They also provide an assistance program for deployed guard members and their families online at www.guardassist.mhn.com.

❖ **Enlisted Association of the National Guard of the United States: www.eangus.org**
3133 Mt. Vernon Avenue
Alexandria, VA 22305
Phone: (703) 519-3846 or (800) 234-EANG

❖ **National Guard Association of the United States: www.ngaus.org**
1 Massachusetts Avenue, NW
Washington, DC 20001
Phone: (202) 789-0031

❖ **Army Reserve Headquarters Hotline Phone: (800) 359-8483, ext. 464-8995/8947**

❖ **National Guard Family Programs Office**
To inquire about your state's family program coordinator, contact:
National Volunteer Coordinator
6848 S. Revere Parkway
Englewood, CO 80112-6709
Phone: (303) 397-3034; DSN: 877-2034

❖ *You Belong to the National Guard Family*
Available from your Family Support Center, your chaplain, or:
Channing L. Bete Co. Inc.
200 State Road
South Deerfield, MA 01373-0200
Phone: (800) 477-4776
www.channing-bete.com

❖ **Air National Guard: www.ang.af.mil**

❖ **Army National Guard: www.arng.army.mil**

❖ **Army One Source: www.armyonesource.com (user ID: army; password: onesource)**
Phone: (800) 464-8107 (United States) or (484) 530-5889 (international collect)
Air Force One Source: www.airforceonesource.com (user ID: airforce; password: ready)
Phone: (800) 707-5784 (United States) or (484) 530-5913 (international collect)

These Web sites are interactive and are meant to help reach families who are unable to come to Family Support Programs at installations.

APPENDIX: ACRONYMS

ACS	Army Community Services
AER	Army Emergency Relief
AFB	Air Force Base
AFHA	Armed Forces Hostess Association
AFTB	Army Family Team Building
ANG	Air National Guard
AOR	Area of Responsibility
ARNG	Army National Guard
ATM	Automatic Teller Machine
BAH	Basic Allowance for Housing
BDU	Battle Dress Uniform
BX	Base Exchange
CACO	Casualty Assistance Calls Officer
CAO	Casualty Assistance Officer
CHAMPUS	Civilian Health and Medical Program of the Uniformed Services
CHAMPVA	Civilian Health and Medical Program of the Department of Veterans Affairs
CNO	Chief of Naval Operations
CNT	Casualty Notification Team
CO	Commanding Officer
COMSEC	Communications Security
CREDO	Chaplains Religious Development Operation
DEERS	Defense Enrollment Eligibility Reporting System
DOD	Department of Defense
DPP	Deferred Payment Plan
DSN	Defense Switched Network
FLCL	Family Life Communication Line
FOD	Foreign Object Debris
FRG	Family Readiness Group
FSC	Family Support Center or Family Service Center
HQ	Headquarters
ID	Identification
IG	Inspector General
ISC	Integrated Support Command
ITT	Information, Tickets, and Tours
JTF	Joint Task Force
KUDOS	Kids Understanding Deployment Operations
KVN	Key Volunteer Network
LES	Leave and Earnings Statement
L.I.N.K.S.	Lifestyle, Insights, Networking, Knowledge, and Skills
MAPsite	Military Assistance Program Site
MARS	Military Affiliated Radio System
MCFTB	Marine Corps Family Team Building
MIA	Missing in Action
MOM	Mothers of Military
MOPS	Mothers of Preschoolers
MP	Military Police
MRE	Meal Ready to Eat

MWX	Marine Corps Exchange
NCESGR	National Committee for Employer Support of the Guard and Reserve
NCO	Non-Commissioned Officer
NEX	Navy Exchange
NFI	National Fatherhood Initiative
NMFA	National Military Family Association
NWCA	Navy Wives Clubs of America
OCF	Officers' Christian Fellowship
ODS	Operation Desert Shield/Storm
OPSEC	Operations Security
PCS	Permanent Change of Station
PIN	Personal Identification Number
POA	Power of Attorney
POV	Privately Owned Vehicle
POW	Prisoner of War
PRIMUS	Primary Care for the Uniformed Services
PX	Post Exchange
SAC	Strategic Air Command
SATO	Scheduled Airline Ticket Office
SEAL	Sea, Air, and Land
SF	Security Forces (formerly Security Police)
SSL	Secure Socket Layer
SSN	Social Security Number
TAD	Temporary Active Duty
TAPS	Tragedy Assistance Program for Survivors
TCK	Third Culture Kids
TDY	Temporary Duty
TMO	Traffic Management Office
TSP	Thrift Savings Plan
UCMJ	Uniform Code of Military Justice
USA	United States Army
USAF	United States Air Force
USAR	United States Army Reserve
USAREUR	United States Army in Europe
USO	United Service Organization
USERRA	Uniformed Services Employment and Reemployment Rights Act

NOTES

CHAPTER I/1

1. Dan Vandesteeg, letter to author, August 15, 2003. Used by permission.

2. Ren Vandesteeg, anecdote written for author, October 25, 2004. Used by permission.

3. Mike Vandesteeg, e-mail message to author, November 11, 2004. Used by permission.

CHAPTER I/2

1. Lt. Col. Charles Kelker, "All Troops Responsible for Military Readiness," Lackland *Talespinner,* November 21, 2001, 6.

2. Associated Press, "Military Reserves to Become More Important, Defense Official Says," *Minot Daily News,* January 11 1999, A-7.

3. Water Schumm, D. Bruce Bell, and Giao Tran, "Family Adaptation to the Demands of Army Life: A Review of Findings," US Army Research Institute for the Behavioral and Social Sciences, January 1994, 13.

4. Captain Stan J. Beach, chaplain, US Navy (retired), "Enduring and Prospering in Your Military Calling," in *Deployed, Not Disconnected: Hope and Help For Husbands and Wives Facing Separations Due to Military Assignments* (Englewood, CO: Officers' Christian Fellowship Books, 1991), 3.

5. Sarah Coffey, "Maine Has Third-Highest Percentage of Troops Deployed," http://www4.fosters.com/news2004/January2004/January_12/news.

6. Melba Newsome, "Uncommon Courage: Captain Mom, Major Dad," *Family Circle,* August 7, 2003, 64.

7. Sig Christenson, "Families Say Goodbyes at Fort Hood," *San Antonio Express-News,* January 15, 2003, A-5.

8. Richard Zowie, "12th TRANS Mechanic Reflects on Deployment," Randolph *Wingspread,* January 10, 2003, 4.

9. Lydia Sloan Cline, *Today's Military Wife: Meeting the Challenges of Service Life,* 2nd ed. (Mechanicsburg, PA: Stackpole Books, 1992), 200.

10. Ibid., 202.

11. Seth Hettena, "Thousands of GIs Ship Out for Gulf," *San Antonio Express-News,* January 7, 2003, A 4.

CHAPTER I/4

1. USAF Chaplain Service Institute, *Link: Staying Together While Apart* (Maxwell AFB, AL: USAF Chaplain Service Institute, 1994), 4.

2. Sue Roberts, "Separated!" in *Deployed, Not Disconnected: Hope and Help For Husbands and Wives Facing Separations Due to Military Assignments* (Englewood, CO: Officers' Christian Fellowship Books, 1991), 47.

3. DOD Office of Family Policy, Support & Services, *1992 DOD Surveys of Officers and Enlisted Personnel and Their Spouses: Individual and Family Readiness for Separation and Deployment* (Rockville, MD: Westat, Inc.), 5–7.

4. Lt. Col. (USAF, ret.) Ward Graham, "Fulfilling a Husband's Responsibility," in *Deployed, Not Disconnected: Hope and Help for Husbands and Wives Facing Separations Due to Military Assignments* (Englewood, CO: Officers' Christian Fellowship Books, 1991), 30.

5. Cline, 242.

6. Denise McColl, *Footsteps of the Faithful* (Moscow, ID: Community Christian Ministries, Inc., 1995), 112.

7. See page 11 of *Daddy's Days Away,* produced by the Family Programs Branch Headquarters, US Marine Corps, for ideas about how to do this.

8. Navy Family Services Center, *Navy Family Deployment Guide* (Norfolk, VA, 1987), 49.

Chapter I/8

1. Poem used by permission of Prayer Outreach/Military Prayer Outreach Ministries.

2. Vincent T. Davis, "Home from the Front," *San Antonio Express-News*, April 2, 2004, B-1.

3. Anne Davis, "Our Hardest Task," December 6, 2001, www.militarywivesandmoms.org.

4. Scott Huddleston, "The GI's Mom," *San Antonio Express-News*, August 18, 2003, B-1.

Chapter I/9

1. Roger Croteau, "Families Say Goodbye to 'the Magnificent 34,'" *San Antonio Express-News,* August 20, 2004, 5B.

2. Robert Burns, "Army Reserve Call-Ups May Become a Sure Thing," *San Antonio Express-News,* January 22, 2004, 4A.

3. Ibid.

4. Master Sgt. Bob Haskell, "It Takes Three Legs to Make the Guard a Stable Force," *The On Guard,* September 2003, 10.

5. Ronald S. Hunter, MSG Gary L. Smith, USA (retired), and Debra M. Gordon, eds., *1996 Reserve Forces Almanac* (Falls Church, VA: Reserve Forces Almanac, 1996), 63.

6. USAR, *What's Next?,* 6.

Chapter I/10

1. Deuteronomy 24:5 (Modern Language Bible).

2. USAF Capt. Dolly Garnecki, "God's Blessings—An Oasis in the Desert," *Command,* April 2004, 2.

3. McColl, *Footsteps,* 109.

Chapter II/2

1. Beth Blase, "Mother's Visit" and "Frustration," used by permission.

Chapter II/3

1. Brenda Pace and Carol McGlothlin, *Medals Over My Heart* (Nashville: Broadman & Holman Publishers, 2004), 79.

2. Margaret Krajeski, "Keeping It Together When You're Apart," in *Married to the Military,* supplement to *Army Times, Navy Times,* and *Air Force Times,* May 16, 1994, 46.

3. Ibid.

4. David A. Paap, *Caring For Military Families* (St. Louis, MO: Stephen Ministries, 1991), 19.

CHAPTER II/5

1. Marshele Carter Waddell, *Hope For the Home Front* (Virginia Beach, VA: One Hope Ministry, 2003), 139.

CHAPTER II/6

1. Used with permission from the *Stars and Stripes,* a DOD publication. © 1996 *Stars and Stripes.*

2. Amelia Jackson, "Caring for the Troops' Kids," *San Antonio Express-News,* August 5, 2004, 3B.

3. US Air Force, *Balancing Work & Life in the U.S. Air Force* (Elkins Park, PA: Educational Publications, Inc., 1993), 52.

4. Cline, 213.

5. Mikell G. Calkin, "Take Care of Mom," *Command,* October 2003, 7.

6. Used with permission from the *Stars and Stripes,* a DOD publication. ©1996 *Stars and Stripes.*

7. Used with permission from the *Stars and Stripes,* a DOD publication. © 1996 *Stars and Stripes.*

8. Used with permission from the *Stars and Stripes,* a DOD publication. © 1996 *Stars and Stripes.*

9. Zowie, 4.

10. Kathie Hightower and Holly Scherer, "Staying Connected Takes Creativity," *Air Force Times,* January 19, 2004, 29.

11. Dan Vandesteeg, letter to author, August 15, 2003. Used by permission.

12. Mike Vandesteeg, letters to author, November 11, 2004, and September 9, 2003. Used by permission.

13. Used with permission from the *Stars and Stripes,* a DOD publication. © 1996 *Stars and Stripes.*

14. Karen H. Whiting, "On the Road Again," *Command,* November 2003, 6.

CHAPTER II/7

1. Peggy Sue Wells and Mary Ann Froelich, *Holding Down the Fort* (Minneapolis: Bethany House Publishers, 1998), 26.

2. Waddell, 52.

3. Paul T. Bartone, *U.S. Army Families in USAREUR: Coping With Separation: Deployment Experiences of Army Spouses In Their Own Words.* US Army Medical Research Unit-Europe, 3.

4. Interview with author, September 16, 1999.

CHAPTER II/9

1. Barbara B. Dahl, Edna J. Hunter, and Hamilton I. McCubbin, eds. *Families in the Military System* (Beverly Hills: Sage Publications, 1976), 162.

2. Amy B. Alder, Paul T. Bartone, and Mark A. Vaitkus, *USAMRU-E Technical Report 95-1: Family Stress and Adaptation During a U.S. Army Europe Peacekeeping Deployment.* US Army Medical Research Unit-Europe, April 1995, 5.

3. Ibid., 19.

4. Paap, 20–25.

5. Ibid., 80.

CHAPTER II/10

1. Oliver North with Sara Horn, *A Greater Freedom: Stories of Faith from Operation Iraqi Freedom* (Nashville: Broadman & Holman Publishers, 2004), 20.

2. USAF Chaplain Service Institute, *Link,* 29.

3. Beach, "Enduring and Prospering in Your Military Calling," 5.

4. Psalm 91:1 (King James Version).

5. Psalm 91:2 (King James Version).

6. Paap, 29.

7. North, 54.

8. Ibid., 93.

9. Ibid., 82.

10. Capt. Stan J. Beach, chaplain, US Navy (retired), "Praise the Lord Anyway," *Command,* Fall 1989, 3.

11. Denise McColl, "Making the Most of Deployments: A Wife's Perspective," *Command,* Fall 1989, 12.

12. Roberts, 45.

13. Adm. Grady Jackson, "President's Letter," *Command,* Fall 1989, 1.

14. Garnecki, 2–3.

15. North, 89.

16. Ibid.

17. Maj. D.R. Heinle, US Marine Corps, "Marital Fidelity in Far-Away Places," in *Deployed, Not Disconnected: Hope and Help for Husbands and Wives Facing Separations Due to Military Assignments* (Englewood, CO: Officers' Christian Fellowship Books, 1991), 100-101.

18. Used with permission from the *Stars and Stripes,* a DOD publication. © 1996 *Stars and Stripes*.

19. 2 Corinthians 4:8–9 (New King James Version).

20. North, 80.

Chapter III/1

1. Ren Vandesteeg, anecdote written for author, November 22, 2004. Used by permission.

Chapter III/2

1. Richard D. Thompson, "Homecoming: A Period of Adjustment," *Military Chaplains' Review,* Winter 1991, 29.

2. Ibid., 21.

3. Craig Storti, *The Art of Coming Home* (Yarmouth, ME; Intercultural Press, Inc., 2001), 85, ff.

4. Huddleston, Scott. "For some, real fight is here," *San Antonio Express-News.* March 18, 2005; 1A, 9A.

Chapter III/4

1. McColl, *Footsteps,* 137.

2. Beverly Moritz, *Service Separations: A Wife's Perspective* (Englewood, CO: Officers' Christian Fellowship Books), 14.

3. Robert M. Hicks, *Returning Home* (Tarrytown, NY: Fleming H. Revell Company, 1991), 109.

Chapter IV/1

1. Bonnie Carroll, Lisa Hudson, and Diane Ruby, "Complicated Grief in the Military," in *Living With Grief After Sudden Loss* (Bristol, PA: Taylor & Francis, 1996), 73.

2. Lauren, Internet chat room, October 9, 2001, http://www.parentcenter.com.

3. Capt. Scott O'Grady, *Return With Honor* (New York: Doubleday, 1995), 90.

4. Edna J. Hunter, *Families Under the Flag* (New York: Praeger Scientific CBS Educational and Professional Publishing, 1982), 24.

Chapter IV/2

1. Eva J. Moore, letter to author, November 8, 1996.

2. Mike Glenn, "Former Prisoner Advises POWs to Concentrate on Staying Alive," *Air Force Times,* April 19, 1999, 24.

3. Ibid., 24.

4. Edna Hunter, 66.

5. Gary L. Bauer, "Let's Go Home Again," *Focus on the Family,* October 1992, 2.

6. Edna Hunter, 69.

7. Ibid., 71.

8. Interview with author, September 16, 1999.

Chapter IV/3

1. Dianne Collier, *My Love, My Life* (Ontario; Creative Bound, Inc., 2004), 74.

Chapter IV/4

1. Victoria Cummock, "Journey of a Young Widow: The Bombing of Pan Am 103," in *Living With Grief After Sudden Loss* (Bristol, PA: Taylor & Francis, 1996), 6.

Chapter IV/6

1. Helen Fitzgerald, *The Mourning Handbook* (New York: Simon and Schuster, 1994), 148.

2. Carroll, Hudson, and Ruby, 76.

Chapter IV/7

1. Dan Schaefer and Christine Lyons, *How Do We Tell the Children?* (New York: Newmarket Press, 1986), 120.

2. Ibid., 211.

3. Ibid., 21.

4. Ibid., 92.

5. Ibid., 93.

Chapter IV/8

1. Jeffrey Gettleman, "Deaths Taking a Toll at Home," *San Antonio Express-News*, November 2, 2003, A-14.

2. Huddleston, "For some, real fight is here," 9A.

Chapter V/2

1. Shelley Bishop, "Meeting Its Mission—And More," *Military Officer*, August 2003, 29–33.

Chapter V/3

1. Hunter, Smith, and Gordon, 63.

2. Jack Spencer and Larry Wortzel, "The Role of the National Guard in Homeland Security," January 22, 2004, www.heritage.org/research/Homeland Defense.

Chapter V/4

1. Jack Spencer and Larry Wortzel, "It Never Gets Any Easier to Leave," *Air Force Times*, October 27, 1997, 11.

2. Collier, 77.

The Word at Work Around the World

A vital part of Cook Communications Ministries is our international outreach, Cook Communications Ministries International (CCMI). Your purchase of this book, and of other books and Christian-growth products from Cook, enables CCMI to provide Bibles and Christian literature to people in more than 150 languages in 65 countries.

Cook Communications Ministries is a not-for-profit, self-supporting organization. Revenues from sales of our books, Bible curricula, and other church and home products not only fund our U.S. ministry, but also fund our CCMI ministry around the world. One hundred percent of donations to CCMI go to our international literature programs.

CCMI reaches out internationally in three ways:

• Our premier International Christian Publishing Institute (ICPI) trains leaders from nationally led publishing houses around the world.

• We provide literature for pastors, evangelists, and Christian workers in their national language.

• We reach people at risk—refugees, AIDS victims, street children, and famine victims—with God's Word.

Word Power, God's Power

Faith Kidz, RiverOak, Honor, Life Journey, Victor, NexGen — every time you purchase a book produced by Cook Communications Ministries, you not only meet a vital personal need in your life or in the life of someone you love, but you're also a part of ministering to José in Colombia, Humberto in Chile, Gousa in India, or Lidiane in Brazil. You help make it possible for a pastor in China, a child in Peru, or a mother in West Africa to enjoy a life-changing book. And because you helped, children and adults around the world are learning God's Word and walking in his ways.

Thank you for your partnership in helping to disciple the world. May God bless you with the power of his Word in your life.

For more information about our international ministries, visit www.ccmi.org.

Additional copies of this or other Life Journey books
are available wherever good books are sold.

ℭℛ

If you have enjoyed this book,
or if it has had an impact on your life,
we would like to hear from you.

Please contact us at:

LIFE JOURNEY BOOKS
Cook Communications Ministries, Dept. 201
4050 Lee Vance View
Colorado Springs, CO 80918

Or visit our Web site: www.cookministries.com

LIFE JOURNEY®
Bringing Home the Message for Life